# LET'S GO BUDGET
# BERLIN

**Research Manager**
Dorothy McLeod

**Managing Editor**
Sarah Berlow

**Editor**
Mary Potter

# Contents

POLITIK IST DIE FORTSETZUNG DES KRIEGES MIT ANDEREN MITTELN

# Discover Berlin

So you've decided to visit Berlin. Congratulations. Your pretentious friends went to Paris. Your haughty friends went to London. And your lost friends went to Belarus. But you decided on Berlin. You've probably heard that Berlin is the coolest city in the world, or that it has one of the best clubs in Europe, or that it sleeps when the sun comes up. Well, don't believe the hype. It's not the coolest city in the world; it's several of the coolest cities in the world. It doesn't have one of the best clubs in Europe; it has 10. To top it off, Berlin never sleeps.

Berlin's rise began with some normal history, taken to epic heights. King Friedrich II and his identically named progeny ruled from canal-lined boulevards, built palaces like middle-fingers to all the haters, and developed Prussia into an Enlightened European powerhouse, with Berlin at the helm. But after centuries of captaining Europe, Berlin went crazy in the 20th. As the seat of Hitler's terror, and with WWII drama in its streets, Berlin rebooted in the '50s, only to become a physical manifestation of Cold War divisions. The Wall rose in '61, slicing the city and fostering the enmity of a radical student and punk population. Ten years after the Wall crumbled in '89, the German government decided to relocate from Bonn to Berlin. And from there, Berlin became today's European champion of cool.

Sorry about your friends.

# Budget Berlin

## CHEAP EATS

Welcome to the land of Cheap and Awesome. Stick to the inexpensive restaurants and food stands in Friedrichsain, Kreuzberg, and Prenzlauerberg, and you just might save enough to buy a coffee and pretend to be rich in the posh cafes in Charlottenburg, Schöneberg, and Wilmersdorf. And while there's plenty of wurst and schnitzel to be had for travelers on a budget, Berlin's ethnic cuisine is some of the tastiest and cheapest on offer. So dive into that falafel, or make your way to the corner Thai or Vietnamese place—you won't be disappointed, and your wallet will thank you.

▶ **MUSTAFA'S:** Mustafa's flavorful *dürüm* is a little Turkish miracle. At just €4, it's undoubtedly the best fast food in town (p. 91).

▶ **MONSIEUR VUONG:** Vietnamese restaurants are among the most common cheap, sit-down lunch places in Berlin, but Monsieur Vuong (p. 82) beats them all with a constantly changing menu of its own tasty creations.

▶ **SCHWARZES CAFE:** This 24hr. cafe (p. 76) serves food at any hour, so plan on washing down an omelette with absinthe at 3:34am on a Sunday.

## Freebies

▶ **WELCOMECARD:** Pick up a WelcomeCard for €17 at any tourist office to get unlimited Metro travel for 48hr. and discounts at 130 sights (p. 155).

▶ **NEW BERLIN:** This walking tour covers Berlin's major sights—for free. Use it to get acquainted with the city when you first arrive (p. 157).

▶ **THE WEINEREI FORUM:** Make The Weinerei (p. 105) in Prenzlauer Berg your first nightlife stop. Pay €2, drink as much as you can, and then pay "what you think you owe" before you leave.

▶ **BEERLIN:** Berlin's annual Bierfestival (p. 178) is free to enter. Sample hundreds of beers from around the world.

▶ **FREE SAMPLES:** Need a quick refuel? Wander through the Turkish Market (p. 124) in Kreuzberg and fill up on free fruit.

▶ **CAFÉ MORGENLAND:** The weekend morning brunch buffet (€9.50) has such an extensive selection of breakfast staples that it blows away competing slim hostel breakfast buffets (p. 92).

▶ **FRITTIERSALON:** Made to look like a '50s American diner, this burger joint's (p. 88) mostly vegetarian menu lists refreshing takes on greasy, meaty German cuisine.

## BUDGET ACCOMMODATIONS

From zany themes to hostel bars to rooftop patios to institutional places that cost next to nothing and impose crazy curfews—you name it, Berlin's got it.

▶ **CIRCUS HOSTEL:** All the fun of a circus, minus the creepy clowns. The only thing bigger than the huge, colorful rooms is the extensive breakfast buffet (p. 35).

▶ **PFEFFERBETT:** A tremendous brick building with a cathedral-sized common room holds chapel-sized rooms and a hip and helpful staff (p. 39).

► **COMEBACKPACKERS HOSTEL:** Refreshing hostel humor, a window-lined common room, and a long outdoor patio overlooking a busy square make this a light and bright hostel experience (p. 44).

► **SUNFLOWER HOSTEL:** Freaky murals featuring icons in American nerd culture line the way to a comfy bunk in a quiet, spacious, and clean dorm (p. 41).

► **JETPAK:** Located remotely far to the southwest in the whispering Grünewald, JetPak channels your favorite childhood summer camp memories with a grassy compound filled with fun and games and a main building that feels like a mountain lodge (p. 32).

## SIGHTSEEING ON THE CHEAP

Fortunately for the budget traveler, many of Berlin's best sights are free to see, if not necessarily to enter or climb. Students will have a particularly easy time of sightseeing on a budget, thanks to the 50% student discount at most sights and museums.

► **TOPOGRAPHY OF TERROR:** This free museum (p. 59), which opened in May 2010, tracks the origins, development, and deployment of Nazi terror.

► **TACHELES:** This bombed-out department store (p. 60) has become a living, breathing street-art metropolis. Chances are you'll never again experience anything like it. The best part? It's completely free.

► **REICHSTAG:** Climb to the Reichstag (p. 56) roof to marvel at the "openness" of German government, symbolized by the glass ceiling. A stunning view of the Berlin skyline awaits.

► **PARK IT:** Berlin's parks (free, of course) are often nothing less than extensive, grassy museums, as some of them, like Volkspark Friedrichshain (p. 69) and Tempelhofer Park (p. 72), feature impressive historical artifacts among the sunbathers and joggers.

# What To Do

## COLD WAR KIDS

Berlin's Cold War history is all around. While you could spend a fortune on entry to certain tourist traps (ahem, **Checkpoint Charlie**), there are plenty of cheaper options that allow you to get up close and personal with Berlin's Cold War relics. The **Berliner Mauer Dokumentationszentrum** (p. 68) covers an entire block in Prenzlauer Berg with a comprehensive collection of all things Wall, including original recordings, telegrams, and photos. The **Stasi Museum** (p. 70), the headquarters of East Berlin's secret police, is now a museum dedicated to Stasi artifacts that is a must for Cold War buffs and fans of *The Lives of Others* (2006). Last but not least, the massive **Soviet Memorial** (p. 58), built by the Soviets in 1945, contains haunting photo exhibits of desolate post-war Berlin and Soviet battlefields.

## GLBT BERLIN

Until 1969, homosexuality was outlawed in both East and West Berlin under a law passed by the Nazis. Since then, Berlin has become one of the world's most GLBT-friendly cities. The **Schwules Museum** (p. 73), the world's only state-funded museum on persecution of homosexuals, showcases fascinating temporary exhibits. Come nightfall, head to **Hafen** (p. 99), a landmark for Berlin's gay community. Stop by if you're in town on April 30th for a huge party celebrating the Queen of the Netherlands—we've heard she always makes an appearance. Alternatively, in a neighborhood dominated by male gay clubs, low-key **Begine** (p. 100) is a welcome retreat for women with readings and live music.

## BEYOND TOURISM

Ready to learn more about Berlin and give back to the community? Take your debating skills to the next level with an internship at **The Bundestag** (p. 185), Germany's national parliament. If you're looking to volunteer, consider **International Cultural Youth Exchange** (p. 183), which places volunteers with a host family and a volunteer job. For more opportunities, see **Beyond Tourism** (p. 179).

### Student Superlatives

▶ **BEST PLACE TO BUY BOOKS YOU CAN ACTUALLY READ:** St. George's Bookstore (p. 129).

▶ **BEST U-BAHN:** All of them, because you can drink beer on the subway and it never ever gets old.

▶ **BEST STROBE LIGHT:** Club Tresor (p. 113) in Kreuzberg.

▶ **MOST LIKELY TO HAVE SUPERPOWERS:** Berliner Philharmoniker (p. 119).

▶ **BEST PLACE TO FIND A HIPSTER HUSBAND:** Hackescher Markt (p. 63)—or really anywhere in Berlin.

# Planning Your Trip

## WHEN TO GO

Tourists visit Berlin year-round. The summer months (May-September) offer the best weather and the highest concentration of tourists. Summer visitors to Berlin can also look forward to beer gardens, cookouts in the park, sprawling flea markets, and floating pubs. The summer is also the most difficult time to find cheap accommodations, but it also brings the most entertainment: bars and clubs will be hopping, many sights and attractions will stay open later, and festivals (many of them free) will be off the Richter. To avoid the crowds, spring and autumn are better bets; spring has calmer and more consistent weather. The winter can be bitterly cold and precipitous in Berlin; if you must visit then, be sure to pack your Mitte-ns.

## NEIGHBORHOODS

### Charlottenburg

Should you forget that Berlin is an old European capital, venture into Charlottenburg. Originally a separate town founded around the grounds of Friedrich I's palace, it became an affluent cultural center during the Weimar years and the Berlin Wall era thanks to

## Icons

First things first: places and things that we absolutely love, sappily cherish, generally obsess over, and wholeheartedly endorse are denoted by the all-empowering ⚑ **Let's Go thumbs-up.** In addition, the icons scattered at the end of a listing can serve as visual cues to help you navigate each listing:

| ⚑ | Let's Go recommends | ☎ | Phone numbers | ⚓ | Directions |
|---|---|---|---|---|---|
| *i* | Other hard info | Ⓢ | Prices | ⏰ | Hours |

Anglo-American support. The neighborhood retains its original old-world opulence, from the upscale Beaux-Arts apartments to the shamelessly extravagant **Kurfürstendamm,** Berlin's main shopping strip. **Ku'damm,** as the locals call it, runs from east to west through southern Charlottenburg. It's home to Europe's largest department store, **KaDeWe,** which comprises five massive floors that keep patrons expertly dressed and lavishly fed with gourmet delicacies. Close to central Charlottenburg is the elephantine **Bahnhof Zoo,** a favorite among families, cute animal enthusiasts, and taxidermists (R.I.P., Knut). Along with the zoo, the Ku'damm, and its never-ending flow of teenagers darting in and out of H and M, is one of the youngest and liveliest areas in Charlottenburg. Other popular sights include the Spree River in the northwest and the absurdly splendiferous **Schloß Charlottenburg** to the north. Otherwise, the neighborhood's high rents keep out most young people and students, so the Charlottenburg crowd tends to be old and quiet, and prefers the sidewalk seating of an expensive Ku'Damm restaurant to crazy ragers in one of the area's few clubs.

## Schöneberg and Wilmersdorf

South of Ku'damm, Schöneberg and Wilmersdorf are primarily quiet residential neighborhoods, remarkable for their world class cafe culture, bistro tables, relaxed diners, and coffee shops spilling onto virtually every cobblestone street. There's a reason that no Starbucks has popped up in Schöneberg: the coffee here is delicious, cheap, and sometimes made with so much love that a heart appears in the foam. Also, nowhere else in Berlin, and perhaps in all of Germany, is the GLBT community quite as spectacularly ready to party as in the area immediately surrounding **Nollendorfplatz.** Here, the gay nightlife scene varies from chill to crazy, and the various bars scattered across the northern part of Schöneberg are often packed beyond capacity. To the west lies one of Berlin's most convenient outdoor getaways: **Grunewald** rustles with city dwellers trading their daily commute for peaceful strolls with the family dog among the pines. But if you don't have the time for the 20min. bus or tram ride—or a palm reader once predicted that you would be mauled by dogs in a German forest—then Schöneberg and Wilmersdorf offer a gracious handful of shady parks scattered among their apartment facades where you can sit back in the grass and kick back the cups of joe.

## Mitte

True to its name ("center" in English), Mitte is without a doubt Berlin's political, historical, cultural, and tourist-ical center. Boasting the **Brandenburg Gate,** the **Reichstag,** the **Jewish Memorial,** the **Rotes Rathaus,** the **Victory Column,** and the **Berliner Dom,** Mitte is crawling with tourists wearing the names of other cities on their T-shirts, passing through to get a glimpse of some of the world's worthiest sights. The area also has Berlin's best cultural institutions; **Museum Island** piles some of the world's most awe-inspiring museums practically on top of each other, with the too-well-preserved-to-be-true **Pergamon Museum** atop the heap. Some of the world's most famous performance halls, including the **Berlin Philharmonic** and the **Deutscher Staatsoper,** grace this cultural capital with their cultural capital. Then, of course, there's the forest-like **Tiergarten** at the center of Mitte, which shelters sunbathers, barbecuers, pensive wanderers, and probably several breeds of magical creatures. The main street cutting through the Tiergarten, **Straße des 17 Juni,** serves as a popular gathering place where carnivals, markets, protests, and public viewings of the World Cup take precedent over constant traffic.

What's perhaps most fun about Mitte is tracing the history of Berlin down its streets and through its buildings. One of the most common phrases in relation to every Mitte sight is "heavily damaged in WWII," and constructions and reconstructions are often difficult to distinguish. The **Berlin Wall** once ran directly through Mitte, and, though the signs of the divide fade with every passing year, there are still many remnants of a more

## Mitte in the Middle

Mitte didn't become the center of Berlin by accident. A historically important borough before the 20th century and once a center of Kaiser Wilhelm's Reich empire, Mitte continued its rise to the top after WWII, when it hosted East Germany's architecturally atrocious (and now thankfully destroyed) Palace of the Republic.

    As a symbol of reunification after the fall of the Berlin Wall, the West Berlin city government moved from Schöneberg Town Hall into the former home of the communist city government. The red bricks and tower of **Rotes Rathaus** (Red Town Hall) in Mitte, now make for a convenient landmark, in case you get lost in the middle of Berlin's urban jungle.

fragmented Berlin, like the DDR-built **Fernsehturm,** which, for better or worse, is Mitte's most incessantly visible landmark. One of the longest still-standing stretches of wall deteriorates in the south, an unsightly sign of unsettling recent times.

    But Mitte ain't just about the capital-S Sights: it also burns brightly from night until morning with some of Berlin's most prized techno clubs, many of which are named after baked goods for whatever reason (e.g. **Cookies**). Plus, with shopping centers both ritzy (**Friedrichstraße**) and intimidatingly hip (**Hackescher Markt**), Mitte can serve as a pricey place to replace your threads with something more flannel or form-fitting; that way, entry into the sometimes exclusive nightlife options is only a flashy strut away.

## Prenzlauer Berg

Like the history of all things trendy, the history of Prenzlauer Berg in the 20th century is reversal after reversal after reversal. When the Wall fell, Prenzlauer Berg was in ruins. Though it had suffered little damage from Allied bombs compared to its neighbors during WWII, its early DDR days were as filled with neglect as Hansel and Gretel: buildings fell into piles of graffitied bread crumbs, and it wasn't until the '70s that people started sweeping up the mess. But as any home-owner with a neighbor who doesn't mow their lawn knows, neglect means lower rents, and lower rents draw students and the younger in years. By the current millennium, Prenzlauer Berg had become the hippest of the hippest, populated by dreadlock-laden grungesters shopping at secondhand clothing stores, tight-jeaned post-teens drinking cheap black coffee from sidewalk cafe tables, and enough flannel to make a lumberjack chuckle. But hip, by definition, never lasts, and as the noughts progressed, Prenzlauer Berg steadily began to gentrify: students became parents, hippies gave way to yuppies, and parks became playgrounds. Today, Prenzlauer Berg is overrun with toddlers and has one of the highest birth rates in the country. Jungle gyms, strollers, and daycares share the streets with the vestiges of a younger, edgier age, like the tiny, pricey fashion and secondhand stores that line **Kastanienallee** and the countless cafes spilling onto every sidewalk around **Helmholtzplatz**. Though it's changed, Prenzlauer Berg hasn't completely lost its cool: with the best bar scene of any of the neighborhoods, including a wine place where you choose how much to pay, a ping-pong bar, and more vintage sofas than *Mad Men,* P'Berg can still be pretty unbelievable. One recommendation for maximizing your time here: rent a bike. With only about four Metro stations, this Berg is most accessible on two wheels.

## Friedrichshain

Friedrichshain's low rents and DDR edge draw a crowd of punks and metal-heads ever eastward. From the longest still-standing remnant of the Berlin Wall, which runs along the Spree, to the stark, towering architecture of the neighborhood's central axis, **Frankfurter Allee,** the ghost of the former Soviet Union still haunts the 'Hain. Fortunately, this ghost only seems to scare the population out into the night, when any crumbling factory, any cobwebbed train station, and any complex of graffiti and grime is fair game for F'Hain's sublimely edgy nightlife. Some locals complain that gentrification has found its way even here, as traditional residential buildings pop up, clubs become tame and touristy, and chic 20-somethings set up shop on the cafe-ridden **Simon-Dach-Strasse** and **Boxhagenerplatz.** Nonetheless, Friedrichshain is still wonderfully inexpensive and unique. Travelers should keep a lookout at night, though, because Friedrichshain's often desolate infrastructure can hide shady characters.

## Kreuzberg

If Mitte is Manhattan, Kreuzberg is Brooklyn. Graffiti adorns everything, and the younger population skulks around while chowing down on street food fit for a last supper. The parties start

later, go later, and sometimes never stop. Kreuzberg was spawned during the 1860s, when industrialization crammed the previously unpopulated area to Berlin's southeast with dense, low-income housing and brick factories, many of which still stand today. During its 20th-century teens, Kreuzberg ruled as the center of punkdom and counterculture in Berlin. Its old warehouses and factories housed *Hausbesetzer* (squatters) in the 1970s, until a conservative city government forcibly evicted them in the early '80s. Riots ensued, and, during Reagan's 1985 visit to the city, authorities so feared protests in Kreuzberg that they locked down the entire district. While time has tamed Kreuzberg, the neighborhood's alternative soul sticks around like an especially persistent squatter. Underground clubs in abandoned basements, burned-out apartment buildings, and oppressive warehouse complexes shake off their dust when the sun disappears and rage until well after it reappears; the clubs that party the hardest, the latest, and the best in Berlin all find shelter in Kreuzberg. Kreuzberg is also home to most of Berlin's enormous Turkish population (hence the nickname "Little Istanbul"). Döner kebabs, the salty scraps cut from those gigantic meaty beehives in every other storefront, go for €2-3 all across this district, and the **Turkish Market** along the southern bank of the **Landwehrkanal** is one of the most exciting, raucous, cheap, and authentic markets in Western Europe. If you want to learn about Berlin, head to Mitte. If you want to not remember what you learned, come to Kreuzberg.

## SUGGESTED ITINERARIES

### Cheap Date

In cheap and hipster Berlin, no date need be expensive—or mainstream. Free museums and great nightclub cover deals make this city a fun, inexpensive dating spot.

**1. DOUBLE EYE:** Start the day off with a €2 cappuccino topped with latte art in nearby Schöneberg (p. 80). Get a little foam heart (or something way cooler) drawn on top to impress that Berliner babe.

**2. GRUNEWALD:** Show off your rugged side at this forest (p. 52), which is outfitted with a restored royal hunting lodge; a peaceful lake; and the highest point in Berlin, Teufelsberg, which is constructed from WWII rubble piled over a Nazi military school.

**3. TACHELES:** This bombed-out department store (p. 60) is a street-art metropolis. It may smell like an outhouse, but the writing on the walls is sure to impress. The best part? It's free to enter and most of the galleries are also free.

**4. KAFFEE BURGER:** Hit the dance floor with the hip 20-some-things at Kaffee Burger (p. 102), where the cover is just €1 Monday through Thursday. The "Drunken Rihanna" cock-tail will have you asking them to not stop the music.

## Walking Tour

When you just can't take the sight of another hipster, escape to the quiet paths and gardens of Berlin's **Tiergarten,** which stretches from the Brandenburg Gate in the east to the Bahnhof Zoo in the west and contains some of the city's most iconic monuments.

**1. ZOOLOGISCHER GARTEN:** The oldest and most popular zoo (p. 52) in Germany is home to almost 1500 species of flora and fauna. Frederick William IV, King of Prussia, donated animals from the pheasantry and menagerie of the Tiergar-ten to comprise the zoo's starter collection.

**2. VICTORY COLUMN:** Heinrich Strack designed the column (p. 65) to commemorate Prussian victory in the Danish-Prussian War. The 35-ton bronze statue of Victoria was later added to celebrate victories in the Austro-Prussian and Franco-Prussian Wars.

**3. NEUE NATIONALGALERIE:** The "temple of light and glass" (p. 59) houses a collection that ranges from early modern art to pieces from the 1960s—more than just light and glass. Plan ahead if you're hoping to see a particular work; the permanent collection is closed when temporary exhibi-tions are on.

**4. CULTURAL FORUM:** This building complex, which com-prises the Philharmonic Hall, the Musical Instrument Museum, and the Chamber Music Hall, near Potsdamer Pl. is the perfect place to get your groove back (p. 119).

**5. REICHSTAG:** After German reunification, intensive restoration brought the meeting place of the German Parliament (p. 56) to its present-day splendor. Climb to the roof and peer through the building's 1200-ton glass dome to witness some democracy.

**6. BRANDENBURG GATE:** On November 9, 2009, 1000 foam dominoes were lined up along the former route of the Berlin Wall, and converged here (p. 65) to celebrate the "Festival of Freedom"—the 20th anniversary of the Wall's fall.

# Three-Day Weekend: Best Bezirke on a Budget

Only in Berlin for three days? Pity. But don't worry—we've got you covered. While most would stick to Mitte for all three days, we've done you one, er, two better. Get your fill of major sights in Mitte, cheap ethnic grub in Kreuzberg, and techno bass in Friederichshain.

## Day One: Mitte

**1. GREATEST HITS:** Mitte is a one-stop shop for some of Berlin's most important museums, memorials, and historic landmarks. Start with the harrowing **Memorial to the Murdered Jews of Europe** (p. 57), then spin through the **Pergamon Museum** or the **Neue Nationalgalerie** (p. 59). If you just can't get enough, purchase a **Tageskarte pass** (p. 141) and hit as many galleries as possible on Mitte's museum island.

**2. HACKESCHER MARKT:** When you've had your fill of museums, pop into a hip cafe on the Hackescher Markt (p. 63) and then dodge flannel-clad Berliners as you bob in and out of cool bookstores, cinemas, and art galleries.

**3. BERLINER PHILHARMONIE:** Be sure to book a ticket in advance for a chance to see this world-renowned symphony orchestra, led by Sir Simon Rattle. Tickets for this one-of-a-kind Berlin experience start at just €7 (p. 119).

**4. KAFFEE BURGER:** A stop at Kaffee Burger (p. 102) will satisfy all of your post-concert needs. Shake it on the dance floor with hip 20-somethings in band T-shirts, or just grab a burger.

## Day Two: Friederichshain

**1. VOLKSPARK:**  Friederichshain's enormous Volkspark (p. 69) will give you the chance to recover and sightsee at the same time. Look for the Märchenbrunnen, a fountain depicting characters from the Brothers Grimm, and check out Mount Klemont, built from the rubble of two enormous WWII bunkers that were demolished in 1950.

**2. EAST SIDE GALLERY:**  The world's largest open-air gallery (p. 69) contains the longest remaining portion of the Wall and one of the best Wall-related sights Berlin has to offer.

**3. TECHNO, PLEASE:**  Friederichshain may look like block after block of deserted warehouses, but any techno aficionado knows that behind these brick walls and past intimidating bouncers lie some of the world's foremost nightclubs. Start with house music at the indoor-outdoor Rosi's (p. 109), pay a visit to the Transformers action figures at Astro-Bar (p. 109), and brace yourself for the trip out to K-17 (p. 109), a massive Diskothek that the tourists haven't discovered yet.

## Day Three: Kreuzberg

**1. CAFÉ MORGANLAND:**  Restorative croissant, anyone? Grab a €5 Parisian breakfast to fuel up for a day of... relaxation? Don't worry, we've built a lot of sitting-on-your-bum into Day Three (p. 92).

**2. TURKISH MARKET:**  Open-air markets are everywhere in Berlin, but this is the real deal. Pick up a cheap new wardrobe or a bunch of free fruit samples as you wander its stalls (p. 124).

**3. ARENA POOL:**  This is a pool (p. 72) that floats in the Spree. Hope you brought your Speedo.

**4. TEMPELHOFER PARK:**  Once the drop point for the Berlin

Airlift, the Tempelhofer Airport was closed in 2008 and converted into a park. So go ahead—work off that wurst with a jog on a former runway (p. 72).

**5. WE'RE NOT IN BERLIN ANYMORE:** Phew. That runway was longer than it looked, huh? Refuel post-jog with a bite from one of Kreuzberg's many ethnic eateries. Try Middle Eastern at Restaurant Rissani (p. 93) or Mexican at Santa Maria (p. 92).

Planning Your Trip

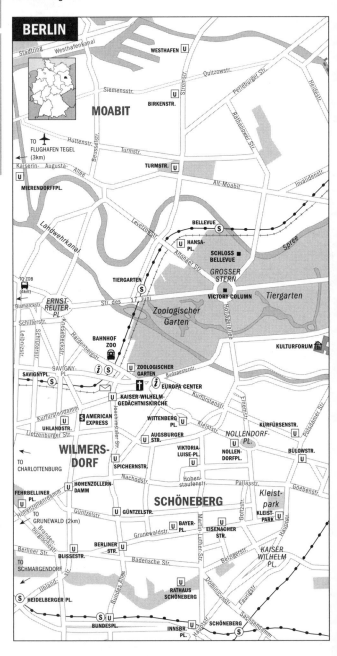

BERLIN

Westhafenkanal

Städtring

WESTHAFEN Ⓤ

Siemensstr.

Quitzowstr.

Perleburger Str.

Stomstr.

BIRKENSTR. Ⓤ

MOABIT

Hüttenstr.

TO ✈ FLUGHAFEN TEGEL (3km)

Turmstr.

Beusselstr.

TURMSTR. Ⓤ

Kaiserin- Augusta- Ⓤ

Alt-Moabit

Invalidenstr.

MIERENDORFFPL.

Landwehrkanal

Levetzowstr.

BELLEVUE Ⓢ

Spree

Ⓤ HANSA-PL.

SCHLOSS BELLEVUE ■

TIERGARTEN Ⓢ

GROSSER STERN

TO ZOB (4km)

ERNST-REUTER-PL.

Str. des 17 Juni

Altonaer Str.

Hofjägeralee

VICTORY COLUMN ■

Tiergarten

Bismarckstr.

Schillerstr.

Leibnizstr.

Schlüterstr.

Knesebeckstr.

Hardenbergstr.

Zoologischer Garten

BAHNHOF ZOO 🚂

KULTURFORUM 🏛

SAVIGNY-PL.

ⓘ Ⓢ

Ⓢ ZOOLOGISCHER GARTEN

Budapesterstr.

SAVIGNYPL. Ⓢ

✉

ⓘ EUROPA CENTER

Ⓤ KAISER-WILHELM-GEDÄCHTNISKIRCHE

Kurfürstenstr.

Joachimstaler Str.

Kurfürstendamm

$ AMERICAN EXPRESS

WITTENBERG PL. Ⓤ

Kleiststr.

Einemstr.

KURFÜRSTENSTR. Ⓤ

Potsdamer Str.

UHLANDSTR. Ⓤ

Lietzenburger Str.

AUGSBURGER STR. Ⓤ

VIKTORIA-LUISE-PL. Ⓤ

NOLLENDORF-PL. Ⓤ

BÜLOWSTR. Ⓤ

WILMERS-DORF

TO CHARLOTTENBURG

SPICHERNSTR. Ⓤ

NOLLENDORFPL. Ⓤ

Goebenstr.

Nachodstr.

Hohenstaufenstr.

Pallasstr.

FEHRBELLINER PL. Ⓤ

HOHENZOLLERN-DAMM Ⓤ

SCHÖNEBERG

Kleist-park

Hohenzollerndamm

Güntzelstr.

GÜNTZELSTR. Ⓤ

Grunewaldstr.

BAYER-PL. Ⓤ

Martin-Luther-Str.

EISENACHER STR. Ⓤ

KLEIST-PARK Ⓤ

Gothar.

Hauptstr.

KAISER WILHELM PL.

TO GRUNEWALD (2km)

Brandenburgischestr.

Berliner Str.

BERLINER STR. Ⓤ

Belziger str.

TO SCHMARGENDORF

Uhland-

BLISSESTR. Ⓤ

Badensche Str.

Bundes Allee

Dominicusstr.

Sachsendamm

HEIDELBERGER PL. Ⓢ

RATHAUS SCHÖNEBERG Ⓤ

Ⓢ Ⓤ

BUNDESPL.

INNSBR. PL. Ⓤ

SCHÖNEBERG Ⓢ

Hauptstr.

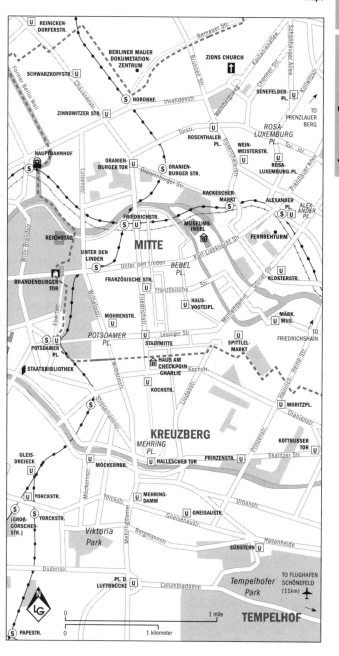

# CHARLOTTENBURG

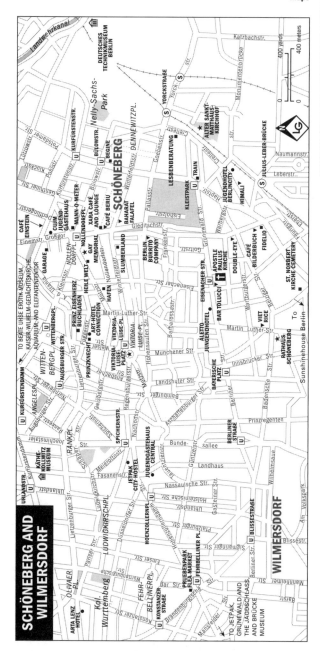

## SCHÖNEBERG AND WILMERSDORF

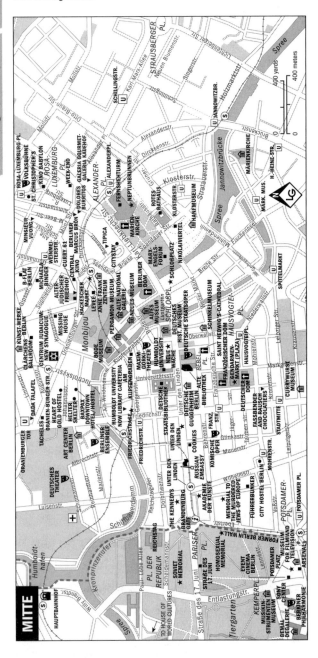

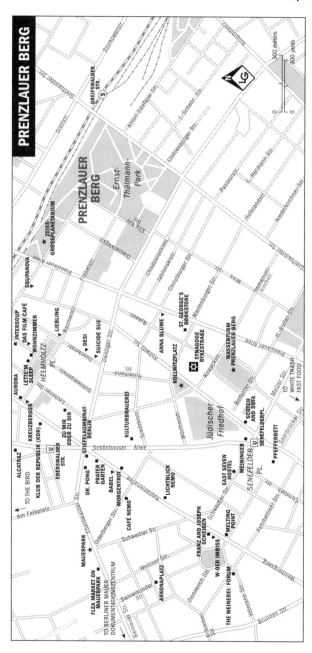

**PRENZLAUER BERG**

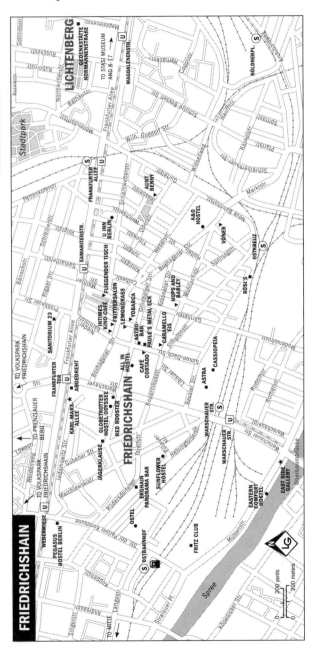

**FRIEDRICHSHAIN**

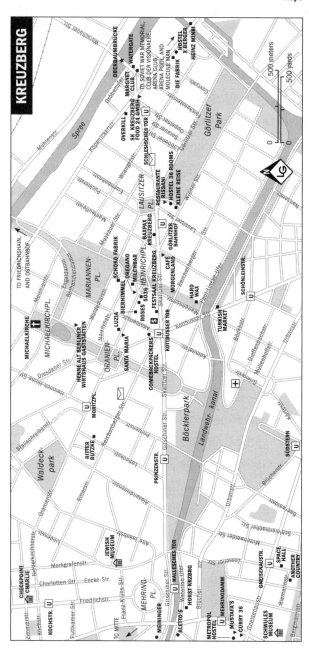

KREUZBERG

TO FRIEDRICHSHAIN, AND OSTBAHNHOF

Spree

OBERBAUMBRÜCKE

WATERGATE

MAGNET CLUB

To SOVIET WAR MEMORIAL, CLUB DER VISIONAERE, ARENA CLUB, ARENA POOL, AND MOLECULE MAN

DIE FABRIK

HOSTEL X-BERGER

HEINZ MINKI

OVERKILL

SK KREUZBERG

FOOD 24 GMBH

SCHLESISCHES TOR

Görlitzer Park

RESTAURANTE RISSANI

HOSTEL 36 ROOMS

KLEINE REISE

GÖRLITZER BAHNHOF

SCHOKO FABRIK

OREGANO

MILCHBAR

HEINRICHPL.

BAXPAX KREUZBERG

ROSES SO36

BIERHIMMEL

LUZIA

FESTSAAL KREUZBERG

CAFÉ MORGENLAND

SANTA MARIA

KOTTBUSSER TOR

HARD WAX

TURKISH MARKET

SCHÖNLEINSTR.

MARIANNEN-PL.

MICHAELKIRCHE

MICHAELKIRCHPL.

HENNE ALT BERLINER WIRTSHAUS GASTSTÄTTEN

ORANIEN-PL.

COMEBACKPACKERS HOSTEL

MORITZPL.

Böcklerpark

Landwehr-kanal

SÜDSTERN

RITTER BUTZKE

PRINZENSTR.

Waldeck-park

JEWISH MUSEUM

MEHRING-PL.

HALLESCHES TOR

HORST-KRZBRG

SPACE HALL

ANOTHER COUNTRY

CHECKPOINT CHARLIE

KOCHSTR.

TO MITTE

MEININGER

ALETTO'S

MEHRINGDAMM

METROPOL HOSTEL

MUSTAFA'S

CURRY 36

SCHWULES MUSEUM

GNEISENAUSTR.

500 meters

500 yards

0

0

LG

# Accommodations

Berlin's accommodations run the gamut from trashy to classy, so it's all up to you (and your wallet) to decide where you fall. And in this big, booming metropolis, most neighborhoods will guarantee you something to do or see—or at least a convenient U-Bahn stop. Travelers with just a few nights in Berlin should consider shelling out for a room in Mitte to be nearby the city's major sights and nightlife. Central Charlottenburg is dotted with cheap pensions and hostels, and the neighborhood's relative affluence practically ensures that you won't stumble into a shady part of town. Schöneberg and Wilmersdorf can be pricey for a solo backpacker, so come with your wolf pack (not the one-man kind) to get the most for your money. Prenzlauer Berg's few hostels are among the best in town: for only a couple bucks more than their counterparts down south in Mitte, you can claim a bed in one of several hostels with a hip staff, spacious rooms, and great proximity to the neighborhood's world-class bars and cafes as well as public transportation that can take you quickly south. A variety of cheap options for backpackers in Friedrichshain provide more than a place to crash after dancing yourself clean—even though that's probably all you'll be doing at the neighborhood's techno clubs. If you're looking to meet fellow travelers, the hostels in Kreuzberg have a great sense of community, and they're just a quick leap to Mitte's sights and an even quicker leap to Berlin's best clubs come nightfall.

## Budget Accommodations

Finding cheap housing in Berlin isn't too difficult—the city is used to the young, broke traveler. **Friedrichshain,** in East Berlin, may be your best bet for inexpensive housing. As a mecca of student life for Berliners and travelers alike, Friedrichshain offers community and affordability—just keep an eye out for the neighborhood's seedier side.

# CHARLOTTENBURG

### 🏨 Berolina Backpacker                    HOSTEL $$

Stuttgarter Pl. 17

☎030 327 09 072; www.berolinabackpacker.de

This quiet hostel rejects the generic with pastel walls and bunk-free dorms. The high ceilings and big windows are a necessary foil to the narrow rooms, some of which even have balconies and intricate molding. Surrounding cafes and close proximity to the U-Bahn and S-Bahn make up for its distance from the rush of the city. Relax and enjoy a breakfast buffet (€7), or the "backpackers' breakfast" (a roll with sausage, cheese, and coffee; €3) in the popular, pale blue dining area, or cook your own food in one of the hostel's many kitchens (communal €1 per day, private €9.50).

▶ 🚊 S3, S5, S9, or S75: Charlottenburg or U7: Wilmersdorfer Str. *i* Free Wi-Fi. Internet access on the hostel computer first 30min. free, €0.50 per 15min. thereafter. Ⓢ Dorms €17; singles €30-36; doubles €37-47; triples €40-55; quads €46-60. 🕐 Reception 8am-1:30am.

### Hotel Pension Cityblick                    PENSION $$$

Kantstr. 71

☎030 323 03 282; www.hotel-cityblick.de

Rich ochre decor, surprisingly large rooms, and exposed timbers make this cheap, conveniently located pension a pleasant surprise. The dark wood paneling that lines the classy breakfast room will make you feel like you're kickin' it in a posh Ku'damm hotel rather than an upper Charlottenburg faux-tel. Just be aware that prices may vary steeply from one week (or even day) to the next. To avoid surprises, email ahead to verify rates at hotel-cityblick@gmx.de.

▶ ⚝ S3, S5, S7 or S75: Charlottenburg, or U7: Wilmersdorfer Str. Ⓢ Singles from €35; doubles from €58; triples from €75; quads from €100. 🕐 Reception 8am-10pm.

## A & O Hostel
HOSTEL $

Joachimstaler Str. 1-3

☎030 809 47 5300; www.aohostels.com

On a busy, commercial street, A & O may not have an ideal location unless you plan on visiting the Erotik Museum 40m away. Its cheap and spacious rooms, dominated by boxy furniture and low ceilings, are reliable despite their surroundings. After all, A & O owns several hostels in Germany, so any possible personality is wiped clean by standardization. The lobby and bar are packed nightly, as is the roof patio despite its resemblance to a dilapidated minigolf course.

▶ ⚝ 30m from Bahnhof Zoo. *i* Breakfast buffet €6. Linens €6. Wi-Fi €5 per day. Ⓢ 8-10 bed dorms from €10; smaller dorms from €15. Singles from €78; doubles from €50. Prices may change significantly in busy months. 🕐 Reception 24hr.

## Frauenhotel Artemisia
HOTEL $$$$

Brandenburgische Str. 18

☎030 873 89 05; www.frauenhotel-berlin.de

This quiet hotel for women was the first of its kind in Germany. Located four flights up in a modern apartment building, its enormous carpeted rooms peek through wide windows onto a silent courtyard. But the city is never far: the rooftop terrace attached to the breakfast room allows a priceless view of the trees and towers of lower Charlottenburg. Named after Italian painter Artemisia Gentileschi, the hotel hosts rotating art exhibitions.

▶ ⚝ U7: Konstanzer Str. *i* Breakfast buffet €8. Free Wi-Fi. Ⓢ Singles €98-108, with bath €128-158; doubles €78-108. Extra bed €20. 🕐 Reception daily 7am-8pm.

## Jugendhotel Berlin
HOSTEL $$$$

Kaiserdamm 3

☎030 322 10 11; www.sportjugendhotel-berlin.de

Though mostly booked by traveling school groups, Jugendhotel Berlin is an uninteresting option that benefits from its proximity to public transportation. Clean, small rooms with lots of light suffer from an unfortunate lack of decoration and character, exemplified by the bare, boxy furniture that looks like it came from an IKEA shopping spree gone wrong. All rooms have full baths and more than half have balconies.

▶ ✈ U2: Sophie-Charlotte-Pl. *i* Breakfast and linens included. Substantial discounts for groups of 10 or more, email for details. Ⓢ Singles €36-49 per person; doubles €32-35 per person; triples €23-30 per person. 🕐 Reception 24hr.

## City Pension Berlin                                                  PENSION $$$$

Stuttgarter Pl. 9

☎030 277 410; www.city-pension.de

The value of proximity to public transportation can never be underestimated, and this hotel is directly across the street from the Charlottenburg U-Bahn/train hub. Oh, and there are rooms too! Travelers at City Pension get ensuite baths, televisions, and small carpeted rooms sans bunk beds. The pension itself is tiny and quiet, and walking through its yellow-lit halls is like eating toffee with your eyes. Also only a block away from the strip mall-lined Wilmersdorfer Pl., City Pension is a convenient and intimate non-hostel option for groups that can keep you all under budget.

▶ ✈ S3, S5, S7, or S75: Charlottenburg, or U7: Wilmersdorfer Str. *i* Breakfast included. Free Wi-Fi. Ⓢ Singles €54; doubles €76; triples €89; quads €104. 🕐 Reception 24hr.

# SCHÖNEBERG AND WILMERSDORF

## 🏨 Jugendhotel Berlincity                                          HOSTEL $$$$

Crellestr. 22

☎030 787 02 130; www.jugendhotel-berlin.de

Jugendhotel Berlincity, which does not offer dorms, is quite a splurge for solo travelers. Fortunately, it's an unforgettable one. Sky-high brick ceilings, wall-consuming windows, stained wood floors, colorful furniture, and quirky paintings make it a real charmer. Check out the painting in the huge breakfast room to see what we mean: it's *The Last Supper,* staged with Disney and Looney Tunes characters, featuring Mickey as Jesus. The hostel strictly prohibits smoking and alcohol, and it's popular with younger groups, but the mere 5min. walk to the U-Bahn provides a quick escape. Plus, the employees tend to be absurdly charismatic, so seek them out if you want some over-20 conversation.

▶ ✈ U7: Kleistpark. *i* Linens and large breakfast buffet included. Wi-Fi €1 per 30min., €5 per 24hr. (can be used over several days). Ⓢ Singles €38, with bath €52; doubles from €60/79; triples €87/102; quads €112/126; quints €124/150; 6-person rooms €146/168. Ⓩ Reception 24hr., although sparse in the late morning and early afternoon.

## JetPAK
HOSTEL $

Pücklerstr. 54

☎030 832 501; www.jetpak.de

You might need a jetpack to reach it, but JetPAK is definitely the most unique hostel you'll find in Schöneberg or Wilmersdorf. Hidden in the Grunewald (Berlin's own extensive forest) and secluded from the city by a 15-minute bus ride and seven-minute hike, JetPAK resembles the summer camp where you lost your virginity more than it does the hostel in which you contracted bedbugs. JetPAK comes complete with long tables and bench seating, a collection of bikes, a woodpile, and a small field where you can emulate your favorite *Fußball* players. Originally an old German army camp, the hostel has been warmed up with colorful walls, comfortable beds, and ubiquitous sofas. And with showers heated by the hostel's own solar panels, JetPAK is also one of Berlin's most environmentally conscious places to kick back and reap the benefits of nature.

▶ ✚ U3: Fehrbelliner Pl. or U9: Güntzelstr. Then, bus #115 (dir. Neuruppiner Str.): Pücklerstr. Follow the signs to Grunewald, and turn left on Pücklerstr. Turn left again at the JetPAK sign, just before the road turns to dirt. *i* Breakfast, linens, and internet included. Ⓢ 8-bed dorms €14; doubles €23.

## JetPAK City Hostel
HOSTEL $$

Pariserstr. 58

☎030 784 43 60; www.jetpak.de

There's nothing like large rooms with pine bunks, big windows, and brightly colored walls to lessen the institutional hostel feel. Owned by the same people who started JetPAK in the Grunewald, this hostel is much more practical and central, if not as one-of-a-kind. The bathrooms are newly tiled, and the common room has couches and a foosball table (they call it "Kicker" in Deutschland). There's even a small cafe on the first floor that serves as the reception area during the day. The rates make this place popular with backpackers, so be sure to book ahead online.

▶ ✚ U3 or U9: Spichernstr. *i* Most breakfast items (including croissants) €1. Linens included. Ⓢ 8-bed dorms from €17; 6-bed from €19; 4-bed from €20. Ⓩ Reception 8am-midnight.

## Jugendgästehaus Central                    HOSTEL $$

Nikolsburger Str. 2-4

☎030 873 01 88 89; www.jugendgaestehaus-central.de

With around 450 beds, Jugendgästehaus is one of Berlin's largest hostels. Due to a heavy student demographic—think the younger, field-trip-taking kind—this hostel is very helpful for the newly arrived, complete with a courteous English-speaking staff, a huge street and train map of Berlin on one of its entrance walls, and its own ATM. Breakfast is included, and seven separate dining rooms cater to the hostel's tremendous population. The rooms are tiny, forgettable, and around 50 years old, but, at these prices, we'll forgive them.

▶ ⚑ U3: Hohenzollernpl. or U9: Güntzelstr. *i* Linens €2.50 for stays of under 3 nights, included for stays of 3 nights or more. ⓢ Mar-Oct dorms with breakfast €24, with ½-board €28, with full board €31; singles €30/34/37. Nov-Feb dorms with breakfast €20, with ½-board €24, with full board €26; singles €26/30/32. ⓩ Reception 24hr.

## Sunshinehouse Berlin                    HOSTEL $$

Wexstr. 8

☎030 826 20 79; www.sunshinehouse-berlin.de

Three three-story buildings and a reception house dot the grassy grounds of Sunshinehouse Berlin, which means that there is, appropriately, plenty of sunshine to be had. Unfortunately, the hostel lies right next to the freeway, so a morning jaunt will leave your ears ringing. But Sunshinehouse provides a solution: common kitchens on every floor of every building allow you to stay inside all day, making yourself breakfast after breakfast. And though you're about as far south as you can get in Schöneberg, a nearby U-Bahn stop keeps you connected to the city above.

▶ ⚑ U4: Innsbrucker Pl. *i* Bathrooms with showers shared between 2 rooms. ⓢ 2- to 3-bed dorms €20; singles €30. ⓩ Reception 9am-9pm.

## Art-Hotel Connection                    HOTEL $$$$

Fuggerstr. 33

☎030 210 21 8800; www.arthotel-connection.de

With deep purple walls, crystal chandeliers, chairs so silver you can nearly see your reflection, and dark wood floors, this hotel is (almost) nothing but class. A gay hotel that describes itself as "hetero-friendly," Art-Hotel boasts some of the most sophisticated style in Schöneberg, especially after recently outfitting all rooms with flatscreens and DVD players. Lest we get too serious, this hotel also offers "playrooms," with slings and other

Accommodations

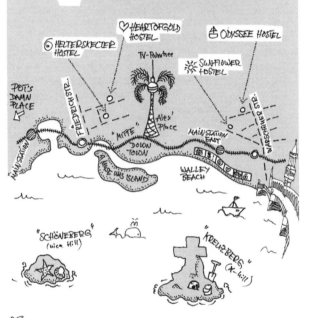

sex toys. Plus, with breakfast offered until 4pm, you can stay in and enjoy the furnishings without missing a meal.

▶ ⚡ U1, U2, or U15: Wittenbergpl. *i* Free Wi-Fi. Ⓢ Singles €49-70, with bath €59-80; doubles with shower €79-120, with full bath €89-130; suites €99-130. Ⓩ Reception 8am-10pm.

# MITTE

### ◾ Circus Hostel                                    HOSTEL $$

Weinbergsweg 1A

☎030 200 03 939; www.circus-berlin.de

You'll know this hostel by the lobby's red-and-white-striped circus tent of a ceiling. Especially clean and colorful rooms are far more fun than their namesake, featuring tremendous wood floors, couches, tables, and a line of wide windows looking down on a broad and bustling intersection. Rooms come with a ton of "extras": podcast audio tours, jogging route maps, quality food recommendations, and outstandingly helpful staff really do make a difference. Plus, a huge basement bar with lounge space may spare you the cost of a U-Bahn ride to find nightlife. The breakfast buffet (€5) is probably the freshest and biggest you'll find in Mitte's hostels.

▶ ⚡ U8: Rosenthaler Pl. It's visible right as you exit the Metro. *i* Lockers €10 deposit. Linens included. Towels €1. Ⓢ 8- to 10-bed dorms €19; 4-bed €23. Singles €86; doubles €56. €2 service charge when paying with credit card. Bikes €12 per day. Segways €35 per day. Ⓩ Reception 24hr.

### ◾ Helter Skelter                                    HOSTEL $

Kalkscheunenstr. 4-5

☎030 280 44 997; www.helterskelterhostel.de

The receptionist's warning: "The bar's open all day, but if you're too drunk at breakfast, we cut you off." Though the furniture is worn and the sheets are old, this hostel is so drunkenly social that you probably won't mind (or notice). Every night, a huge common room fills to the brim with booze-thirsty backpackers, joining the partying skeletons painted on the wall. Rooms are spacious and colorful, and a lack of individual door keys makes the hostel feel more communal (but less secure) than most. If hostel-wide drinking games and late nights are your thing, then take a chance on this place, and years from now (though perhaps not the morning after) you'll remember it as a Berlin highlight.

▶ U6: Oranienburger Tor. From the Metro, head south on Friedrichstr. and take a left on Johannisstr. The hostel is on the 3rd floor through a courtyard. Follow the signs. *i* Breakfast €3; free for stays longer than 3 days. Linens, towel, coffee, and tea included. Free Wi-Fi. Smoking allowed in common area. Kitchen available. 1st 10min. of computer use free, €1 per 30min. thereafter. $ Megadorm €10-14; singles €34; doubles €22-27. ⏰ Reception 24hr.

### Wombat's City Hostel — HOSTEL $$$

Alte Schönhauser Str. 2

☎030 847 10 820; www.wombats-hostels.com

Mod, spotless, comfortable, and with a rooftop bar and terrace—if Wombat's is wrong, we don't want to be right. Though the prices are only a bit higher than average, every detail screams nice hotel, from cushy furniture to sparkling ensuite bathrooms. Relax on the beanbags in the lobby and enjoy the feeling of cleanliness. And if the higher price is still nagging you, keep in mind that your first beer at the rooftop bar is free once you book a bed.

▶ U2: Rosa-Luxemburg-Pl. From the Metro, head through the alleyway across from a small grassy area. *i* Breakfast €3.70. Linens, lockers, and luggage storage included. Free Wi-Fi. Towels €2, free in doubles and apartments. Laundry €4.50. Internet stations €.50 per 20min. Guest kitchen. Non-smoking. $ 4- to 6-bed dorms €22-24; doubles €58-70; apartments €40-50 per person. ⏰ Reception 24hr.

### Heart of Gold Hostel — HOSTEL $

Johannisstr. 11

☎030 290 03 300; www.heartofgold-hostel.de

This isn't a hostel to which you'll simply say, "So long, and thanks for all the fish," but a place that will last especially long in your memory bank, even relative to the rest of Mitte's distinctive offerings. Deeply space-ious rooms, each with a window that actually takes the place of an entire wall, provide all the joys of the final frontier, while an open courtyard and some rooms with balconies provide a perfect vantage point for stargazing. If your nerd powers haven't kicked in by now, this hostel is based entirely on Douglas Adams's *The Hitchhiker's Guide to the Galaxy,* which we hope is your second favorite travel guide. The breakfast and common room may contain more than 42 references to this beloved sci-fi series.

▶ S1, S2, or S25: Oranienburger Str. From the Metro, head south on Tucholskystr., then right on Johannisstr. *i* Breakfast €3.50, free for stays over 3 days. Lockers and towels included. Linens deposit €5. Laundry €4. Key deposit €5. Free Wi-Fi. Padlock deposit €10. $ Megadorms from €10; 7- to 8-bed €12; 4-bed €16. Singles €32; doubles €56. ⏰ Reception 24hr.

### Baxpax Downtown Hotel/Hostel

HOSTEL, HOTEL $

Ziegelstr. 28

☎030 278 74 880; www.baxpax.de

Baxpax Downtown has a bag full of fun hostel tricks. Two above-ground pools are revealed in the summer (one on the lower patio, the other on the roof, where there's a sweet minibar and a spectacular view of the skyline). Downstairs there's a bar with lots of cheap food (€2-9) and there's a club in the basement. Like everything else in the building, the rooms are brightly colored, and spotless wood floors provide a reassuringly classy click to your step. Plus, in a location that manages to be both quiet *and* just a few minutes' walk from iconic Mitte attractions (like Museum Island!), baxpax Downtown promises both a great night and an easy sleep.

▶ 🚇 U6: Oranienburger Tor. From the Metro, head south on Friedrichstr., then turn left on Ziegelstr. ℹ Breakfast €5.50. Linens €2.50. Towels €1, free in doubles and singles. Laundry self-service €5, full-service €8. Key deposit €5. Non-smoking. $ 20-bed dorms €8-31; 8-bed-dorms with showers €12-33; 5-bed dorms with ensuite bathrooms and showers €15-36. Singles €29-92; doubles €54-132. ⏰ Reception 24hr.

### CityStay

HOSTEL $$

Rosenstr. 16

☎030 236 24 031; www.citystay.de

A central location, a beautiful, well-kept courtyard, and an expansive cafe lounge separate this hostel from the pack. Rooms are small, smell like several generations of backpackers, and lack any furniture or decoration other than a couple of plastic chairs, but they benefit from huge windows and cushy beds. You know what really seals the deal? A 2min. walk to Museum Island, Unter den Linden, and Alexanderpl.

▶ 🚇 U5, U8, S5, S7, S9, or S75: Alexanderpl. From the Metro, head south on Karl-Liebknecht-Str., then turn right halfway down the block onto Rosenstr. ℹ Lockers €10 deposit. Linens €2.50, with ISIC free. Laundry €5. Towels €5 deposit. 5 computers in lobby €3 per hr. $ 8-bed dorms €17; 4-bed €21. Doubles €50, with private shower €65. ⏰ Reception 24hr.

### St. Christopher's

HOSTEL $

Rosa Luxembourg Str. 41

☎030 814 53 960; www.st-christophers.co.uk

It's rare you find a hostel bar with €1 Jager shots, but St.

Christopher's delivers this and the inevitable crazy Jager nights. A roomy bar complemented by indoor and outdoor seating and a broad loft space with a pool table and loads of lounging space ensure that your stay won't lack social time. Rooms, though, are small and boring, with cheesy plastic furniture and fuzzy blue carpeting that scream "hostel." Still, it's a bargain for backpackers, and apartments with kitchens are a cheap option for long-term stays.

▶ ✿ U2: Rosa-Luxemburg-Pl. Right next to the Metro. *i* Breakfast, luggage storage, lockers, and linens included. Towels €1. Internet €2 per hr. Non-smoking. Ⓢ Dorms €9-20; doubles €35-50; quads €60-96. Prices can vary by day based on availability. ☾ Reception 24hr. Bar open daily until 3am. Happy Hour daily 5-10pm.

## Three Little Pigs Hostel                                    HOSTEL $

Stresemannstr. 66

☎030 326 62 955; www.three-little-pigs.de

An enormous century-old former abbey serves as this hostel's lobby. Hidden far back in a silent courtyard, Three Little Pigs guarantees a quiet place to sleep, although consequently provides little in the way of nightlife. Tremendously spacious and bright rooms gain some color with floral designs, and large windows allow you to gaze quietly on the beautiful brick complex that surrounds you. Unfortunately, with a 3min. walk between the hostel and a non-central S-Bahn station, staying here will require a hefty commute to reach prime Mitte destinations (20min. or so).

▶ ✿ S1, S2, or S25: Anhalter Bahnhof. From the Metro, head south on Stresemannstr. and turn left into a long courtyard. *i* Breakfast €5. Linens €2.50. Towel €1. Lockers included. Free Wi-Fi. Laundry €5. 4 computers with Internet access €2 per hr. Bike rental €12 per day. Guest kitchen. Parking available. Ⓢ 6- to 8-bed dorms €11-17; singles €34-36; doubles €44-48. ☾ Reception 24hr.

## Baxpax Mitte                                                HOSTEL $

Chausseestr. 102

☎030 283 90 965; www.baxpax.de/mittes-backpacker

Recently refurbished and repainted rooms make Baxpax Mitte one of the most interesting places to catch some zzzs. Hallways covered from floor to ceiling with mystical murals, including a glittery mountainscape, lead to some of the quirkiest themed dorms and private rooms you'll find. The "Beetle Room" features a tangled, metal sculpture in the center of its ceiling; the

"Miró Room" hides a jittery mural based on the abstract work of its namesake; and the "Fruit of the Loom" room may make you crave fruit-snacks more than underwear with its fruity, neon stripes. A small common room with a tiny kitchen fails to match the social spaces of other Mitte hostels, and the area is too far north to guarantee nearby nightlife, but you may be too busy studying the wall behind your roommate's bed to notice.

▶ U6: Naturkundemuseum. From the Metro, head north on Chausseestr. *i* Guest kitchen available. Breakfast €5.50. Linens €2.50. Towels €1. Full-service laundry €7. 2 Internet kiosks €2 per hr. Key deposit €10. Happy hour at small in-house bar 7-8pm. Non-smoking. $ 10- to 12-bed dorms €6-31; 8-bed €7-33; 6-bed €9-34. Doubles €50-86, with private toilet €56-92. ⏰ Reception 24hr.

# PRENZLAUER BERG

## Pfefferbett — HOSTEL $

Christinenstr. 18-19

☎030 939 35 858; www.pfefferbett.de

This 19th-century brick building features high, arched ceilings, giant pillars, exposed beams, and a cathedral-sized common room. This may sound a little scary and impersonal, but, fortunately, green walls, two patios (one in a shaded garden), a fireplace, and an energetic staff with a taste for house music fill this huge space with a requisite amount of warmth. The rooms feature some of the highest brick ceilings you'll have seen in a hostel and accommodate massive metal bunks. Some fun features, including sports projected on the common room wall, a pool table, and a fully stocked bar, promise constant entertainment between your assaults on the town.

▶ U2: Senefelderpl. From the Metro, exit through the southernmost exit. Look immediately to your right, and there will be a sign in a large doorway directing you to Pfefferbett. Go up the left flight of stairs, turn right at the top, and walk to the back of the shaded, cluttered courtyard. Turn left at the back. The hostel is just around the corner. *i* Breakfast €4. Linens €2.50. Free Wi-Fi in common room. Women-only dorms available. $ 8-bed dorms from €12; 6-bed from €15, with shower from €19; 4-bed from €20. Singles with bath from €47; doubles with bath €64. ⏰ Reception 24hr.

Accommodations

### East Seven Hostel

HOSTEL $$

Schwedter Str. 7

☎030 936 22 240; www.eastseven.de

A strict no-bunk policy makes this retro hostel an especially comfortable place to lay your head. The indoor lounge area and the gorgeous, grill-bedecked back patio are popular hangouts for backpackers who appreciate cold beer specials (€1) and the finer things. Rooms are spacious, with hardwood floors, old windows, and subtle-hued stripes that would make Martha Stewart proud. The young, personable staff even make checking in and out a real treat; be sure to take advantage of their refreshingly opinionated expertise on the city.

▶ U2: Senefelderpl. From the Metro, exit through the northernmost entrance, and you'll be near Schwedter Str. Cross Schönhauser Allee to the west side, then walk west on Schwedter Str. The hostel is on the right. *i* Linens included. Free Wi-Fi. Internet terminals €0.50 per 20min. $ Mar-Oct 8-bed dorms €18; 4-bed with bath €22. Singles €38; doubles €52; triples €68. Nov-Feb 8-bed dorms €14; 4-bed with bath €19. Singles €31; doubles 44; triples €57. Bike rental €10 per day. ⏰ Reception 7am-midnight.

### Lette'm Sleep Hostel

HOSTEL $$

Lettestr. 7

☎030 447 33 623; www.backpackers.de

As one of Berlin's very first hostels, Lette'm Sleep knows what it's doing. A huge amount of floor space ensures that you won't awkwardly brush up against your dorm-mates in the morning, and wide windows admit the sights and sounds of Helmholtzpl., which is home to a shady park and P'Berg's highest concentration of cool cafes. The fluorescent paint job, a communal kitchen with mattress-like couches, and a staff that actually enjoys conversing with guests make this far more than just a place to crash.

▶ U2: Eberswalder Str. From the Metro, head east on Danziger Str., turn left on Lynchener Str., then turn right on Lettestr., which is immediately past the park. The hostel will be on your left. *i* Linens included. Each room has a sink. Free Wi-Fi. $ Apr-Oct 3- to 7-bed dorms €17-21; doubles with kitchenette €49; triples with kitchenette €84. Nov-Mar 4- to 7-bed dorms €16-20; doubles with kitchenette €40; triples with kitchenette €75. ⏰ Reception 24hr.

## Alcatraz
HOSTEL $$

Schönhauser Allee 133a

☎030 484 96 815; www.alcatraz-backpacker.de

Don't worry: Alcatraz is no island prison. It has a great, accessible location, and your roommates will only have committed several murders *in your imagination.* Plus, a cozy "Chill-Out Room," outfitted with a foosball table, a TV, and several couches will make you feel far more comfortable than that time you spent the night in jail for "public drunkenness." Unfortunately, the rooms are so small and bare that you might begin to suspect that the name has more accuracy than you'd hoped. Instead of sitting in your room contemplating your remorse, check out the beautiful central courtyard and the bright, cartoonish murals lining the halls, or bake a cake in the common kitchen.

▶ ✪ U2: Eberswalder Str. From the Metro, head north on Schönhauser Allee. The hostel will be on the left. *i* Free Wi-Fi. Fully equipped kitchen. Breakfast €2. Linens €2. Bike rental €10 per day. Ⓢ Mar-Oct 8-bed dorms €16; 4-bed €18. Singles €40; doubles €50; triples €69. Nov-Feb 8-bed dorms €13; 4-bed €15. Singles €35; doubles €44; triples €57. Cash only. ◷ Reception 24hr.

# FRIEDRICHSHAIN

### ▨ Sunflower Hostel
HOSTEL $

Helsingforser Str. 17

☎030 440 44 250; www.sunflower-hostel.de

In one hall, Darth Vader kicks an arcade game. In another, Sesame Street characters and pixelated Space Invaders battle for your attention. The lobby's young, personable staff and indie electro mix are all just one Habermas book away from a college cafe. The sum of all of these elements? A real blossom of a hostel. Each room and hallway is ecstatically and hilariously painted with the best breed of Berlin quirkiness. Yet with tremendous windows and a wealth of floor space that just invites cartwheels, these rooms aren't only about the walls. Seven minutes from the Simon-Dach restaurant strip, and about five from the club scene, this hostel is only somewhat off the beaten path but far enough off its rocker to make a lasting impression.

▶ ✪ U1, S3, S5, S7, S9 or S75: Warschauer Str. From the Metro, walk north on Warschauer Str., turn left on Helsingforser Str., and the hostel will be on your right. *i* Breakfast €3. Linens and padlocks €3 deposit. Laundry €4.50. Free Wi-Fi. Ⓢ 7- to 8-bed dorms €10-15; 5- to 6-bed

€13-17. Singles €30-37; doubles €38-48; apartments €70-75. Bikes €12 per day. ⏰ Reception 24hr.

### Globetrotter Hostel Odyssee

HOSTEL $$

Grünberger Str. 23

☎030 290 00 081; www.globetrotterhostel

Hi-scary-ous medieval statues and walls covered in jagged fragments of old wooden crates greet you as you enter Globetrotter Hostel's spacious lobby, where a chalkboard calendar lists the concerts and parties in Berlin for every day of the week. Though some of these details, along with the dark brown paint job, may seem disconcertingly metal at first, they are only part of this bright and busy hostel. Muraled walls, an ivy facade, and a shaded courtyard out back are highlights, along with a 22-bed dorm, which, by virtue of well-placed barriers and clever bed positioning, actually feels far more private than most 8-bed dorms.

▶ 🚏 U5: Frankfurter Tor. From the Metro, walk south on Warschauer Str., then turn right on Grünberger Str. The hostel will be on your right, halfway down the block. ℹ Breakfast €8. Linens €3 deposit. Free Wi-Fi. Internet terminals €0.50 per 20min. $ 22-bed dorms €13-19; 8-bed €14-20; 6-bed €16-22; 4- to 5-bed €18-24. Singles €36-49; doubles €47-59, with shower €54-69. Prices vary, so check the calendar on the website for precise rates. Credit card min. €25. ⏰ Reception 24hr.

### U Inn Berlin Hostel

HOSTEL $$

Finowstr. 36

☎030 330 24 410; www.uinnberlinhostel.com

The crowning detail of this tiny hostel is probably that every Friday at 7pm, the employees and guests come together to cook organic food in the guest kitchen. If this is your idea of a memorable Friday evening, then this is definitely the hostel for you. U Inn Berlin doesn't consider itself a party hostel: there's a no-alcohol policy, and quiet hours start at 10pm. But with only two floors, a beautiful little common room, and potted plants galore, it's a wonderfully homey community to join for a couple days. Plus, the small and somewhat dim rooms benefit from eclectic paint coats based on different U- and S-Bahn lines.

▶ 🚏 U5: Frankfurter Allee. From the Metro, walk west on Frankfurter Allee, then turn left on Finowstr. The hostel is hidden to the left. ℹ Breakfast €2. Linens €2. Hostel internet terminals €1 per 20min. Daily supplement to pay for "greening" the cleaning supplies and buying fair trade, organic coffee €0.50. $ Apr-Oct 8-bed dorms €15; 5-bed €18; 4-bed €19. Singles €29; doubles €50; triples €69. Nov-Mar 8-bed dorms €13; 5-bed €16; 4-bed €17. Singles €25; doubles €46; triples €63. ⏰ Reception 7am-1am.

## All In Hostel

HOSTEL $

Grünberger Str. 54

☎030 288 76 83; www.all-in-hostel.com

Right in the midst of the Simon-Dach restaurant strip, this hostel has the best location of any on the list, but not by quite enough of a margin to make up for otherwise underwhelming facilities. Dorms are some of the tiniest: bunks are actually pressed up against each other, and moving around with several other people in the room is a tight squeeze. Though the rooms may be small, the massive common room contains a fleet of spotless tables, a bar, a pool table, two TVs, and a smoking room.

▶ 🚇 U5: Frankfurter Tor. From the Metro, walk south on Warschauer Str., turn left on Grünberger Str., and look for a slightly inconspicuous, orange-lettered sign on your right. The hostel is set back from the street by a small courtyard. ℹ Breakfast €5. Linens €3 for 1st night. Wi-Fi €1 per hr., €5 per 24hr. Hostel internet terminal €1 per 20min. [$] 10-bed dorms €10; 6-bed with bath €18. Singles with bath €39; doubles with bath €44. ⏰ Reception 24hr.

## Ostel

HOSTEL $$

Wriezener Karree 5

☎030 257 68 660; www.ostel.eu

No, it's not a typo. "Ost" means "east" in German, and this hostel delivers more east than Easter. Located in a DDR flat and filled with original DDR furniture and wallpaper (think glossy, boxy bookshelves and orange-striped walls that are so 1950s, they'll make you want to mow your lawn and have seven kids), Ostel is a respectable attempt at recreating daily life from before the wall's fall. Though a bit of a splurge, a stay in the "Pioneer Camp" dorm is like living in a condo with people you don't know: it consists of two huge six-bed rooms with large tables and ensuite bathrooms. Perhaps the only detail that will remind you you're still living in a post-wall Berlin is the beach volleyball court out front.

▶ 🚇 S3, S5, S7, S9, or S75: Ostbahnhof. From the Metro, walk north on Str. der Pariser Kommune, and turn right at the Ostel Restaurant. Follow the sidewalk to the next building, and turn left into the narrow street with the beach volleyball court. ℹ Breakfast €6.50. Linens and towels included. [$] "Pioneer Camp" 12-bed dorms €15; singles €33; doubles €54. Bikes €9 per day. ⏰ Reception 24hr.

### Eastern Comfort Hostel
HOSTEL $$

Mühlenstr. 73-77

☎030 667 63 806; www.eastern-comfort.com

Grab your swim trunks and your flippy-floppies, 'cause this hostel-boat is straight flowin' on the Spree. Guests rent rooms in cabins, with fold-down beds and portals for windows. Rooms are closet-sized, but you're on a boat, backpacker! The truly adventurous can rent a tent and sleep on the top deck for the cheapest view of the big blue watery road. Every Wednesday, travelers enjoy a Language Party, where guests get together to enjoy the hostel's international clientele.

▶ 🚇 U1, S3, S5, S7, S9, or S75: Warschauer Str. ℹ Breakfast €4.50. Linens €5. Free Wi-Fi. Internet €1 per 30min. 2-night min. stay on weekends. $ Tents €12; 4- or 5-bed dorms €16; singles with bath €50; doubles with bath €58; triples with bath €69; quads with bath €76. ⏰ Reception 8am-midnight.



## KREUZBERG

### 👍 Comebackpackers Hostel
HOSTEL $$

Adalbertstr. 97

☎030 600 57 527; www.comebackpackers.com

In a long, curved building on a busy square, this hostel looks futuristic but delivers a refreshing dose of the basics: light, space, and entertainment. Windows take up nearly three walls of the common room and an entire wall of each spacious bedroom, so there's plenty of sunlight to wake you up when you accidentally set your phone's alarm clock to PM. The roof terrace that lines the common room has only dead plants, rocks, and a bird cage with plastic birds, but it provides a great view of the bustle below, a perfect place to smoke or drink, and, in the summer, grill. Jittery wall murals and couches in the hall add some interest, as does a funny, young staff with an affinity for hardcore punk. Let's hope this is what hostels are like in the future.

▶ 🚇 U1 or U8: Kotbusser Tor. From the Metro, walk up Adalbertstr. and turn into the curved alleyway to your left. The hostel is on the left. ℹ Continental breakfast €3. Coffee and linens included. Free Wi-Fi. Full-service laundry €5. Towel €2. Key deposit €10. $ Dorms €14-20. Cash only. ⏰ Reception 24hr.

## Metropol Hostel

HOSTEL $

Mehringdamm 32

☎030 259 40 890; www.metropolhostel-berlin.com

So you're in a total food coma from eating *zwei Würste ohne Darm* at **Curry 36** and then wandering about 5 ft. and downing a dürüm (Turkish wrap filled with döner kebab) at **Mustafa's.** Where, oh, where can you sleep this off? Well, turn around, my friend, because Metropol Hostel is right behind you. Don't let the century-old doors fool you: this hostel opened in July 2010 and as mod as they come. The long common room overlooks the busy Mehringdamm, and a bar, some booths, and fleets of cushy seats add hominess. The rooms are almost too spacious, but wide wood floors make you appreciate the emptiness. Almost universally ensuite bathrooms, Wi-Fi everywhere, and spotless rooms make this huge hostel feel more like a hotel.

▶ U6 or U7: Mehringdamm. From the Metro, cross to the west side of Mehringdamm and walk south past the building that looks like a cartoon version of a Medieval castle. The hostel is on the 4th floor of a well-labeled building. *i* Breakfast, lockers, luggage storage, safe, and towels included. Linens €2. Free Wi-Fi. Shower and toilet in every room. $ 6-to 10-bed dorms €9-21, with bath €12-29; singles €39-69; doubles €50-79. ⏰ Reception 24hr.

## Hostel X Berger

HOSTEL $

Schlesische Str. 22

☎030 695 31 863; www.hostelxberger.com

For the quickest jump to the coolest clubs in Berlin, no one outdoes Hostel X Berger, which is right along the canal. The rooms are small, the bunks old, and the mattresses frayed, but thick curtains block out the sun from your inevitably blood-shot eyes. A foggy downstairs smoking room with a pool table feels like an underground club filled with punks, potheads, and people with pink hair. Some unique extra features let you play hard, like a late check-out time (2pm), free coffee for your after-party blues, and a communal kitchen where you can grab a snack before you hit the hay.

▶ U1: Schlesisches Tor. From the Metro, head southeast on Schlesische Str. The hostel is on the right, just before the canal. *i* Linens €2. Laundry €4. Towel €1. Luggage storage included. 2 internet computers. Lock rental €1. Key deposit €10. Free Wi-Fi. $ 16-bed dorms €8-13, 4-bed €15-19. Singles €30-37; doubles €38-48. ⏰ Reception 24hr. Guest kitchen open 24hr.

## baxpax Kreuzberg                                            HOSTEL $$

Skalitzer Str. 104

☎030 695 18 322; www.baxpax.de

If we were measuring by common space, baxpax Kreuzberg would take the proverbial hostel cake. A huge lobby with a bar and couches; a venti-sized interior common room with all sorts of cushy lounge furniture, foosball, and a flatscreen; and a long, bright common kitchen connected to a frighteningly agreeable roof terrace guarantee some space to converse. Each room has a different country as a theme, and, like countries, not all rooms are created equal: while the Italian room is spacious, bright, and covered in football posters, most of the German room is taken up by a vintage Volkswagen Bug with a bed inside. The Wi-Fi can be unreliable, but otherwise this fun, colorful hostel is a real rose.

▶ ♯ U1: Görlitzer Bahnhof. From the Metro, cross to the north side of Skalitzer Str. and walk about halfway down the block. Enter the labeled courtyard to the left; the hostel will be at the end of the courtyard, to the right, on the 3rd floor. *i* Breakfast €1-2.50. Linens and towel €2.50. Internet terminals €2 per hr. Laundry €7. Lockers, luggage storage, and safe included. Guests can smoke in the common room after 6pm. $ 32-bed dorms €8-28; 8-bed €12-33. Singles €25-54; doubles €40-98, with bath €48-120; quads €64-176. ☼ Reception 24hr.

## Meininger                                                   HOSTEL $

Hallesches Ufer 30

☎030 983 21 075; www.meininger-hotels.com

Meininger can only approximate the sense of community at some of its Kreuzberg peers, but it does provide top-notch service and plenty of common space. Graffiti-lined walls lead to a quaint guest kitchen that never closes, all-you-can-eat breakfast graces a roomy roof terrace, and a relaxed bar serves drinks daily after 7pm. The rooms definitely beat the mean: each has a TV and the carpets are as spotless as a summer sky. With proximity to a vertical/horizontal U-Bahn crossroads, this hostel ensures that Mitte is just a quick hop away, assuming you can figure out which train to take.

▶ ♯ U1 or U6: Hallesches Tor. From the Metro, head west on Gitschiner Str., cross Mehringdamm, and continue heading west on Hallesches Ufer. *i* Linens and lockers included. Breakfast €4. Laundry €5. Towel €1, plus €5 deposit. Lock deposit €5. Late riser fee €5. $ 8-bed dorms €12-18; 4-bed €14-21. Singles €42-55; doubles €54-66. ☼ Reception 24hr. Roof terrace open daily until 10pm.

## Aletto's

HOSTEL $$$$

Tempelhofer Ufer 8-9

☎030 259 30 480; www.aletto.de

In spite of a logo that resembles a dildo with a boomerang through its head (ouch!...ouch!), Aletto keeps it clean for groups of travelers. Though rooms accommodate multiple guests, each is private and must be booked in its entirety. The Hostel Oscar (Hoscar?) nominees for Best Amenities at an Aletto in Kreuzberg are: large free breakfast, starring eggs; the mini-cinema, starring free DVD rentals; and the huge common spaces, starring free Wi-Fi, a full service bar, and a foosball table. Light pine bunks and proud pictures of that rascally dildo enchant every room.

▸ 🚇 U1 or U6: Hallesches Tor. From the Metro, cross to the south side of the canal, then head west, crossing over Mehringdamm to reach Tempelhofer Ufer. The hostel will be about halfway down the block. *i* Linens, luggage storage, and towels included. Internet terminals €2 per hr. ATM available in lobby. [$] Singles €35-55; doubles €39-75; quads €64-124. ⏰Reception 24hr.

## Hostel 36 Rooms

HOSTEL $$

Spreewaldpl. 8

☎030 530 86 398; www.36rooms.com

A preserved 1878 townhouse is the site of this gorgeous hostel, with wood floors, high ceilings, and beautiful molding. Large, bright rooms and an outdoor patio are robbed of some fun by the hostel's no-outside-alcohol policy, but guests can get a beer at the hostel bar or wait until Thursday, Friday, and Saturday, when an underground club rocks in the hostel's basement. Hot travelers (like you) can also dip in the wave pool across the street at the hostel's discounted price (€4 per hr., students €3 per hr.). The Old-World rooms are adorned with chandeliers and vintage furniture but unfortunately may carry a similarly Old-World smell.

▸ 🚇 U1: Görlitzer Bahnhof. From the Metro, head east on Skalitzer Str. Turn right on Spreewaldpl., just before the park. *i* Locker rental €2. Linens €2.50. Towels €2. Key deposit €10. [$] 8-bed dorms €14-16; 4-bed €18-20. Singles €35-38; doubles €50-56. Bike rental €10 per day. ⏰ Reception 24hr. Patio and kitchen open daily until 10pm.

# Sights

Berlin is bursting at the seams with memorable sights, most of which won't even cost you a euro. All of the memorials, picturesque streets, and most of the churches are open for your unlimited and untaxed viewing pleasure. Check Mitte for by far the greatest concentration of sights, many of which are free. Head to Charlottenburg if it's a Baroque palace you're after, or retreat to Schöneberg's Grunewald for a pastoral escape. Prenzlauer Berg is better known for hip shops and cafes than sights, but the city's premier Wall museum, Berliner Mauer Dokumentationszentrum, is a must-see. Friederichshain offers more Cold War era sights, including the Stasi Museum and the East Side Gallery, which contains the longest remaining portion of the Berlin Wall. Kreuzberg is less known for its sights, but there are a handful of memorials, museums, and parks worth visiting if you're in the area. So grab a map and get going.

## Budget Sights

As in most European cities, it won't bust your budget to visit many of Berlin's museums. Most, if not all, offer student discounts and some—like many on the **Museum Island** in Mitte—have combined pass options that can save you a lot of dough. Also, half of the sights to see in Berlin are parts of the city itself, like parks and monuments, and are a completely free way to spend your free time. Check Prenzlauer Berg for the hippest park in Berlin, **Mauerpark.**

# CHARLOTTENBURG

Most of Berlin's sights are located outside of the more residential Charlottenburg, closer to the center of the city. That said, Charlottenburg has certain sights that recommend themselves to the traveler with more than a day or two to spend in Berlin. Unique museums, grand palaces, and one of the world's most historic stadiums are spread out all over the neighborhood—and we mean *all* over.

### 🔲 Schloß Charlottenburg                          PALACE

Spandauer Damm 10-22

☎030 320 92 75

This expansive Baroque palace, commissioned by Friedrich I in the 1600s as a gift for his wife, Sophia-Charlotte, could have been one of the more indulgent summer homes featured on 17th-century *Cribs.* **Altes Schloß,** the Schloß's oldest section (marked by a blue dome in the middle of the courtyard), flaunts historic furnishings (much of them reconstructed after WWII), elaborate gilding, and neck-strainingly splendid ceiling murals. **Neuer Flügel** (New Wing) will make you feel poor and tiny with basketball-court-sized receiving rooms and the more somber royal chambers. **Neuer Pavillon** houses a museum dedicated to Prussian architect Karl Friedrich Schinkel. Other sections include the **Belvedere,** a small building containing the royal family's obscenely extensive porcelain collection, and the **Mausoleum,** where the remains of most of the family, well, remain. Behind the palace you'll find the exquisitely manicured Schloßgarten, full of small lakes, fountains, and those secretive, forested paths you've always wanted to walk along.

▶ 🚌 Bus #M45 from Bahnhof Zoo to Luisenpl./Schloß Charlottenburg or

**Sights**

U2: Sophie-Charlotte Pl. Ⓢ Altes Schloß €12, students €8; Neuer Flügel €6/5; Belvedere €3/2.50; Mausoleum free. A Tageskarte (day ticket; €15, students €11) covers them all. Audio tours (available in English) included with admission. 🕐 Altes Schloß open Apr-Oct Tu-Su 10am-6pm; Nov-Mar Tu-F 10am-5pm, Sa-Su noon-4pm. Neuer Flügel open year-round M and W-Su 10am-6pm. Belvedere open Apr-Oct daily 10am-6pm, Nov-Mar daily noon-5pm. Mausoleum open Apr-Oct 10am-6pm.

### 🖼 Käthe-Kollwitz-Museum                                    MUSEUM
Fasanenstr. 24
☎030 882 52 10; www.kaethe-kollwitz.de

Through both World Wars, Käthe Kollwitz, a member of the Berlin *Sezession* (Secession) movement and one of Germany's most prominent 20th-century artists, protested war and the situation of the working class with haunting sketches, etchings, woodcuts, sculptures and charcoal drawings of death, poverty, and starvation. The series of works entitled "A Weaver's Revolt" on the second floor are the drawings that skyrocketed Kollwitz to fame. The death of the artist's own son, who was killed in Russia in WWII, provides a wrenching emotional authenticity to her depictions of death, pregnancy, and starvation as well as her bleak self-portraits. Her almost entirely black works contrast powerfully with the museum's bright, all-white interior.

▶ ⚇ U1: Uhlandstr. Ⓢ €6, students €3. 🕐 Open daily 11am-6pm.

### Museum Berggruen                                            MUSEUM
Schloßstr. 1
☎030 326 95 80

Think Picasso is a jerk whose art doesn't deserve the hype? This sunny museum will obliterate your anti-Picasso sentiments. The first and second floors are Picasso-packed, with the occasional foray into Matisse and African masks. The third floor showcases intensely abstract paintings by Bauhaus teacher Paul Klee, as well as Alberto Giacometti's super-skinny sculptures of the human form. A wide spectrum of works from across Picasso's career allows you to track the development of the big-lipped, warped-faced figures that have always confounded you, displayed most beautifully in *Le matador et femme nue* (The matador and the nude woman).

▶ ⚇ Bus #M45 from Bahnhof Zoo to Luisenpl./Schloß Charlottenburg or U2: Sophie-Charlotte Pl. 𝑖 Ticket covers entry to Berggruen Museum, Bröhan-museum, and Sammlung Scharf-Gerstenberg on the same day. Ⓢ €8, students €4, children free. Audio guide included. 🕐 Open Tu-Su 10am-6pm.

## Olympiastadion

STADIUM

Olympischer Pl. 3 (Visitors Center)

☎030 250 02 322; www.olypiastadion-berlin.de

This massive Nazi-built stadium comes in a close second to Tempelhof Airport in the list of monumental Third Reich buildings in Berlin. It was erected for the infamous 1936 Olympic Games, in which African-American track and field athlete Jesse Owens won four gold medals. Hitler refused to congratulate Owens, who has since been honored with a Berlin street, Jesse-Owens-Allee. Owens' name has also been engraved into the side of the stadium with the other 1936 gold medal winners. The six stone pillars flanking the stadium were originally intended to signify the unity of the six "tribes" of ethnicities that Hitler believed fed into true German heritage. Recent uses have included the 2006 World Cup final. The independently operated **Glockenturm** (bell tower) houses an exhibit on the history of German athletics and provides a great lookout point.

▸ 🚏 S5, S7, or U2: Olympia-Stadion. For Glockenturm, S5 or S7: Pichelsburg. $ €4, students €3. Guided tour €8, students €7, under 6 free. Audioguides €3.50. ⏰ Open daily Apr-May 9am-7pm, from June to mid-Sept 9am-8pm; from mid-Sept to Oct 9am-7pm; Nov-Mar 9am-4pm. Last entry 30min. before close. Glockenturm open daily 9am-6pm.

## Bröhanmuseum

MUSEUM

Schloßstr. 1A

☎030 326 90 600; www.broehan-museum.de

If you're wondering where all the stuff you couldn't sell at your great-aunt's estate sale went, here it is. Though a museum dedicated to bro version of Dragonball Z might have been more captivating, these Art Nouveau and Art Deco paintings, housewares, and furniture will still wow you. Along with figurines and lampshades that resemble the knicknacks you sneered at (and now regret not buying) at neighborhood garage sales, the ground floor also pairs several groupings of period furniture with paintings from the same era (1889-1939). However, don't expect the highest of the high: these paintings, like the household objects that surround them, are sometimes absurdly grounded in their time, including giggle-worthy idealizations of factory workers. The second floor is a small gallery dedicated to the modernist Berlin *Sezession* painters, and the top floor houses special exhibitions, like a recent all-silver exhibit.

▸ 🚏 Bus #M45 from Bahnhof Zoo to Luisenpl./Schloß Charlottenburg or U2: Sophie-Charlotte Pl. The museum is next to the Bergguen, across from the

Schloß. $ €6, students €4. Ticket covers entry to Berggruen Museum, Bröhanmuseum, and Sammlung Scharf-Gerstenberg on the same day. ⏰ Open Tu-Su 10am-6pm.

### Zoologischer Garten — ZOO

8 Hardenberg Pl.

☎030 254 010; www.zoo-berlin.de; www.aquarium-berlin.de

Germany's oldest zoo houses around 14,000 animals of 1500 species, most in open-air habitats connected by winding pathways under dense cover of trees. Unfortunately, the zoo's biggest asset, über-cute polar cub 📷 **Knut,** recently died, but there are still some fluffy options, like the white wolf, who somehow pulls off a dangerous combination of adorable and badass. Also, there is highly contested talk that Knut may be stuffed in the near future, so keep your eyes peeled. With a few uninteresting tanks (and one obese shark), the **Aquarium**, which lies inside the zoo, proves that fish may actually be boring after all.

▶ 🚏 U2 or U9: Zoological Garten, or S5, S7 or S75: Bahnhof Zoo. Main entrance is across from the Europa Center. $ Zoo €13, students €10, children €6.50. Aquarium €12, students €9, children €6. Combination to zoo and aquarium €20/15/10. ⏰ Open daily Jan 1-Mar 19 9am-5pm; Mar 20-Oct 3 9am-7pm; Oct 4-Dec 31 9am-5pm. Last entry 1hr. before close.

## SCHÖNEBERG AND WILMERSDORF

Schöneberg sights are a mix of pastoral parks and whatever cultural tidbits ended up in this largely residential neighborhood. Travelers with limited time in Berlin should note that attractions here are few and far between, and aren't easily and efficiently visited. If you want to visit them all, or at least the majority, map them and attack them in groups.

### 📷 Grunewald and the Jagdschloß — PARK

Am Grunewaldsee 29 (Access from Pücklerstr.)

☎030 813 35 97; www.spsg.de

This 3 sq. km park, with winding paths through wild underbrush, gridded pines, and a peaceful lake, is popular dog-walking turf and a great change from the rest of bustling Berlin. About a 1km walk into the woods is the **Jagdschloß,** a restored royal hunting lodge that houses a gallery of portaits and paintings by German artists like Anton Graff and Lucas Cranach the Elder. The lodge is the picture of understated elegance, surrounded by even more blooming botany. The one-room hunting lodge is worth skipping, unless you find pottery shards particularly earth-shattering. Instead, walk around the grounds, or take a hike north in the forest to **Teufelsberg** ("Devil's Mountain"), the highest point in Berlin, made of rubble from WWII piled over a Nazi military school.

▶ 🚏 U3 or U7: Fehrbelliner Pl., or S45 or S46: Hohenzollerndamm, then bus #115 (dir. Neuruppiner Str. of Spanische Alle/Potsdamer): Pücklerstr. Turn left on Pücklerstr., follow the signs, and continue straight into the forest to reach the lodge. *i* Check the Jagdschloß visitors center for a map. $ Hunting lodge €4, students €3. Tours in German (€1) offered on the weekends. ⏰ Open in winter Sa-Su 10am-4pm; in spring-fall Tu-Su 10am-6pm. Last entry 30min. before close.

## Brücke Museum — MUSEUM

Bussardsteig 9

☎030 831 20 29; www.brueckemusuem.de

Die Brücke (The Bridge) was a short-lived but influential part of German Expressionism, a period when figuration had begun to break down into thick lines and simple patterns, creating disorienting and intricate abstractions. What resulted were the energetic colors and the fierce brushstrokes jutting out from the canvases of this museum, which makes up for its lack of a permanent exhibition with engaging special exhibitions, like the gripping landscape works of Karl Schmidt-Rottluff that will grace the walls into 2012. The museum is tiny and requires a substantial trek to find, but it is a rare privilege to enjoy these paintings in an angular modern building nestled in the whispering woods of the Grunewald.

▶ 🚏 U3 or U7: Fehberlliner Pl., then bus #115 (dir. Neuruppiner Str. to Spanische Allee/Potsdammer): Finkenstraße, then walk back up Clayallee for about 50 ft. and turn left on the footpath leading into the woods; signs will lead you from there. $ €5, students €3. Cash only. ⏰ Open M 11am-5pm, W-Su 11am-5pm.

## Alter Sankt-Matthäus-Kirchhof — CEMETERY

On Großgörschen Str., right next to the lower Yorckstr. S-Bahn Station entrance.

This expansive, sloping cemetery isolated from the city by tall trees and hushed gardens conceals the graves of some of Germany's most famous, including renowned linguists, folklorians, and general academic badasses the Brothers Grimm and Romantic composer Max Bruch. A grand, mid-19th-century chapel juts out from the shrubbery, as do a number of gigantic and increasingly impressive structures that old Berlin families built for their deceased. On your way out, stop by the cafe and flower shop to freshen up from all that grave hunting.

▶ U7, S2, S25: Yorckstr. ⏰ Hours vary by month, but approximately: winter M-F 8am-4pm, Sa-Su 9am-8pm; summer M-F 8am-8pm, Sa-Su 9am-8pm. Cafe open M-Sa 9am-6pm.

# MITTE

If you're anything like us, 95% of your time in Mitte will be spent screaming obscenities at Segway tours. For the other 5%, here's a modest list of suggestions for the sights that make Mitte a way to Seg.

## Architecture and Landmarks

### Fernshehturm — TOWER

Panoramastr. 1A

☎030 242 33 33; www.tv-turm.de

At 368m, the Fernshehturm (literally "TV Tower") trumps all other sky-pokers in the EU. It's shaped like a lame 1950s space probe on purpose: the East Berliners wanted their neighbors to the west to remember Sputnik every time they looked out their windows in the morning. For better or worse, capitalism has since co-opted the DDR's biggest erection, giving you the chance to rocket up into the tower's crowning Christmas ornament for a steep fee. Fortunately, in spite of the hordes of tourists that will inevitably get in your way, the view is incredible, and especially worth checking out at the end of your stay once you have a working vocabulary of Mitte's sights. Otherwise, it's just a big, beautiful mess of towers and roofs.

▶ U2, U5, or U8: Alexanderpl. $ €11, ages 3-16 €7, under 3 free. ⏰ Open daily Mar-Oct 9am-midnight; Nov-Feb 10am-midnight.

### Berliner Dom — CHURCH

Am Lustgarten

☎030 202 69 119; www.berlinerdom.de

You may cringe upon paying to enter a church (damn it), but in this case it's completely worth it. Though *Dom* means "cathedral" in German, this 1905 church belongs to the Protestants, so it's technically not a cathedral. Nonetheless, when it comes to grandeur, it crushes most of the cathedrals you've seen. A museum upstairs shows various failed incarnations of the church, and if you climb some back stairs that seem to get sketchier and sketchier as you proceed, you can actually get to a spectacular roof terrace lookout. Don't forget the basement with the most splendiferous crypt you've ever seen, which houses the ghosts of lightweights like the Hohenzollern kings.

▶ ✚ U2, U5, or U8: Alexanderpl. From the Metro, walk southwest on Karl-Liebknecht-Str. Ⓢ €5, students €3. 🕐 Open Apr-Sept M-Sa 9am-8pm, Su noon-8pm; Oct-Mar M-Sa 9am-7pm, Su noon-7pm.

## Rotes Rathaus                                        CITY HALL
Rathausstr. 15
☎030 90 260

Fortunately not quite as horrifying as a house for rats, this "Red Town Hall" used to be East Berlin's city hall. Today it houses the Berlin Senate. Berlin, after all, is its own state, so each district has individual state senators who meet at the Rathaus every week. Inside, there are rolls of red carpet and a few small, loosely related exhibits for intrepid tourists, like a series of aerial photographs of central Berlin from 1943 to 2004. Make sure to check the place out at night: its four brightly glowing clock faces make it look like a robot owl monster.

▶ ✚ U2: Klosterstr., then head north. Or U2, U5, or U8: Alexanderpl. 🕐 Open daily 8am-6pm.

## Marienkirche                                          CHURCH
Karl-Liebknecht-Str. 8
☎030 242 44 67; www.marienkirche-berlin.de

The oldest still-standing medieval church in Berlin (built in 1270) has one of the most frightening murals you'll ever see: in it, a line of saints and kings perform the dance of death alongside a line of skeletons who look more like *X-Files* aliens than Christian iconography. There's a Dan Brown novel here just waiting to be written.

▶ ✚ U2, U5, or U8: Alexanderpl. From the Metro, walk southwest along Karl-Liebknecht-Str. Ⓢ Free. 🕐 Open daily in summer 10am-8pm; in winter 10am-6pm.

## Saint Hedwig's Cathedral                            CATHEDRAL
Hinter der Katholischen Kirche 3
☎030 203 48 10; www.hedwigs-kathedrale.de

Named after Harry Potter's owl (okay, maybe not), the biggest and oldest Catholic cathedral in the city is like no cathedral you've seen before: with a billowing dome and an angled overhang, it looks more like God's baseball cap. Due to money troubles, it took about 140 years to build (1747-1887), only to be destroyed about 60 years later by British bombs and eventually reconstructed in the 1960s. As a result, it's got '60s written all over the interior, with long strings of glowing glass balls and abstract stained glass. It's a beautiful cathedral to see, both inside and out, and due to some acoustic miracle, it might be the quietest place you'll find to read this book.

▶ 🚏 U2: Hausvogteipl. From the Metro, walk north along Oberwallstr. Look for the copper dome. $ Free. ⏰ Open M-F 10am-5pm, Su 1-5pm.

## Neptunbrunnen FOUNTAIN

Alexanderpl.

Located in the wide square just southwest of the Fernshehturm, this fountain, built in 1891, depicts the Roman god Neptune getting in a water fight with slimy creatures of the deep, including a crocodile and a snake—gross. He's also surrounded by four women, each of whom represents one of the main rivers of Prussia: the Elbe, the Rhine, the Vistula, and the Oder. Fun activity: move around until the Fernshehturm is sticking out of Neptune's head!

▶ 🚏 S3, S5, S75, U2, U5, or U8: Alexanderpl. $ Free—it's a fountain. ⏰ Open 24hr.

## Reichstag PARLIAMENT

Pl. der Republik 1

☎030 227 32 152; www.bundestag.de

Visitors to the German parliament building can climb the roof's 1200-ton glass dome that looks down into the main chamber to symbolize the "openness" of German democracy. It also serves to focus sunlight into the government chambers via an aggressive spire of mirrored fragments that juts down toward the floor. A free, automated audio tour tracks your movements up and down the nearly 300m ramp—fortunately it's not yet advanced enough to follow your furtive eye movements. Stop off at the top for a swell view of the Berlin skyline and to marvel at the fact that this dome—and therefore the Reichstag—is roofless. Rain, snow, and sleet all fall into the building and land in a giant "cone" located on the dome's floor. Visitors can trek around the roof terrace while avoiding the solar panels that make the Reichstag the world's only zero-emission congress.

▶ 🚏 Bus #100: Pl. der Republik. U55: Reichstag. ℹ To access the roof, you must reserve an appointment online at least 2 days before. $ Free. ⏰ Open daily 8am-10pm.

## Memorials

### Memorial to the Murdered Jews of Europe MEMORIAL

Cora-Berliner-Str. 1

☎030 263 94 311; www.stiftung-denkmal.de

Stark concrete blocks arranged in a grid pattern across an entire city block commemorate the Jews killed by the Nazis. Though the commotion of the busy streets surrounding the memorial may seem to discourage reflection, as you walk deeper into the gradually growing blocks, the city recedes into silence. Lose yourself on the uneven paths of the memorial, then head below ground for a moving, informative exhibit on the history of Judaism during WWII. Especially devastating is the "family" room, which presents pre-war Jewish family portraits and then investigates the individual fates of the family members. The last room continuously plays one of thousands of compiled mini-biographies of the six million individuals killed in the Holocaust. To read the bios of every murdered Jew would take over six years.

▶ 🚇 U2: Potsdamer Pl. From the Metro, walk north on Ebertstr. $ Free. ⏰ Open daily Apr-Sept 10am-8pm; Oct-Mar 10am-7pm.

### Homosexual Memorial MEMORIAL

On Ebertstr.

www.stiftung-denkmal.de/en/homosexualmemorial

While Berlin's acceptance of homosexuality is matched by few other places in the world, it wasn't so until 1969. Before that, homosexuality was illegal in both East and West Germany under a law passed by the Nazis. As a result, homosexuals were not included in many WWII memorials. This memorial, which opened in 2008, consists of a giant block of gray stone, like a misplaced part of the Memorial to the Murdered Jews of Europe across the street, but with one big difference: if you gaze fixedly into a small window, you can watch a video of two men kissing in slow motion projected on a permanent loop. While containing a definite middle-finger-to-Hitler message, the looped video is also intensely humanizing, and worth looking into, quite literally.

▶ 🚇 U2: Potsdamer Pl. From the Metro, walk north on Ebertstr. The memorial will be on your left, in the garden. ⏰ Open 24hr.

### Soviet Memorial                                          MEMORIAL
Str. des 17 Juni

WWII tanks and anti-aircraft guns flank this memorial, which was built by the Soviets in 1945. A larger-than-life-sized copper soldier reaches out to the air before him on the peak of a gate held up by rectangular pillars and covered in Cyrillic. After taking several photos of a writing system you can't even sound out, make sure to check out the tiny outdoor exhibit behind the memorial to get some historical context that has been translated into English. Haunting photos of a desolate post-war Berlin (the Reichstag, the Soviet Memorial, and the Brandenburger Tor stand spookily on a barren field now covered by the trees of the Tierpark) and of Soviet battlefields covered with bodies make this memorial more than just an overbearing sign of Soviet militarism.

▶ 🚌 Bus #100: Pl. der Republik. Head south through Tiergarten to Str. des 17 Juni and take a right. Ⓢ Free. 🕐 Open 24hr.

### Neue Wache                                               MEMORIAL
Unter den Linden 4
☎030 250 025

Neue Wache was built as a guard house for the nearby city palace (hence, "New Watch"). Since then, it's been used as a number of different memorials, and in 1969 the remains of an unknown soldier and an unknown concentration camp victim were laid to rest here. Since 1993, the Neue Wache has served as the central memorial of the Federal Republic of Germany for the Victims of War and Tyranny, and it now contains a sculpture by Käthe Kollwitz depicting a mother holding her dead son inside of a hauntingly empty room. An open skylight that exposes her to the elements symbolizes civilian suffering under Nazism.

▶ 🚇 U2: Hausvogteipl. From the Metro, walk north along Oberwallstr. Ⓢ Free. 🕐 Open daily 10am-6pm. The interior of the monument is still visible when the gate is closed.

## Museums

### 🏛 Pergamon Museum                                       MUSEUM
Am Kupfergraben 5
☎030 209 05 577; www.smb.museum

As long as it kept its two main exhibits, the Pergamon Altar and the Ishtar Gate, the rest of this museum could display cotton balls, and it'd still be worth it. Pergamon was the capital of a Hellenistic kingdom of the same name, and the museum reconstructs its temple to nearly its full size, so that you can walk up its steep steps. The battle relief on the wall displays jagged-toothed snakes ripping off heroes' arms while titans rip lions' mouths apart, so epic-leptics beware. The Mesopotamian Ishtar Gate, reconstructed tile-by-original-tile, rises 30m into the air, then stretches 100m down a hallway. You'll hardly believe it.

▶ 🚏 S5, S7, S9, or S75: Hackescher Markt. From the Metro, head south on Burgstr., turn right on Bodestr., and then right again on Kupfergraben after crossing the bridge. $ €10, students €5. A Tageskarte (€16, students €8) grants entry to all museums on Museum Island on the day of purchase. ⏰ Open M-W 10am-6pm, Th 10am-10pm, F 10am-6pm.

## 🏛 Neue Nationalgalerie — MUSEUM

Potsdamer Str. 50

☎030 266 424 510; www.smb.museum

With some of the most famous and inspired works of the early German Modernists, this museum is a rare look at the masterpieces of early 20th-century painting. Works by Franz Marc, Max Ernst, and Ernst Ludwig Kirchner are just a few of the highlights. Sadly, key works were labeled "degenerate" by the Nazis in the 1930s and have since disappeared from the collection. Missing works appear as black-and-white photocopies throughout the gallery. The permanent exhibition fills the basement, while the spacious "Temple of Light and Glass" that greets you on the ground floor holds spectacular contemporary exhibits.

▶ 🚏 U2: Potsdamer Pl. From the Metro, head west on Potsdamer Str. and follow it as it curves south. $ €10, students €5; with Tageskarte €16/8. Admission includes audio tour. ⏰ Open M-W 10am-6pm, Th 10am-10pm, F-Su 10am-6pm.

## 🏛 Topography of Terror — MUSEUM

Niederkirchner Str. 8

☎030 254 50 950; www.topographie.de

This exhibit opened in May 2010 and tracks the origins, development, and deployment of Nazi terror from 1930 to 1946. Spreading across the first floor of a glassy modern building, the exhibit consists of an extended series of maps, graphs, photographs, and an enormous amount of context—you could spend an entire afternoon reading through all the captions and explanations, which are fortunately provided in both German and English.

Travelers with weak stomachs be warned: no detail or image is deemed off-limits. That said, the images are so consistently powerful—and the exhibition so unbelievably exhaustive—that it is a must for any nuanced understanding of the development of Nazi terror. Outside, a newer exhibition of the development of Nazi influence in Berlin runs along the block-long remaining segment of the Berlin Wall: it too, is tremendously affecting, especially when many of the sights you've just seen are shown in ruins or surrounded by Hitler-heiling mobs.

▶ 🚇 U6: Kochstr. or U2: Potsdamer Pl. From the Metro, head east on Leipzigerstr. and take a right on Wilhelmstr. $ Free. ⏰ Open daily 10am-8pm.

### Neues Museum — MUSEUM

Bodestr. 1

☎030 266 424 242; www.neues-museum.de

One of the top museums in the city, this collection of Egyptian and Greek antiquities contains a variety of unbelievably well-preserved artifacts from the ancient world, from jewelry to sculpture to the most intricate coffins you've ever seen. Mummies run rampant, sarcophagi multiply, and somewhere in it all, that famous bust of Nefertiti—yeah, that one—sits glowing in her own gallery. The building was heavily damaged in WWII, and this new New Museum incorporates the old collection into a spectacularly modern complex. Wander into the central chamber on the second floor, and you might just feel like the slab of granite you're standing on is floating through some esoteric Egyptian incantation. To avoid the lines, reserve a ticket online.

▶ 🚇 U6: Friedrichstr. S5,S7,S75, or S9: Hackescher Markt. From the S-Bahn, head south on Burgstr., then turn right on Bodestr. The museum will be on your right, but the ticket office is on the left before the river. ℹ Tickets correspond to a time; once they've been purchased, visitors must return at the time printed on their ticket. $ €10, students €5; with Tageskarte €16/8. ⏰ Open M-W 10am-6pm, Th-Sa 10am-8pm, Su 10am-6pm.

### Tacheles — GALLERY

Oranienburger Str. 53

☎030 282 61 85; www.tacheles.de

An unforgettable experience day or night, this bombed-out department store has become a living, breathing street-art Metropolis. Bars, galleries, a movie theater, a faux beach exterior, and a sculpture garden and workshop are all covered in graffiti art, human piss, or both. *But it's worth it.* Though it no longer

## Jelly Doughnut Conspiracy

In the days of the Berlin Wall, any US president worth his salt had to give some dramatic speech about it. One of the most famous was JFK's *"Ich bin ein Berliner"* ("I am a Berliner") speech, delivered in 1963 to express US support for West Berlin in the wake of the Wall's construction. West Berliners lived on an island in the sea of Soviet-dominated East Germany. To drive his point home, Kennedy claimed to be a symbolic citizen of Berlin, pronouncing *"Ich bin ein Berliner!"* in his Boston accent. Afterward, several journalists claimed that by including the word *"ein"* Kennedy had mistakenly said "I am a jelly-filled doughnut," since *Berliner* could also refer to this jam-filled confection. The amusing argument that followed between linguists over whether or not Kennedy had indeed claimed to be a delicious pastry ultimately concluded that regardless of the wording, JFK had gotten his point across. But with all the debate, maybe it would have been better to stick to English.

has quite the revolutionary artsiness it once had now that the original artists have uprooted for other digs, recent political developments toward tearing Tacheles down should force it toward the top of your Berlin bucket list. It may smell like an outhouse, but you'll probably never experience something like this anywhere else.

▶ ⚇ U6: Oranienburger Tor. From the Metro, head east on Oranienburgerstr. Tacheles will be on your right. Ⓢ Free to enter; most galleries also free. ⏲ Open 8am-late.

### The Kennedys                    MUSEUM

Pariser Pl. 4A

☎030 206 53 570; www.thekennedys.de

An exhibit of photographs and rare memorabilia follows this little-known family that had such strong ties to Berlin. You may end up learning more about the Kennedys than you ever wanted to know, and the exhibition can often seem far too starry-eyed for its handsome protagonist, but the photographs are engaging, especially the ones you don't already recognize. The other artifacts that grace the exhibit, like original letters and notes, are also rare enough to invite a look. One paper even shows the first time Kennedy scrawled out his (in)famous phrase, "Ich bin ein Berliner."

Sights

▶ ☇ S1, S25, or U55: Brandenburger Tor. From the Metro, walk west toward Brandenburg Gate, then turn right in the square immediately before the Gate. Ⓢ €7, students €3.50. ⓩ Open daily 10am-6pm.

## Hamburger Bahnhof Museum                       MUSEUM
Invalidenstr. 50-51
☎030 397 83 439; www.hamburgerbahnhof.de

This massive museum, stretching the entire length of the old station house, pairs modern masterworks, like gigantic Andy Warhol prints (a very colorful Chairman Mao included) and several pioneering Minimalist works, with boldly (and often annoyingly) conceptual works. You may find yourself playing a Guitar Hero version of a one-note Lamont Young piece. You may find yourself lost and trembling in the back of a dark tunnel. Wherever you are, it will take a lot of walking to get back to the entrance, because this museum stretches for leagues in every direction. A unique home for a unique collection, it's full of old people with sweaters around their necks looking to get their culture back.

▶ ☇ S5, S7, S9, or S75: Hauptbahnhof. From the Metro, exit through the northern exit, then walk northeast on Invalidenstr. On the left, the museum is set back in a small court hidden by vegetation. Ⓢ €12, students €6. ⓩ Open Tu-F 10am-6pm, Sa 11am-8pm, Su 11am-6pm.

## Museum Nightlife

If you find yourself craving culture when the sun goes down, Berlin's got your back. Besides the bevy of clubs and concerts, over 100 museums across the city open from 6pm to 2am twice per year (usually in late January and August) for the **Long Night of the Museums.** Stay up all night with special programs, guided tours, readings, and performances, but don't expect a quiet evening: sleepless locals crowd the exhibits. Tickets include entry to all museums and a free shuttle service that connects them.

## Alte Nationalgalerie                           GALLERY
Bodestr. 1-3
☎030 209 05 577; www.smb.museum

This wide collection of mostly German *fin de siècle* and early 20th-century art does special justice to masters like Adolph

Menzel, whose Realist canvases are all over the first floor, including a grotesque painting of his own feet. The exhibition is also very Romanticism-heavy, so you may get a little tired of the same idealized golden cliffs and imaginary castles after you've seen them several times over. Music fans will note the famous portrait of Richard Wagner. One of the museum's main strengths is its small assortment of French Impressionism on the second floor, including absolute beauts by Monet, Manet, Munet (okay, maybe not Munet), and Renoir.

▶ 🚉 S3, S5, or S75: Hackescher Markt. From the Metro, head south on Burgstr. and turn right on Bodestr. The museum will be the 1st on your right. $ €10, students €5; with Tageskarte €16/8. ⏰ Open M-W 10am-6pm, Th 10am-10pm, F-Su 10am-6pm.

### Altes Museum — MUSEUM

Am Lustgarten
www.smb.museum

This "old" museum, smiling widely with its pillar teeth next to the Berliner Dom, is filled with Roman and Etruscan antiquities, including a wide range of pottery, sculpture, jewelry, and other artifacts from the daily lives of the long dead. After seeing the Pergamon and the Neues Museum, you might feel a little relieved once a gilded bronze victory goddess waves goodbye at the end of this permanent exhibition. But don't let this museum be overshadowed by its flashier neighbors. Its rebuilt central hall, with imposing marble busts surrounding you at every angle, may induce euphoria.

▶ 🚉 U2, U5, or U8: Alexanderpl. From the Metro, head southwest on Karl-Liebknecht-Str., and turn right after the Berliner Dom. $ €10, students €5; with Tageskarte €16/8. ⏰ Open M-W 10am-6pm, Th 10am-10pm, F-Su 10am-6pm.

## Parks, Squares, and Streets

### Hackescher Markt — SQUARE

Hackescher Markt

Guitarists strum and didgeridooers drone for cash. Restaurants spill their outdoor seating far out onto the cobblestones, heavily flanneled 20-year-olds play badminton at 2am, and hip storefronts extend in every direction from this bee-hive-busy square along the S-Bahn tracks. If the square isn't enough for your massive appetite for culture, check out the quiet shops and cafes of the **Hackesche Höfe** (that is, courts) just up Rosenthaler Str., as well as the little courtyard next-door, where film houses, restaurants, bookstores, cafes, and art exhibitions join together in a heavily graffitied, Tacheles-like complex.

▶ 🚇S5, S7, S9, or S75: Hackescher Markt.

## Friedrichstraße           STREET

Friedrichstr.

About as unpretentious as its Hohenzollern namesake, Friedrich-straße is Mitte's Fifth Avenue, where marble collonades cover the sidewalks and high-end franchises fight for your attention and your wallet. A block-wide Mercedes Benz showroom and a five-floor behemoth of a music and bookstore are only two of the jewels in this tremendous corporate crown. Come for the glass facades, but don't stay very long—otherwise, you might have to buy something.

▶ 🚇 S1, S2, S3, S5, S75, or U6: Friedrichstr.

## Tiergarten           PARK

Tiergarten

www.berlin.de/orte/sehenswuerdigkeiten/tiergarten

Stretching from the Brandenburg Gate in the east to the Bahnhof Zoo in the west, this enormous park at the heart of Berlin contains some of its most iconic monuments, including the Victory Column and the **Soviet Memorial.** Str. des 17 Juni bisects the park from east to west, and frequently hosts parades, celebrations, and markets. During the 2010 World Cup, the city blocked off the entire street in June and July and broadcast the World Cup on 10 enormous screens to thousands of fans. The park also contains some beautiful paths, ponds, and gardens that can offer solace from the heat and the hordes of hipsters.

▶ 🚇 Bus #100, #200, S1, or S2: Brandenburger Tor. From the Metro, head west on Unter den Linden.

## Gendarmenmarkt           SQUARE

Gendarmenmarkt

This plaza contains Konzerthaus Berlin, where the Berlin Philharmonic Symphony performs, and the Französischer Dom, an 18th-century church built for French Huguenots (Protestants). In July, the Berlin Symphony Orchestra plays free night concerts outside, while in December, the Markt hosts one of Berlin's most popular Christmas markets, guaranteed to make you feel like a kid again. Regardless of the season, it's a broad, bustling, and beautiful square. For a kick, read some of the menus of the fancy cafes around the square that try to be "bourgeois hip" and offer such pairings as currywurst and champagne.

▶ ⚲U2: Hausvogteipl. ⓢ Französischer Dom Tower €2.50. ⏲ Tower open daily 10am-6pm.

---

## Vistas

### Brandenburg Gate                                    MONUMENT

Pariser Pl.

☎030 226 33 017

You've already seen its image obnoxiously covering the windows of every U-Bahn train, but upon approaching the real Brandenburg Gate for the first time, trumpets may still blare in your head. During the day, tourists swarm this famous 18th-century gate; however, the wise traveler will return at night to see it ablaze in gold. Friedrich Wilhelm II built the gate as a symbol of military victory, but Germans these days prefer to shy away from that designation, due to their weak 20th-century batting average. A system of gates once surrounded it, but today only this most famous gate remains.

▶ ⚲ S1, S2, or S25: Brandenburger Tor.

### Humboldt University                                 UNIVERSITY

Unter den Linden 6

www.hu-berlin.de

Home to some of the greatest thinkers of the modern age, including Freud and Einstein, this university is closed to the public and doesn't make much of a tourist sight, but it's neat to stop by and feel like you're somehow involved in something. During the day, vendors sell used books out front. Maybe you'll find Einstein's old unread copy of *The Mayor of Casterbridge*.

▶ ⚲ U2: Hausvogteipl, then walk north along Oberwalstr. and turn left on Unter den Linden. Or U6, S3, S5, or S7: Friedrichstr., then walk south on Friedrichstr.

### Victory Column                                      MONUMENT

Großer Stern 1

☎030 391 29 61; www.monument-tales.de

This 27m monument celebrates Prussia's victory over France in

Sights

1880. The statue of Victoria at the top is made of melted-down French cannons, and during WWII, Hitler had the statue moved to its present location to increase its visibility. Inside, you can now find a worthless exhibit on world monuments, complete with a fleet of mundane miniatures, but the real value of the price of admission is the view from the top of the column. Though your calves will protest against the 250+ stairs that spiral up a narrow shaft, your eyes will thank you for the spectacular view of the entire Tiergarten and the skylines of practically every Berlin neighborhood.

▶ ✚ U9: Hansapl. From the Metro, walk southeast on Altonaer Str. *i* Present your ticket at the cafe to get a €0.50 drink discount. Ⓢ €2.20, students €1.50. Ⓘ Open Apr-Oct M-F 9:30am-6:30pm, Sa-Su 9:30am-7pm; Nov-Mar M-F 10am-5pm, Sa-Su 10am-5:30pm.

## Schloßplatz SQUARE
Schloßpl.

Schloßpl. is a sight where even the castles themselves feud. The Berliner Schloß (the Hohenzollern imperial palace) stood on this spot until the Communists tore it down in 1950 to build the Palast der Republick. After reunification, the Palast der Republick was torn down, this time to make way for a replica of the Berliner Schloß. Construction is set to start in 2013 and finish in 2019. Currently, the field sits open, divided by a network of boardwalks accessible to the public, while some sections are under archaeological excavation. Placards mounted around the boardwalk provide information in German and English about the building-to-be, while a free tour of the dig site (in German) is offered every Friday at 2pm.

▶ ✚ U2: Hausvogteipl. From the Metro, walk north along Oberwalstr. and take a right on Französische Str. Stay on Französische Str. and cross the canal bridge. *i* Meet in front of Schlosspl. 1 for the tour.

## Dorotheen Municipal Cemetery CEMETERY
Chausseestr. 126

Hegel, one of the most notorious haunts of college syllabi, has reached synthesis with the earth here, as has Bertolt Brecht, whose grave unfortunately does not force you to take a position. A map near the entrance points out graves of interest, so you won't have to keep searching past nightfall.

▶ ✚ U6: Oranienburger Tor. From the U-Bahn, head north on Chausseestr. Ⓘ Open daily 8am-dusk.

Sights

## High Sights

The only thing better than seeing Berlin? Seeing Berlin high. Conquer your fear of heights and scale these landmarks for the best views in town.

- **Get Closer to Your Maker:** Climb the spiral stairs of the **Franzosischer Dom,** Berlin's French Cathedral. You will see Mitte and the surrounding square, but views of heaven are not guaranteed.

- **Politicize** at the **Reichstag.** To some, Norman Foster's modern glass dome may stick out like an anachronistic eyesore, but the top of the Reichstag still has dazzling views of the city and less-dazzling views of the parliamentary debates below.

- **Celebrate** the 1871 German victory over France atop the **Victory Column.** From 66m up, you can also celebrate the calories you've burned going up the stairs.

- **Climb** Berlin's tallest hills for the 30m **Muggelturm**. Originally planned as a TV tower, this ugly building ended up serving as a listening post for East Germany's Stasi. You don't have to be a spy (or a wizard) to trek up the steps and enjoy distant views of Berlin, framed by suburbs and greenery.

- **Unleash your inner Olympian** at **Glockenturm,** the Bell Tower at the Olympiastadion. Thanks to the 2006 World Cup, the tower sports a new glass lift and a historical exhibition. Want 24/7 eyes on Berlin? Check out the live webcam at www.olympiastadion-berlin.de.

# PRENZLAUER BERG

Tourists who can't shake the itch to take snapshots tend to flock to the brick-tastic but yawn-sensational **Kulturbrauerei** on Schönhauser Allee, the actually interesting **Berliner Mauer Dokumentationszentrum** in the north, and the towering **Wasserturm.** Generally, other than our two thumbpicks, P'Berg's sights are only worth a brief pass by between buying shoes and drinking brews.

### ▨ Mauerpark                                                    PARK

Extends north of the intersection between Eberswalder Str. and Schwedter Str.

Like Berlin, Mauerpark on a hot afternoon is an amalgam of

a thousand different things that shouldn't exist in the same world, let alone on the same flat surface, but somehow do so in the most colorful way possible. Hipsters, punks, goths, hippies, bros, drunkards, lovers, the shirtless, and everything in between flatten the dry grass with blankets, lawn chairs, card tables, portable barbecues, African drums, and enough bottles to fill the stadium next door. Footballs, tennis balls, basketballs, and clouds of smoke soar through the air. Every inanimate surface (and several animate ones) are coated with thick graffiti. A rock climbing wall crowns one end, while a gigantic, multicolored edifice of logs writhes with the adventurous children of the hip at the other. Taken in full, Mauerpark is contemporary Berlin's thesis statement spoken through a distorted megaphone.

▶ 🚏 U2: Eberswalder Str. From the Metro, walk west on Eberswalder Str. Mauerpark will extend far to the north after you pass the stadium. $ Free.

### 🏛 Berliner Mauer Dokumentationszentrum MUSEUM, MEMORIAL

Bernauer Str. 111

☎030 464 10 30; www.berliner-mauer-gedenkstaette.de

A remembrance complex, museum, chapel, and entire city block of the preserved Berlin Wall come together as a memorial to "victims of the Communist tyranny." The church is made of an inner oval of poured cement walls, lit from above by a large skylight and surrounded by a see-through skeleton of two-by-fours. The museum has assembled a comprehensive collection of all things Wall, including original recordings, telegrams, blueprints, film footage, and photos. Climb up a staircase to see the wall from above.

▶ 🚏 U8: Bernauer Str. From the Metro, walk north on Brunnen Str., then turn left on Bernauer Str. The church and memorial are on the left before Ackerstr., and the Dokumentationszentrum and exhibition are on the right immediately after Ackestr. $ Free. ⏰ Open Tu-Su Apr-Oct 9:30am-7pm; Nov-Mar 9:30am-6pm.

### Kollwitzplatz PARK, MONUMENT

Directly below Wörther Str.

This little triangle of greenery is one big playground, with toddlers climbing over tree stumps, jungle gyms, and even the lap of Käthe Kollwitz's statue. Nearby, a magical little playground with a small bridge, stream, and willow trees is another popular destination for young moms with energetic kids. Non-parents are drawn by the upscale market on Saturdays, where vendors sell everything from boar meat sausage to handmade ravioli.

▶ ⚇ U2: Senefelderpl. From the Metro, walk north on Kollwitzstr. until you reach Knaackstr. The park is on the left. Ⓢ Free.

# FRIEDRICHSHAIN

### 🏛 Volkspark Friedrichshain                                PARK

Volkspark Friedrichshain may lose out to the Tiergarten in a battle of bulk, but as Berlin's oldest park, it makes the Tiergarten look like a youthful dabbler. It's huge too: with 52 hectares, it's too large to feel crowded, even with masses of dog-walkers and suntanners filling the paths and lawns. Since opening in 1840, monuments and memorials have cropped up here and there; today it seems part-park, part-museum. In 1913 the **Märchenbrunnen** or "Fairy Tale Fountain" was completed, depicting 10 characters from the tales of the Brothers Grimm around a tremendous cascade of water. **Mount Klemont,** which now occasionally serves as a platform for open-air concerts and movie screenings, gains its mass from the enormous pile of rubble swept beneath it in 1950 from two bomb-destroyed, WWII bunkers. With perhaps too much history for its own good, the park still draws thousands from their homes on nice days, so people-watching provides several afternoons' worth of entertainment.

▶ ⚇ S8 or S10: Landsberger Allee or U5: Strausbgr. Pl. From Strausbgr. Pl., walk north on Lichtenberger Str. Bounded by Am Friedrichshain to the north, Danziger Str. to the east, Landsberger Allee to the south, and Friedenstr. Str. to the south.

### 🏛 East Side Gallery                          GALLERY, MONUMENT

Along Mühlenstr.

www.eastsidegallery.com

The longest remaining portion of the Berlin Wall, this 1.3km stretch of cement slabs has been converted into the world's largest open-air art gallery. The Cold War graffiti no longer exists; instead, the current murals hail from an international group of artists who gathered in 1989 to celebrate the wall's fall. One of the most famous contributions is by artist Dmitri Wrubel, who depicted a wet, wrinkly kiss between Leonid Brezhnev and East German leader Erich Honecker. The stretch of street

**Sights**

remains unsupervised and, on the Warschauer Str. side, open at all hours, but vandalism is surprisingly rare.

▶ U1, U15, S3, S5, S6, S7, S9, or S75: Warschauer Str. or S5, S7, S9, or S75: Ostbahnhof. From the Metro, walk back toward the river. $ Free.

### Stasi Museum

MUSEUM

Ruschestr. 103, Haus 1

☎030 553 68 54; www.stasimuseum.de

This Lichtenberg suburb harbors perhaps the most hated and feared building of the DDR regime: the headquarters of the East German secret police, the **Staatssicherheit** or **Stasi.** During the Cold War, the Stasi kept dossiers on some six million of East Germany's own citizens, an amazing feat and a testament to the huge number of civilian informers in a country of only 16 million people. Since a 1991 law made the records public, the "Horror Files" have rocked Germany, exposing millions of informants and wrecking careers, marriages, and friendships at every level of German society. Officially known today as the Forschungs-und Gedenkstätte Normannenstrasse, the building retains its oppressive Orwellian gloom and much of its worn 1970s aesthetic. The museum exhibition, housed until 2012 in a temporary space across a courtyard from the actual headquarters during renovations, presents a wide array of original Stasi artifacts, among which is the mind-blowing collection of concealed microphones and cameras. All we want to know is how nobody noticed the bulky microphone concealed in a tie.

▶ U5: Magdalenenstr. $ €4, students €3. Exhibits in German; English info booklet €3. ⏰ Open M-F 11am-6pm, Sa-Su 2-6pm.



## KREUZBERG

Most of Kreuzberg's sights are skippable, especially in comparison to their glamorous cousins up north, but if you're in the area during the day, there are several museums, parks, and buildings you should definitely stop by. In addition to the sights we've listed, Kreuzberg also has several beautiful 19th-century churches that are worth a look, including **Saint-Michael-Kirche** (Michaelkirchpl.), the **Heilig-Kreuz-Kirche** (Zossener Str. 65), and **Saint Thomas-Kirche** (Bethaniendamm 23-27).

## Deutsches Technikmuseum Berlin MUSEUM

Trebbiner Str. 9

☎030 902 54 0; www.sdtb.de

Don't tell the National Air and Space Museum about this place. With 30 full-sized airplanes, 20 boats—including a full-sized Viking relic—and a train from every decade since 1880, this museum could be a city in itself. Though the prime demographic that enjoys these behemoths of progress includes your five-year-old brother and your dad, there's something to appeal to anyone's sense of awe in this absurdly large collection. Five floors of large machinery include an original WWII German rocket (hopefully deactivated), a U-boat (the last haven for Kreuzberg squatters), and a turn-of-the-century model for a balloon that would carry an entire city (what we dub the "Balloon of Babel.") You won't have dropped your jaw this much since the Pergamon Museum.

▶ 🚇 U1 or U2: Gleisdreieck. From the Metro, head east on Luckenwalder Str. and turn right on Tempelhofer Ufer. Walk under the train tracks and turn right onto Trebbiner Str. The entrance is about ¾ of the way down Trebbiner Str. ℹ Many exhibits in English. $ €6, students €3. ⏰ Open Tu-F 9am-5:30pm, Sa-Su 10am-6pm.

## Soviet War Memorial MEMORIAL

Treptower Park

This 20,000 sq. m memorial, built in 1949 to commemorate the Soviet soldiers lost in the Battle of Berlin, makes Mitte's **Soviet Memorial** seem teeny in comparison. Two jagged triangular slabs, each bearing the hammer and sickle, guard a tremendous rectangular square lined by exquisitely cut shrubs and surrounded by marble reliefs of Soviet soldiers helping the poor and the huddled. Quotations from Stalin in the original Russian and in German translation encircle you at every step. But the most impressive piece stands at the end of the square: a tremendous grassy mound bears a giant bronze statue of a Soviet soldier, crushing a broken swastika and lugging a sword. After a jaunt around the place, you'll either be horrified, ready to unite the working classes of the world, or a little bit of both.

▶ 🚇 U1 or U15: Schlesisches Tor. From the Metro, walk southeast on Schlesische Str. Cross both canals, and continue until you reach a fork in the road, between Puschkinallee and Am Treptower Park. Take Puschkinallee, and walk along the park until you reach a large semicircular courtyard with an entrance gate. Turn into this courtyard; the memorial is on the left. $ Free. ⏰ Open 24hr.

## Tempelhofer Park                                          PARK

At Columbiadamm and Tempelhofdamm

☎030 700 90 688; www.tempelhoferfreiheit.de

Once an airport (and drop point for the Berlin Airlift), Tempelhof closed forever in 2008. In 2010, it was converted into a park and reopened to the public. Now, this flat, expansive plot of land covered in tall grass and wide runways provides plenty of legroom, and some of the most pastoral paths on which to enjoy a bike ride, a jog, or, appropriately, a kite-fly. Before or after spending a quiet, breezy afternoon on the taxiway, make sure to check out the **Berlin Airlift Memorial** just to the northwest: it looks like a rainbow under construction.

▶ ♯ U6: Pl. der Luftbrücke. From the Metro, walk south on the left side of

---

### Go on a Spree

Forget the fact that it flows past 250 mi. of industrial lands, forests, and fields. The Spree is best known where it hits Berlin, before joining the Havel River in the suburbs. Unfortunately, due to the decrepit drains that support the city's sewage system, occasional torrential rain means that sewage often mixes with river water. Not to worry, though. Since 2008, the Spree 2011 project has worked to contain the overflow waste and clean up the water. For now, here are some ways to enjoy the river without sharing the water with your favorite coliform bacteria.

- **Fancy a float?** Book a river cruise and tour Berlin from the (dis) comfort of your boat. Avid rowers can rent their own rowboats at **Rent-a-Boat** (☎177 299 32 62; www.rent-a-boat-berlin. com) at the entrance to the Abtei Bridge in Treptower Park. Several companies also run tours.

- **How about a dip?** The Spree might be too polluted for casual bathing, but you can still swim on the river if you head to the **Arena Pool.** This converted shipping container holds a clean swimming pool, floating next to a sandy area with a bar and lounge. In the winter, massage areas and two saunas will keep you sweating in the covered pool. If it's too crowded to do your laps, grab a cocktail and lap up views of the Berlin skyline instead.

- **Hit the bar.** The sandbar, that is. Complete with beach chairs, parasols, and exotic palm trees, 30 beaches dot the Spree, so you can work on your tan without leaving the city.

Tempelhofer Damm and pass by the old airport parking lot. There will be signs indicating the park's entrance. $i$ The dog that you brought on your backpacking trip must stay on a leash. $ Free. $\mathbb{Q}$ Open daily dawn-dusk.

## Oberbaumbrücke                                          BRIDGE

At the south end of Warschauer Str.

Massive twin brick towers rise from this late 19th-century double-decker bridge that spans the Spree River. Once a border crossing into East Berlin, it now connects Kreuzberg to Friedrichshain. Residents of the rival neighborhoods duke it out on the bridge every July 27, when thousands of people chuck rotten vegetables at each other in order to establish which 'hood is edgier.

▶ $\maltese$ U1 or U15: Schlesisches Tor. From the Metro, follow Oberbaum Str. as it curves north.

## Jewish Museum                                          MUSEUM

Lindenstr. 9-14

☎030 259 93 300; www.jmberlin.de

Modern, interactive exhibits treat subjects ranging from the Torah to the philosophies of Moses Mendelssohn to discrimination against Jews under Charles V. Architect Daniel Libeskind designed the museum's building to reflect the discomfort, pain, and the inherent voids in Jewish history, including tremendous, triangular shafts, inaccessible rooms, and uneven floors. One tall room is piled with metal faces (Menashe Kadishman's *Fallen Leaves*) that make a terrible racket as you walk across them. It's an amazing museum that actually succeeds at being "experiential": it's disorienting, frightening, and historical.

▶ $\maltese$ U1 or U6: Hallesches Tor. From the station, head east on Gitschiner-str. and take a left at Lindenstr. $ €5, students €2.50, under 6 free. Audio tours €3. $\mathbb{Q}$ Open M 10am-10pm, Tu-Su 10am-8pm. Last entry 1hr. before close.

## Schwules Museum (Gay Museum)                            MUSEUM

Mehringdamm 61

☎030 695 99 050; www.schwulesmuseum.de

This small museum is the world's only state-funded exhibit on homosexual persecution. Temporary exhibits take up over half of the museum, and the permanent exhibition is tiny but packs a big punch with its presentation of interesting, lesser-known history and materials you probably won't find anywhere else. Penises are common, but so are 19th-century canvases; issues of *Der Eigene,* the world's first gay newspaper; and the mug shots of gay men prosecuted by the Nazis. Plus, the temporary exhibitions are actually worth seeing: the most recent, on Wittgenstein, featured everything from the eminent philosopher's thoughts on his tweed blazer to what to do with friends that you haven't talked to for a while.

▸ ⇆ U6 or U7: Mehringdamm. From the Metro, head south on Merhringdamm. The museum will be through a courtyard on the left in the block after Gneisenaustr. *i* English exhibit guide available. $ €5, students €3. ⏰ Open M 2-6pm, W-F 2-6pm, Sa 2-7pm, Su 2-6pm.

# Food

German food may not sound appealing in theory, but in practice, we think you'll find the opposite to be true. It's not just about beer and sausage anymore: check ethnic eateries for great deals on pho, döner, burritos, and more. Wealthy Charlottenburg is not known for its budget-friendly fare, so head north to the neighborhood Moabit for cheap, authentic Turkish or Vietnamese food. Check out Schöneberg's relaxed cafe culture around the intersection of Maaßenstrasse and Winterfeldstrasse. In Mitte, it's best to avoid overpriced restaurants and cafes near major sights. Instead, look north of Alexanderpl. for the best value, where streets like Alte Schönhauserstrasse and Rosa-Luxemburg-Strasse are lined with delicious, modern restaurants that offer all types of cuisine for less than €10. Prenzlauer Berg is another cafe capital: check out Kastanienallee or the streets around Helmholtzplatz for the highest concentration of caffeine. Some of Friedrichshain's narrow cobblestone streets are lined with cheap cafes, ice cream joints, and reasonably priced restaurants, which makes it simple to find something that piques your appetite without stealing too much of your cash. The intersection of Simon-Dach-Strasse and Grünbergerstrasse is a good place to start. For the best international cuisine in a city known for cheap ethnic fare, head to Kreuzberg, where incredible restaurants line Oranienstraße, Bergmannstraße, and Schlesische Straße.

## Budget Food

This tip really just writes itself: Berlin is full of cheap food. From currywurst to döner kebabs, street food will keep you full for under €4. Our researchers report that the best cheap eats can be found at **Mustafa's** in Kreuzberg.

# CHARLOTTENBURG

### 🏷 Schwarzes Cafe                    BAR, CAFE $$$

Kantstr. 148

☎030 313 80 38

Pharmacies, grocery stores, and even whole neighborhoods might close down at night, but Schwarzes will still be open. As you sit on one of the two packed, candlelit floors, you might begin to forget how much of a tab you're building up sampling the extravagant menu. Kick back an absinthe and watch the artistically peeling paint on the exquisitely molded ceilings dance to the folk-rock mix. Then chase your massive drinkage with breakfast when the sun comes up or, if you prefer, at a more bohemian hour: all meals are served around the clock.

▶ ✈ S3, S5, S7, S9, or S75: Savignypl. Ⓢ Weekly specials €7-13 served 11:30am-8pm. Breakfast €5-8.50. Drinks €3-7. Cash only. ⏰ Open M 24hr., Tu 11am-3am, W-Su 24hr.

### Fam Dang                    VIETNAMESE $$

Hutten Str. 5

☎030 755 67 526

Located in a predominantly Vietnamese area, Fam Dang's bright rooms, outdoor patio, and ridiculously inexpensive daily menu make it a must. Drop by in the busy noon hour to watch the waitresses career around with tremendous white bowls as they rapidly rail in accented German at a middle-aged, professional crowd on its lunch break. The soup menu includes a wide variety of Vietnamese favorites, like glass noodle soup. Portions are gigantic, so make sure to come starving and dehydrated.

▶ ✈ Bus M27: Turnstr./Beusselstr. Ⓢ Entrees €5. Cash only. ⏰ Open M-F 11am-9pm, Sa noon-9pm.

Food

## Kastanie
BEER GARDEN $$

Schloßstr. 22

☎030 321 50 34; www.kastanie-berlin.de

Nestled between the high apartment facades that line Schloßstr., Kastanie offers a little piece of Bavaria on the cheap. A changing entree menu (€3.50-6.50) includes all the old German favorites, including delectable Nürnberger sausages and yummy *Käsespätzle* (späzle with cheese and onions). The weathered wooden tables spread across the shaded, gravel grounds exude authenticity, while the colorful wooden masks hanging above suggest a quaint quirkiness. Kastanie is the *echt deutsch* place to enjoy a beer and quiet conversation on a sunny early afternoon.

▶ ♯ U2: Sophie-Charlotte Pl., then walk up Schloßstr. toward the Schloß. Ⓢ Breakfast €4-6. Beer €3. Cash only. ☒ Open daily 10am-1am. Breakfast served 10am-2pm.

## Areperia
COLOMBIAN $

Stuttgarter Pl. 18

☎030 310 10 626; www.la-areperia.de

With only three menu options, it may not have the widest selection, but Areperia delivers in quality and quantity what it lacks in variety. Choose between *arepas* (the root of the title; €3), empanadas (3 for €4), *patacónes* (delicious fried banana patties; 3 for €4), or a combination thereof, all with a variety of tasty and filling options, like avocado or cold cheese. Though it looks like some generic franchise runoff from Wilmersdorfer Str., Areperia is anything but. The neon orange and lime green walls, modern furniture, and photographs for sale on the walls put the cool back in postcolonial.

▶ ♯ S3, S5, S7, S75: Charlottenburg; U7: Wilmersdorfer Str. Ⓢ Cash only. ☒ Open M-Sa noon-9pm, Su 1-6pm.

## Abbas
MIDDLE EASTERN $

Huttenstr. 71

☎030 343 47 770

Abbas and the restaurants around it, like Fam Dang, belong to Middle Eastern and Asian immigrants attracted by the area's low rent. This sprawling sweet and nut shop sells a wide range of authentic Middle Eastern desserts on the cheap, from chocolate-covered lentils to pistachio-cashew pastries. Try the specialty baklava (2 pieces €1.30; sizeable box €3)—you'll be licking your fingers for hours.

Food

▶ Bus M27: Turmstr./Beusseistr. $ Cash only. ⏰ Open M-Th 10am-5pm, F-Sa noon-8pm. Cash only.

## Mensa TU

CAFETERIA $

Hardenbergerstr. 34

☎030 939 39 7439

It's a cafeteria, but the Hardenbergerstr. Mensa offers the cheapest hot meal around, with three entree choices as well as vegetarian options. And our favorite part: your portion size is as much food as you can fit on a plate. Accordingly, it's overrun by university students, who chat in the sunny, modern complex and read on the ubiquitous benches. The food is nothing special, but, like any cafeteria, it's meant for folks on a budget, and it probably won't poison you (fingers crossed!). The slightly higher-priced cafeteria downstairs should be avoided.

▶ U2: Ernst-Reuter-Pl. or bus #245: Steinpl. A 10min. walk from Bahnhof Zoo. $ Meals €4-5, students €2-3. Cash only. ⏰ Upstairs cafeteria open M-F 11:30am-3:30pm. Coffee bar M-F 11am-6pm. Cake shop M-F 7:30am-2:30pm. Downstairs open M-F 11am-2:30pm.

## Paris Bar

BISTRO $$$$

Kantstr. 152

☎030 313 80 52; www.parisbar.de

Formerly one of West Berlin's favorite hip gathering places, the Paris Bar is now a stuffy and formal restaurant (pronounced rest-owe-RAW) that's geared more toward art patrons than artists. The frenzy of Surrealist canvases and quirky posters that line the walls seem misplaced among a collared, older crowd downing entrees with obscene prices. The black and white linoleum floors and dark wood walls are certainly nice, but at what cost? A hefty one, that's what.

▶ U1: Uhlandstr. $ Soups from €5.50. Appetizers €6.50-14.50; entrees €12-25. Drinks €4-12. ⏰ Open daily noon-2am. Kitchen closes at 1am.

## La Petit France Croissanterie

CAFE $

Nürnberger Str. 24A

☎017 817 11 3826

Fresh, inexpensive lunches are sometimes difficult to come by in sprawling Charlottenburg. This pocket-sized French bistro has some stellar baguettes and classic Francophone music to transport you across the Rhine. Try the small baguettes with a variety of toppings, including tomato, mozzarella, and basil.

▶ ⚡ U3 to Ausgburger Str. Ⓢ Baguettes €2.50, large €3.30. Quiche and salad combo €4.50. Cash only. ⏰ Open M-Sa 8am-6:30pm.

# SCHÖNEBERG AND WILMERSDORF

If you manage to burn through all the cafes on **Maaßenstrasse** and **Winterfeldtstrasse,** more popular cafes and inexpensive restaurants crowd the **Akazienstrasse,** which runs from the U-Bahn station at Eisenacherstr. to Hauptstr. All in all, come for the foamy coffee, stay for the eclectic foreign cuisine.

### 🖾 Cafe Bilderbuch                                                   CAFE $$
Akazienstr. 28

☎030 787 06 057; www.cafe-bilderbruch.de

Even if you couldn't eat here, Cafe Bilderbuch's antique cabinets, fringed lamps, deep-cushioned sofas, and adjoining library would still make this a place to visit. Fortunately, their unbeatable Sunday brunch menu, named after different fairy tales, has us shoving grandmothers out of the way to get in the door. Our favorite combo is *"Der Froschkönig "* (The Frog Prince), which includes salmon, trout, caviar, and a glass of prosecco. The menu, printed on their own press, doubles as a weekly newspaper.

▶ ⚡ U7: Eisenacher Str. *i* Free Wi-Fi. Ⓢ Soup from €3.70. Salads from €6. Entrees €8. Coffee €1.50. Cash only. ⏰ Open M-Sa 9am-midnight, Su 10am-midnight. Kitchen closes daily 11pm.

### 🖾 Baharat Falafel                                                  TURKISH $$
Winterfeldtstr. 37

☎030 216 83 01

This isn't your average döner stand. First, it doesn't serve döner. Second, this vegetarian Turkish restaurant makes all of its falafel fried to order, in fluffy pita with lots of tomatoes, lettuce, and mango or chili sauce (€3-4). Wash down Baharat's plates (hummus, tabouleh, and salad) with fresh-squeezed *Gute-Laune Saft* (good-mood juice, €1-2), which tastes sublimely refreshing in a land where even water is a soft drink. Indoor seating with a map of Iraq on the bright walls or an outdoor bench under a striped awning are comfortable settings for your messy nom-nom-nomming.

▶ ⚡ U1, U3, U4, or U9: Nollendorfpl. Ⓢ Entrees €6-8. Cash only. ⏰ Open M-Sa 11am-2am, Su noon-2am.

## 👍 Himali

TIBETAN, NEPALESE $$

Crellestr. 45

☎030 787 16 175; www.himali-restaurant.de

A tandoori oven spits out piping hot Nepali and Tibetan classics. Entrees are never short on spices, either in quantity or variety, which are grown and ground by hand. Himali offers a tremendous range of vegetarian dishes, curried or grilled, with tofu, vegetables, naan and your choice of seasonings. The Nepali tea (€2.50) makes English Breakfast seem like child's play.

▶ 🚏 U7: Kleistpark, walk up (quite literally) Langenscheidtstr. and turn right on Crellestr. [$] Entrees €6.50-10. ⏰ Open daily noon-midnight.

## Double Eye

CAFE $

Akazienstr. 22

☎017 945 66 960; www.doubleeye.de

For coffee purists, this is an inexpensive way to enjoy the best kind of brew. This small and quick coffee bar has a line of locals snaking out the door all day, waiting to order the no-syrup-added daily brews covered in enough bright-white foam to build a Santa disguise. Baristas prepare each espresso with surgical precision and take pride on their top-quality "latte-art": designs traced into the inch-thick crowns of foam. And yes, they've got victory plaques behind the bar to back up that smack.

▶ 🚏 U7: Eisenacher Str. [$] All drinks €1-3. Soup-bowl-sized coffee with milk only €2.20. Cash only. ⏰ Open M-F 8:45am-6:30pm, Sa 9am-6pm, Su 8:45am-6:30pm.

## Café Einstein

VIENNESE CAFE $$$

Kurfurstenstr. 58

☎030 261 50 96; www.cafeeinstein.com

You don't have to be a rocket scientist to enjoy Café Einstein, which is Berlin's premier Viennese coffeeshop and an obligatory stop for tourists, impeccably dressed locals playing hard-to-get in their books, and intelligent, good-looking *Let's Go* travelers alike (oh, we know: we shouldn't have). Large windows refract the light bouncing off of Einstein's private garden, where you can sip a splurge-worthy home-roasted coffee (cappuccino €4.30; *Milchkaffee* €3.80). You'll want time to slow down as you cherish a small cake or an 👍**Apfelstrudel**, which are the least expensive (but perhaps the tastiest) ways to enjoy the cafe's dark wood-paneled walls and detailed molding, and will set you back about €4.

▶ 🚏 U1, U3, U4, or U9: Nollendorfpl. [$] Entrees €15-22. Breakfast from €5.80. Su brunch bar €13. ⏰ Open daily 6am-1am.

## Berlin Burrito Company

BURRITOS $

Pallasstr. 21

☎030 236 24 990; www.berlin-burrito-company.de

Alright, we see you. You're narrowing your eyes and muttering self-righteously to yourself, "Burritos have nothing to do with Berlin." It's okay, we forgive you. Other than the same first syllable, they don't. But for those college kids who have spent an entire year eating a burrito for every meal, locating the nearest cheap burrito place could be life-saving. Plus, this place is cheap and delicious, with a variety of interesting fillings (like lime chicken and spicy tomato habañero sauce) to complicate the usual way you stuff your face. And with see-through barber shop chairs and some dark electro tunes you've never heard before, this little burrito place has a definite Berlin flavor.

▶ 🚏 U1, U2, U3, U4: Nollendorfpl., then walk down Maasenstr. toward the church, and turn right on Pallasstr. [$] Burritos €3.30, with meat €5. Cash only. ⏰ Open M-Sa noon-11pm, Su 1-10pm.

## Bar Tolucci

ITALIAN $$

Eisenacher Str. 86

☎030 214 16 07; www.bar-tolucci.de

With stone-oven-cooked pizzas and outdoor seating on wood-slated bistro tables along the quiet street corner, this restaurant is casual eating and generous portions at their finest. The pizzas are cheap (€5.50-8.20) and eclectic (smoked salmon? Bitte!). Be sure to arrive after the oven starts firing at 5pm; non-pizza

### The Glories of Meat

We can thank Berlin for developing many of the meaty staples of German cuisine, although some may seem more palatable than others. If you are ready to delve into this gastronomical adventure, we must warn you about one of the meats you're likely to encounter: **Eisbein.** Literally "ice legbone," *Eisbein* is a boiled dish made from pickled ham hock (a.k.a. pig knuckles). It's best to order this dish on an empty stomach, since *Eisbein* comes in huge portions, covered in a thick layer of fat with the soft skin left on. You're not supposed to eat that part, though, so be sure to peel the skin off. In order to soften the meat, *Eisbein* must be cooked for many hours, giving it a distinctive and aromatic flavor that makes up for the appearance (or so we hope).

options can be a bit pricier. Double-fist your pizza slices in a warm, red interior or a small garden.

▶ 🪧 U7: Eisenacher Str. [$] Pizzas €5.50-8.20. Entrees €7-12. ⏰ Open M-F 10am-midnight. Garden open noon-midnight. Pizza oven in use M-F 5pm-midnight.

## MITTE

### 👍 Monsieur Vuong — VIETNAMESE $$

Alte Schönhauserstr. 46

☎030 992 96 924; www.monsieurvuong.de

The prices are a little high compared to most Vietnamese places, and the portions are not as fantastically large, but Monsieur Vuong rationalizes its stinginess with some of the tastiest and most beautifully presented Vietnamese food you'll find. With a menu that changes every two days, Monsieur Vuong has developed a wide popularity among regulars who just can't stop coming back for the next fix... er, dish. The delicious and cheap Vietnamese coffee (€2) made with condensed milk and a little bit of 'Nam will prevent you from having to say "Goodnight, Saigon."

▶ 🪧 U2: Rosa-Luxemburg-Pl. From the Metro, take the alleyway from the park across Rosa-Luxemburg-Str., then turn left on Alte Schönhauserstr. [$] Entrees €6-9.80. Vietnamese "shakes" €3.40-5.80. ⏰ Open daily noon-midnight.

### Berliner Marcus Bräu — GERMAN $$

1-3 Münzstr.

☎030 247 69 85; www.brau-dein-bier.de

Though Marcus Bräu has only been brewing since 1982, the *Bier* tastes like what your German grandpa was drinking before German history went crazy. The home-brewed liqueurs (especially the coffee liqueur) taste as good as your mom smells, assuming she smells great. The decor's a little kitschy (as in, framed religious slogans kitschy) and entrees tend to hover around €10, but several delicious varieties of wienerschnitzel from only €9.20 are a rare and belly-filling bargain. Try the beer—it goes down smoother than air.

▶ 🪧 U2, U5, U8, S5, S7, S9, or S75: Alexanderpl. From the Metro, head north on Karl-Liebknecht-Str., then turn left on Münzstr. [$] Entrees €7.50-11. Drinks €1-7. Beer €2.40 per 0.3L, €6.70 per L. ⏰ Open daily noon-late.

## Good Morning Vietnam

VIETNAMESE $$

Alte Schonhauserstr. 60

☎030 308 82 973; www.good-morning-vietnam.de

The name is great. The explanation for the name is even better: "A yesterday's movie title, a salutation that reminds us of the past, a past full of starvation and war..." Brimming with such great food, this restaurant is hardly about starvation, although it may start a war among your friends when you must decide between this place and Monsieur Vuong down the street. Entrees are cheaper than their MV counterparts, and include crispy duck, mango chicken skewers, and tofu platters. While the food may not dance in your mouth quite as wonderfully as at Monsieur Vuong, the larger portions will definitely please your belly.

▶ ⚡ U2: Rosa-Luxemburg-Pl. From the Metro, take the alleyway across Rosa-Luxemburg-Str. from the park. Ⓢ Entrees €7.50. ☒ Open daily noon-midnight.

## Tipica

MEXICAN $$

Rosenstr. 19

☎030 250 99 440; www.tipica.mx

Tipica (pronounced TEE-pee-ca) is built around a DIY taco menu. Large portions of meat, cilantro, onion, and lime come with four tortillas; you add the sides and salsas and roll your own creations. The meats get crazy (veal tacos!), but the portions stay large and the selection crowd-pleasing. Get any meat Alcurbie style—fried with peppers, onions, and bacon—for no extra charge.

▶ ⚡ S5, S7, S9, or S75: Hackescher Markt. From the station, head east and turn right at An der Spandauer Brucke immediately after the Markt. Follow it 100m or so as it curves to the right. Ⓢ Tacos €6-7. Sides €2. Salsa €1. ☒ Open M-Th 11am-11pm, F-Sa 11am-1am, Su 11am-11pm.

## Dolores Burritos

MEXICAN FUSION $

Rosa-Luxemburg-Str. 7

☎030 280 99 597; www.dolores-online.de

Modeled after the Mexican fusion model of Baja Fresh or Chipotle, this "California Burrito" shop sells hulking tubes under €5. While we won't go so far as to call these suckers "Californian," we will say that they're appropriately tremendous, which always tickles our fancy. The place supplies a hefty and distinctive menu of chipotle chicken, spiced *carnitas,* and vegetables and lets you combine them in burrito (€4), bowl (€4), or quesadilla

**Food**

(€3.70). Also, the blown-up map of the Mission District in San Francisco that covers the walls may convince you that you've stepped through a portal to sunnier climes...or it may just baffle your sense of direction more completely.

▶ 🚏 U2, U5, U8, S5, S7, S9, or S75: Alexanderpl. From the Metro, head north on Rosa-Luxemburg-Str. $ Burritos from €5; prices vary depending on your ingredients. Cash only. ⏰ Open M-Sa 11:30am-10pm, Su 1-10pm.

## Dada Falafel

FALAFEL $

Linienstr. 132

☎030 275 96 927; www.dadafalafel.de

Ever stood in line at a falafel place and thought, "This place could use more Duchamp!"? Well, even if you haven't, this is the place for you. The high walls and ceiling of this tiny takeout place are covered in thick multicolored paint swirls, as if to reflect the smear of sauces that will soon cover your face. The falafel (€3.50) is appropriately packed with flavor, the plates (€5) are beautifully and smearfully arranged, and everything just seems to taste better with the classic jazz playing from the speakers. After feasting your belly, feast your eyes on "Derdasdie," the Dada art exhibit next to the restaurant.

▶ 🚏 U6: Oranienburger Tor. $ Cash only. ⏰ Open M-Sa 9am-6pm.

## Fassbender and Rausch Chocolatiers

CHOCOLATE $$$

Charlottenstr. 60

☎030 204 58 443; www.fassbender-rausch.de

To prepare for his fall into Wonka's chocolate river, Augustus Gloop must have jumped into F and R's chocolate volcano (real), took a ride on their chocolate Titanic (real, though it might be the Lusitania), and commented on the Baroque idealism of their chocolate Berliner Dom. Established in 1863, this is a giant bustling chocolate house where every inch is filled with confections so delicious, they make Wonka seem like an amateur. You'll wish that all your friends and family were just chocolate replicas here so you could feast on their delicious flesh. Truffles (€0.50-0.80) come in 100 flavors, and it's hard to go wrong with any of them.

▶ 🚏 U2 or U6: Stadmitte. $ Chocolate €0.50-300. ⏰ Open M-Sa 10am-8pm, Su 11am-8pm.

## Rosenthaler Grill

FAST FOOD $

Torstr. 125

☎030 283 21 53

Outstanding deals and quality Berlin street food at a nice outdoor cafe. Big eaters or families of five, get pumped: an entire chicken costs €5. Gigantic döner kebabs (like a gyro, but made with cabbage; €3.40) and pizzas (€3-5) are also tasty and dirt cheap (without the dirt). Quick tip: the place never closes, and the large döner is the perfect hangover prevention if you eat it on the way home from a crazy night.

▶ 🚏 U8: Rosenthaler Pl. [$] Menu €1-6. Cash only. ⏰ Open 24hr.

## Arabeske

LEBANESE $

Kastanienallee 59

☎030 440 12 770; www.arabeske.berlin.de

A solid meal at a great price with no frills and one thrill (the salad dressing! No joke, it kills). Safe bets include shawarma (€5.50), which comes with hummus and salad, or its sandwich counterpart (€2.70), which is a packed, burrito-sized wrap that can be easily eaten while holding onto a subway railing for dear life. Vegetarians take comfort in falafel (€4) and the fact that they only indirectly contribute to the deaths of millions of innocent animals.

▶ 🚏 U8: Rosenthaler Pl. From the U-Bahn, head northeast up Weinbergsweg. [$] Entrees €4-6. ⏰ Open daily 11am-late.

## Humboldt University New Library Cafeteria

CAFETERIA $

Geschwister-Scholl-Str. 1

☎030 209 399 399; www.ub.hu-berlin.de

Amid the most tourist-bespeckled sidewalks in all of Mitte—where a cup of coffee costs €4—sits the quiet, seemingly off-limits library of Humboldt University. You'll find no one but students inside this absurdly narrow cafeteria in the library's entrance hall (conveniently located before the security checkpoint) that has the lowest prices anywhere in central Berlin. Bockwurst (€1.50), salads with chicken and egg (€2), pastries (€1-2), and coffee (€0.85-1.70) must be state-subsidized at these prices. They even have a tray of powders to construct your very own "curry bockwurst." Frequently packed tables may make you feel like the cafeteria outcast all over again, but there's always a small bar with quick turnover or the steps outside.

▶ 🚏 U6: Friedrichstr. From the station, take Friedrichstr. north and make a right just past the tracks. Ⓢ Entrees €1-2. Cash only. 🕐 Open M-F 9am-8pm, Sa-Su noon-5pm.

# PRENZLAUER BERG

Prenzlauer Berg is smitten with its cafes: nearly every street hides a cafe (or six), so a cheap, tasty cup of joe or a small, inexpensive meal are never hard to come by. If your place is kitchen-equipped, stock up at **Fresh'N' Friends** grocery store. (Kastanienallee 26 ☎030 440 40 670; www.freshnfriends.com 🕐 Open 24hr.)

### 🔳 W—Der Imbiss                                    VEGETARIAN $$
Kastanienallee 49

☎030 443 52 206; www.w-derimbiss.de

Maybe it's Indian food, or maybe it's Mexican. We can't really tell, but one thing we do know: it's tasty. W specializes in fusing ethnic food types to make something novel, extremely popular, and damn good. Its specialty is the *naan* pizza (€2-8)—freshly baked in a tandoori oven and spread with anything from pesto to avocado to chipotle sauce and piled high with arugula and feta or mozzarella. They also sell cold wraps, quesadillas, and burritos to go.

▶ ♯ U8: Rosenthaler Pl. From the Metro, walk north on Weinbergsweg until it becomes Kastanienallee. The restaurant is on the left. Ⓢ Cold or grilled wraps €4-6. Burritos €6. Cash only. 🕐 Open daily May-Aug noon-midnight; Sept-Apr 12:30-11:30pm.

### 🔳 Das Film Café                                    BURGERS, THEATER $$
Schliemannstr. 15

☎030 810 19 050; www.dasfilmcafe.de

Das Film Café serves homemade burgers to fans hungry for a good meal and even better movies. With screenings of indie and international films nearly every night in a small, high-resolution theater downstairs, this cafe proves that you can enjoy burgers while still "understanding" culture. Sometimes they even combine their specialties: "Eat the Movie" film breakfasts (cheese, ham, fruit, prosecco, and movie ticket; €9.90) precede the Sunday 2pm showing, while a monthly "film quiz" is, according to the waitress, a quiz that's about film. Films are never dubbed and are usually in English.

▶ ♯ U2: Eberswalder Str. From the Metro, head north on Pappelallee, turn right on Raumerstr., turn left before the park on Lychenerstr., then turn right immediately so you're walking along the park. Take a left on Schliemannstr.

The cafe will be on the right. Ⓢ Burgers €7. Breakfast €4.90-8.50. Hummus plates €5.50. Cappuccino €2. Tickets €4.50, students €4. Film quiz €5. Cash only. Ⓧ Open M-F 3pm-late, Sa-Su 11am-late.

## Suicide Sue
CAFE $$

Dunckerstr. N2

☎030 648 34 745; www.suicidesue.com

Based on an extended backstory of some *Kill-Bill*-like, samurai-sword-wielding woman who gave up slicing Yakuza brains to slice bread, Suicide Sue is a bright and beautiful place (re: intricate molding) to enjoy some inexpensive internet, coffee, and lunch. Sizable *Stullen* (sandwiches) comprise the main food options, but they're large enough, cheap enough, and varied enough that they transcend the thousands of other sandwiches that Prenzlauer Berg offers. When you're not surfing the web, check out the coffee table books on photography and film.

▶ ⚑ U2: Eberswalder Str. From the Metro, walk east on Danziger Str., then take the 3rd left on Dunckerstr. Suicide Sue is immediately on the right. Ⓢ Stullen €3-5. Breakfasts €2.40-8.50. Cake €2-3 per slice. Cash only. Ⓧ Open M-F 8am-6pm, Sa 9am-6pm, Su 10am-6pm.

## The Bird
BURGERS $$$

Am Falkpl. 5

☎030 510 53 283; www.thebirdinberlin.com

With a bar made of old wood and exposed brick, this seemingly quintessential European restaurant is anything but. Opened by two New York transplants, The Bird makes some of the only honest-to-goodness, criminally huge burgers in Berlin. Everything is made from scratch daily, including the sauce for the aptly named "napalm wings." Locals appreciate "Angry Hour," 6-8pm, when all beer is buy one, get one free. Get it? It's a reference to Angry Birds, right?

▶ ⚑ U8: Bernauer Str. From the Metro, head east on Bernauer Str. and turn left into Mauerpark. Walk along the long grassy area in the park until you reach the gigantic jungle gym of colorful logs. Turn right onto the sidewalk, and walk in front of the stadium until you reach Am Falkpl. on the other side. Turn left onto Am Falkpl., and The Bird will be immediately on your right. Ⓢ Burgers €9.50-13. Wings €6. Cash only. Ⓧ Open M-Th 6-11pm, F 5pm-midnight, Sa noon-midnight, Su noon-11pm.

### Anna Blume

CAFE $$

Kollwitzstr. 83

☎030 440 48 749; www.cafe-anna-blume.de

"Blume" means "flower" in German, and, though "Anna" doesn't mean "coffee," flowers and coffee are this corner cafe's specialties. Outdoor tables blossom out into the street to accommodate a hefty lunch crowd, and multiple coffee blends keep the clientele awake and ready for more. The jam-packed crepes (sometimes quite literally) are a crazy sweet snack; the Alphonso combines mango, orange sauce, peach yogurt, and mango ice cream in one sensational crepacorpia (€6.50). But the real forget-me-not is the flower shop next door, where you can buy some blooms for your loved ones at the height of your coffee buzz.

▶ 🚏 U2: Eberswalder Str. From the Metro, head east on Danziger Str., then turn right on Kollwitzstr. The cafe is on the right, at the southwest corner of Kollwitzstr. and Stredzkistr. $ Breakfast €4-8. Crepes €4-8.50. Coffee €2-3. ⏰ Open daily 8am-2am.

### Kreuzburger

BURGERS $

Pappelallee 19

☎030 746 95 737; www.kreuzburger.de

Okay, so it's not Kreuzberg. Get over it: when you're drunk and stumbling at 2am, you won't give a damn what *Bezirk* you're in anyway. And though we don't want to support your drunk munchies too enthusiastically, there's no better place in P'Berg to prevent a hangover with some tasty fried foods. Bigger and greasier make the morning after easier!

▶ 🚏 U2: Eberswalder Str. From the Metro, head northeast on Pappelallee and take the 1st right onto Raumerstr. Kreuzburger is on the corner of Raumerstr. and Pappelallee. $ Burgers €4-8. Fries €2. Cash only. ⏰ Open daily noon-3am.

## FRIEDRICHSHAIN

If you're staying somewhere with a kitchen, check out **Viv BioFrischeMarkt** (Boxhagener Str. 103 ☎030 521 30 688; www.viv-biofrischemarkt.de ⏰ Open M-Sa 9am-9pm.) to get your grocery fix.

### 👍 Frittiersalon

GERMAN $$

Boxhagener Str. 104

☎030 259 33 906

Yes, we know: ever since you set foot in Berlin, you've been drowning in bratwurst, currywurst, and fried potatoes. Still, this all-organic "frying salon" is unique enough to merit a visit. In addition to a traditional prize-winning Berliner currywurst, this restaurant serves German classics with a twist: try the wheat-based vegetarian currywurst or bratwurst, or a hamburger or veggie burger with strawberries and avocado. All sauces and french fries are homemade, and all dishes are cooked to order.

▶ U5: Frankfurter Tor. From the Metro, walk south on Warschauer Str. and turn left on Boxhagener Str.; the restaurant will be along the 2nd block on the left. $ Bratwurst and currywurst €2.20. Burgers €3.90-7.80. Cash only. ⏰ Open M-Th 5pm-midnight, F-Su 1pm-midnight.

## Aunt Benny — CAFE $

Oderstr. 7

☎030 664 05 300

Frequented by moms who take their children to the playground across the street, students who are wild about Wi-Fi, and anyone who's serious about the art of carrot cake, this cafe is always booming with indie rock and buzzing with caffeine. Regulars are almost aggressive with their enthusiasm for the cafe's *bricher-muesli*—a kind of Swiss cereal, containing nuts, fresh apples, and oats, soaked overnight, served with yogurt, and usually sold out by 4pm. The carrot cake will spoil you for any other attempts at buttercream frosting.

▶ U5: Frankfurter Allee. From the Metro, walk west on Frankfurter Allee, then turn left on Jessnerstr. The restaurant is on the left, opposite the park. $ Smoothies €4.20-4.80. Bagels €1.60. Cake €3.10 per slice. Coffee €1.60. Su brunch €8. Cash only. ⏰ Open Tu-F 9am-7pm, Sa-Su 10am-7pm.

## Vöner — VEGETARIAN $

Boxhagener Str. 56

☎030 992 65 423; www.voener.de

The fries are cut from organic potatoes, the fridge is stocked with more organic smoothies than your spacy aunt's garage, and the employees wear jeans that somehow manage to be skinnier than their legs. Everything on the menu is vegetarian—in fact, most of it is vegan. Veggie döners (vöners), veggie burgers (vurgers?), and veggie currywurst (not even gonna try) all compare quite nicely to their more murderous cousins.

▶ U5: Samariter Str. From the Metro, head south on Colbestr., then turn left on Boxhagener Str., and follow it down until you pass Wühlischstr. $ Vöners €3.40. Veggie burgers €3. Organic soft drinks and smoothies €1.80. ⏰ Open M-F 11:30am-11pm, Sa-Su 1:30-11pm.

## Caramello Eis
ICE CREAM $

Wühlischerstr. 31

☎030 503 43 105; www.caramello-dopamino.de

Caramello Eis scoops some of the best ice cream in town all night long to a following of devoted students. All of Caramello's ice cream is handmade, organic, and vegan, except for the flavor with bacon bits (we kid). Don't leave Friedrichshain without trying the dark chocolate *Eis* with chili powder—the staff says it's the best chocolate ice cream in all of Berlin, and we're not about to argue, as our mouths are too full.

▶ 🚏 U5: Frankfurter Tor. [$] Cones €1. Coffee €1-2.60. Smoothies €2-3. Cash only. ⏰ Open M-Th 11am-10pm, F-Sa 11am-1am, Su 11am-10pm.

## Fliegender Tisch
ITALIAN $$

Mainzer Str. 10

☎030 297 76 489

Though it lacks any of the "flying tables" that its name entails, this cozy, candlelit eatery serves inexpensive Italian food to local devotees. The pizza is cooked fresh in a Dutch oven, like their very own Fliegender Tisch pizza (bacon, onions, pickled peppers, feta cheese, and yumminess; €6.80). The restaurant's fans swear by the risotto (€5.60-6.50), and you just might swear when discussing how great it tastes. A small restaurant with a few small tables, jazz music, and low, brightly lit ceilings, Fliegender Tisch feels a lot nicer than the low prices might suggest.

▶ 🚏 U5: Samariter Str. [$] Pizza €5. Pasta €4.30-6.60. Cash only. ⏰ Open daily 5-11pm.

## Hops and Barley
MICROBREWERY $

Wühlischstr. 22/23

☎030 293 67 534; www.hopsandbarley-berlin.de

This microbrewery makes its own cider, pilsner, and lager on site for hordes of thirsty locals. The bar gets wonderfully packed for German football games, when the bar opens early (3pm) and stays open late enough for the hangovers to kick in. The guys here also make their own bread daily, so you can drink your grain and eat it too.

▶ 🚏 U5: Samariter Str. From the Metro, walk west on Frankfurter Allee, then turn left on Mainzer Str. Follow the same street as it turns into Gärtner Str., then turn left on Wühlischstr. [$] Beer €2.80 per 0.5L. Cash only. ⏰ Open daily 5pm-3am.

## Cafe Cortado                                        CAFE $

Simon-Dach-Str. 9

Flowers and board games on breezy patio tables and a cozy, sofa-covered backroom draw a young crowd with a taste for international coffee blends. Cafe Cortado's mosaic bar serves Turkish and Portuguese coffee by day and beer and cocktails by night. A variety of chai teas, a berry torte, and a handful of deliciously gooey ciabattas prepared fresh daily are highlights best enjoyed simultaneously.

▶ ⚡ U5: Frankfurter Tor. From the Metro, walk south on Warschauer Str., turn left on Grünberger Str., and turn right on Simon-Dach-Str. The cafe is in the long line of restaurants on your left. ⓢ Beer €3. Mixed drinks from €6. Coffee €1.70. Bagels €3.50. Brownies €2. Cash only. 🕐 Open M-F 9am-9pm, Sa-Su 9am-midnight.

## Yobarca                                        FROZEN YOGURT $

Simon-Dach-Str. 40

☎017 096 99 737; www.yobarca.com

This is the first frozen-yogurt place to have opened in Friedrichshain, and while the locals may still be figuring it out, we love it. Try toppings from berries to Haribo fruit snacks and Kinder chocolate. Started by an Italian ice-cream maker, this small and shockingly yellow fro-yo-to-go joint also serves a tasty take on frozen yogurt's hippest cousin: bubble tea. Eat, drink, and be yuppie.

▶ ⚡ U5: Frankfurter Tor. ⓢ Small yogurt with 1 topping €2.50. Extra toppings €0.50. Bubble tea €2.50. Cash only. 🕐 Open daily noon-8pm. Also, closed when it rains, which is sad, because isn't that when we need a sweet treat the most?

# KREUZBERG

## 🔖 Mustafa's                                        MIDDLE EASTERN $

Mehringdamm 32

www.mustafas.de

Some say that this place serves the best döner kebabs in the city—that's debatable, but Mustafa's does undoubtedly have the best dürüm (Turkish wrap filled with döner kebab; €4). Brimming with a spectacular variety of grilled and raw vegetables, plus some tasty cheese and loads of spices, a Mustafa's dürüm is what no other fast food even tries to be: nuanced. Vegetarians who usually scrounge through various falafel

**Food**

options will rejoice at the delicious grilled vegetables in the veggie dürüm (€3.10).

▶ ♯ U6 or U7: Mehringdamm. From the Metro, cross to the west side of Mehringdamm, then walk south past the big building that looks like a cartoon Medieval castle. Mustafa's is in the little stand on the sidewalk immediately past the castle. Ⓢ Entrees €2.50-5. Cash only. Ⓩ Open 24hr.

### 🔲 Santa Maria                                    MEXICAN $$

Oranienstr. 170

☎030 922 10 027; www.lasmarias.de

Started by an Australian and run by a hip, young staff from everywhere but Mexico, this Mexican restaurant defies logic with its amazingly authentic food. A few bites of anything from the long and diverse menu may convince you that you're south of the border, rather than south of the Wall. The *choriqueso* (€6.50) is a pot of melted cheese and sausage...just think about that for a second. The standard issue grub like fat Mexican sandwiches (€6), burritos (€5-7), delicious tacos (€5.50-6.50), and margaritas (€5) are also on hand, and they're all so flavorful that you'll want to savor them for hours. The exposed grill, electro beats, and candlelight make this an unbeatable evening hangout.

▶ ♯ U8: Moritzpl. From the Metro, head southeast on Oranienstr. The restaurant is on the left after Oranienpl. *i* Taco Tu (€1 tacos). Ⓢ Entrees €5-8. Cash only. Ⓩ Open daily noon-late. Happy hour (margaritas; €4) daily 8-10pm.

### 🔲 Café Morgenland                                    CAFE $$

Skalitzer Str. 35

☎030 611 32 91; www.cafemorgenland.eu

The Parisian breakfast—a fresh butter croissant, a large dish of perfect vanilla custard with fresh fruit, and the best milk coffee you've ever had—breaks the laws of economics at just €5. The all-you-can-eat brunch buffet (€9.50) on the weekends will literally make your jaw drop: eight types of meat, five types of bread, 15 spreads, five types of cereal (including German fruit loops), sausages, eggs, curries, potatoes, fish, vegetables, fruits—it's paradise. The few tables packed into this small, bright cafe and lining its sidewalk are predictably full, so unless you want to risk a long wait or an empty tummy, call ahead to make a reservation. Your salivary glands will thank you.

▶ ♯ U1: Görlitzer Bahnhof. From the Metro, walk west on Skalitzer Str. The cafe is in the little square next to the intersection between Skalitzer Str. and Manteufel Str. Ⓢ Entrees €5-15. Cash only. Ⓩ Open M-F 9am-1am, Sa-Su

10am-1am. Brunch Sa-Su 10am-4pm. Business lunch M-F noon-4pm.

### 🍴 Restaurant Rissani MIDDLE EASTERN $

Spreewaldpl. 4

☎030 616 29 433

With a thousand döner places in Kreuzberg to choose from, all of them screaming how "authentic" they are, it's difficult to find the stand-out at which to throw your gold. Well, Rissani doesn't serve döners, only chicken shawarma sandwiches, but they're twice as delicious and half as expensive (€2) as their döner cousins. Dinner plates (€5-6) with shawarma, falafel, tabbouleh, hummus, and salad will make you forget your bad day.

▶ 🚏 U1: Görlitzer Bahnhof. From the station, head east down Skalitzer str. and take a right at Spreewaldpl. [$] Entrees €2-5. Cash only. ⏰ Open M-Th 11am-3am, F-Sa 11am-5am, Su 11am-3am.

### 🍴 Henne Alt-Berliner Wirtshaus Gaststätten GERMAN $$

Leuschnerdamm 25

☎030 614 77 30; www.henne-berlin.de

Henne provides the most German experience imaginable. Inside an antler-lined parlor crammed with plaid tablecloths, sturdy German damsels haul mugs of beer, and the menu bears only a single dinner (€7.90): a piece of bread, creamy potato salad, and enormous, perfectly crispy, internationally renowned chicken that will forever redefine fried food. The chicken skin whispers, "You don't need family, friends, or love in your life. You only need ME!" Frankly, it's got a pretty compelling case.

▶ 🚏 U1 or U8: Kottbusser Tor. From the station, head northwest on Oranienstr. Take a right at Oranienpl. and follow the park about halfway to St. Michael's Church. The restaurant is at the corner of Leuschnerdamm and Waldemarstr. *i* Reservations required for outdoor seating; they're a good idea for indoor seating as well. [$] Sausage €2.40-3.50. Beer €2.60-3.60. Wine €4. Cash only. ⏰ Open Tu-Sa 7pm-late, Su 5pm-late. Kitchen open Tu-Sa 7-11pm, Su 5-10pm.

### Curry 36 CURRYWURST $

Mehringdamm 36

☎030 251 73 68; www.curry36.de

The best currywurst in Berlin means the best currywurst in the world. The standard recipe of sausage, ketchup, and curry spices becomes a holy trinity with some of the most tender, flavorful sausage in *Wurstland* and a uniquely zesty blend of spices—the ketchup's the only ingredient you'll have tasted before. Be brave: take it with fries and an enormous glob of mayo.

▶ ⚇ U6 or U7: Mehringdamm. From the Metro, head south on Mehringdamm. The fast-food stand is on the right just before Yorck/Gneisenaustr. Ⓢ Organic currywurst €1.80. French fries €1.30. Cash only. ⏰ Open daily 9am-5am.

## Oregano                      PIZZA, MIDDLE EASTERN $$

Oranienstr. 19
☎030 614 01 096

This Orianienstr. takeout place serves cheap, delicious pizza baked fresh in a stone oven with toppings prepared before your eyes in gigantic, flaming skillets. Oregano is also a kebab place on the side, so many of its pizza and menu options reflect their "Little Istanbul" surroundings with some distinctly Middle Eastern ingredients. The "Oriental" pizza bears spinach, lamb, and yogurt (€5.30), while the *rolle* (calzone; €3-5) and *pide* (calzone with egg; €3.60-5.80) each hold some infinitely edible combination of cheese, spinach, lamb, and mushrooms.

▶ ⚇ U1 or U8: Kottbusser Tor. From the Metro, head northeast on Adalbertstr. and turn right on Oranienstr. The restaurant is on the left, near the end of the block. Ⓢ Pizzas €3-6. Cash only.      ⏰ Open M-Th 11:30am-3am, F-Sa 11:30am-5am, Su 11:30am-3am.

## Courting the Currywurst

More cult than sausage, currywurst, the fried goodness of pork and beef topped with curry and ketchup, has kept Berliners happy and their stomachs full for over 60 years. As if the city's more than 2000 currywurst stands weren't enough, Berlin also opened the **Currywurst Museum** dedicated to its beloved street food. The ticket includes—no surprise—currywurst in a cup.

Also, look out for the **Grillwalker,** a franchise of currywurst vendors who carry around their grills, freezers, gas tanks, and assorted currywurst condiments and paraphernalia, as they walk around selling the goodies. With so many options, let your gut be your guide, and don't forget to wash the curry concoction down with some champagne, the latest trend in this sausage-obsessed city.

## SK Kreuzberg Food 24 GmbH

STREET FOOD $

Schlesischestr. 1-2

☎030 610 76 000

Home of the amazing €1 personal pizza and the €3 impersonal pizza (so disaffected), SK gets flooded by post-clubbers and pre-clubbers every evening. While the food may remind the careful taster of something pulled from a TV dinner, what matters most is the fact that it's hot, gooey, and filling. No need to look further; this is Kreuzberg's cheapest drunk food.

▶ 🚏 U1: Schlesisches Tor. From the Metro, cross the south lane of Skalitzer Str. along Schlesische Str. The restaurant is on the corner of Schlesiche Str. and Skalitzer Str. [$] Pasta, sandwiches €3-5. Cash only. ⏰ Open 24hr.

# Nightlife

If you're reading this section and thinking "I'm not sure I *want* to go clubbing in Berlin," then stop it. Stop it right now. Take a hint from Lady Gaga, patron saint of Berlin, and just dance... you won't regret it. The true *Diskotheken* await in the barren cityscape of Friederichshain and notoriously nocturnal Kreuzberg. Mitte does not disappoint—its tremendous multi-room clubs filled with exquisitely dressed 20-somethings are generally worth the heftier covers. The major parties in Schöneberg are at the GLBT clubs in the northern part of the neighborhood. For tamer nightlife, try the jazz clubs in Charlottenburg or the bar scene in Prenzlauer Berg.

## Budget Nightlife

Berlin is budget-friendly in most ways, but unfortunately that does not extend to clubs. Sure, it's a mecca of electro-techno-grunge-pop, but you'll have to pay the price. As usual, bars typically ask no cover, while you will be hard-pressed to find a club without one. Some of the best clubs do have designated times during which entry is free, and though you'll probably have to get there a bit before the party does, it may be worth finding this magical window on websites or *Let's Go* listings.

# CHARLOTTENBURG

Charlottenburg's quiet cafes and music venues cater to the 30-something set. The neighborhood is great for a mellow evening or some live jazz, but the real parties are eastward. The **Ku'damm** is best avoided after sunset, unless you enjoy fraternizing with drunk businessmen.

### A Trane
BAR, CLUB

Bleibtreustr. 1

☎030 313 25 50; www.a-trane.de

A Trane is small in size and big in history. With walls covered in signed black and white photographs of past jazz legends who have performed on its stage (Herbie Hancock, Wynton Marsalis) and a rack of albums recorded live there, A Trane has a long reputation as one of Berlin's premier jazz clubs. But, with dying legends and fading interest, the Trane has derailed a bit by pursuing popularity over prowess (Red Hot Chili Peppers jazz covers? No thanks!). Skip the fads and sit in on a Saturday jam session; these tend to extend well into Sunday morning.

▶ ✈ S3, S5, S7, S9, or S75: Savignypl. Ⓢ Cover €10-15, students €8-13. Sa no cover after 12:30am. Cash only. ⏰ Open M-Th 9pm-1am, F-Sa 9pm-late, Su 9pm-1am.

### Cascade
CLUB

Fasanenstr. 81

☎030 318 00 940; www.cascade-club.de

The walk down to the large basement club is bordered by steps flooded by flowing, pink water (hence Cascade). With a high cover, this club might be a bit of a splurge, but in return patrons get a dance floor of underlit blocks (a la *Saturday Night Fever*), a wall-to-wall bar, and a young crowd, which happen to be the three basic ingredients of a good dance party. There are ways to get around the high cover charge: stop by on a Friday and pick up a voucher for free entry, which is good the next evening or even the next weekend.

▶ ✈ U1: Uhlandstr. Ⓢ Cover €10, F no cover until 1am. Beer €3.50. Shots €4. Cash only. ⏰ Open F-Sa 11am-late.

### Quasimodo
CLUB

Kantstr. 12A

☎030 312 80 86; www.quasimodo.de

The upside here is that Quasimodo showcases live music in a

variety of genres, including soul, R and B, folk, and jazz, nearly every night of the week. The music choices are wildly eclectic, but each act guarantees a long night of entertainment. The downside is that the older crowd sometimes gives the club a kind of office-party energy. A spacious basement room with a large bar and stage lets all those awkward coworkers dance right up close to the performers.

▶ U2, S5, S7, S9, or S75: Zoologischer Garten. *i* Check the website for music schedule. $ Cover for concerts €8-30, cheaper if reserved in advance. Drinks €2.50-4.50. Cash only. ⏰ Open daily 12:30pm-late.

## Anda Lucia

BAR, RESTAURANT

Savignypl. 2

☎030 540 271; www.andalucia-berlin.de

So you're wandering around the streets of Berlin after hours, thinking, "Hey, you know what I'm in the mood for? A little Latin flavor! I wonder where I could nosh on tapas and show off my salsa at 2am!" (Don't say we don't know our readers.) We've found the perfect place for you: Anda Lucia may not have a dance floor, but that doesn't keep guests and staff from dancing around tables to salsa tunes blasting late into the heat of the night. There's also outdoor patio seating for those on a dance siesta and in the mood for a late night tapas. If Anda Lucia's not hoppin' on a particular night, there are, eerily, three more tapas places in Savignypl. from which to choose.

▶ S5, S7, or S75: Savignypl. $ Wines from €4 per glass. Tequila €3. Tapas €3.70-5. ⏰ Kitchen open 5pm-midnight. Tapas bar open 5pm-late.

## Salz

CLUB

Salzufer 20

☎017 028 33 504; www.salz-club.de

You'll have to go a little out of your way to find a more upbeat and youthful bunch in low-key Charlottenburg—and by "a little out of your way" we mean a 20min. walk from the nearest U-Bahn station. But if you're looking to stay in the neighborhood and see someone dancing under the age of 32, this is the place to go. Exposed brick walls keep the disco-ball-lit floor looking classy at this salt-warehouse-turned-techno-club. Out front find a beautiful patio lit with multi-colored lights and tiki torches.

▶ U2: Ernst-Reuter-Pl. Walk down Str. des 17 Juni to Satzufer. Turn left and walk along the river to Salz. *i* Check the website for music schedules. $ No cover. Cash only. ⏰ Open Th 8pm-late.

# SCHÖNEBERG AND WILMERSDORF

Schöneberg is still Berlin's unofficial gay district, therefore it's full of GLBT nightlife. A couple of distinctive cocktail bars may be worth visiting in the interest of broadening your buzz, but the neighborhood's real parties happen at the GLBT clubs and bars in northern Schöneberg.

**Nightlife**

### ☒ Hafen                                    BAR, GLBT

Motzstr. 19

☎030 211 41 18; www.hafen-berlin.de

Nearly 20 years old, this bar has become a landmark for Berlin's gay community. The sign outside may only specifically invite "drop dead gorgeous looking tourists," but you'll find plenty of locals all along the spectrum of attractiveness. Dancing neon lights grace the walls of an expansive bar with a large supply of tables and a consistently high level of volume and energy from its clean, drum-machine-heavy tunage. The weekly pub quiz (M 8pm; 1st M of the month in English) is wildly popular, and every Wednesday features a new DJ. On April 30th, Hafen hosts their largest party of the year, in honor of the Queen of the Netherlands. They promise us that the "Queen" makes an appearance.

▶ ✄ U1, U3, U4, or U9: Nollendorfpl. Ⓢ No cover. ⏰ Open daily 8am-4am. Cash only.

### ☒ Slumberland                              BAR

Goltstr. 24

☎030 216 53 49

So normally we like a little more authenticity in our bars, but we're not going to pretend that we don't appreciate an island escape in the middle of land-locked Berlin, and the locals aren't either. So what if you didn't come to Germany for reggae, palm trees, and sand in your shoes? By the way, if you were confused with that last part, the floor is covered with sand. Try an obligatory beach favorite, like a piña colada or a Sex on the Beach (both €6.50), or go tropical in a new direction with a fruit-flavored African beer (DjuDju, €3.90).

▶ ✄ U1, U3, U4, or U9: Nollendorfpl. Ⓢ Most drinks €2-7. ⏰ Open M-Th 6pm-2am, F 6pm-4am, Sa 11am-4am, Su 6pm-2am.

## Prinzknecht

BAR, GLBT

Fuggerstr. 33

☎030 236 27 444; www.prinzknecht.de

A huge wooden bar dancing with disco ball reflections is the beating heart of this ecstatic gay bar. Even with levels upon levels of bar stools and couches extending far back into its neon-lit interior, the bar fills up way past capacity on event nights, and people begin to resemble waves on the street. A mostly male clientele spread between 20-somethings and 50-year-olds nods to the almost oppressively loud beats inside, while others cool off on the long benches that stretch across the pavement outside. Check the website for upcoming events, including an incredibly popular ABBA night.

▶ 🚏 U1 or U2: Wittenbergpl. $ 2-for-1 drinks W 7-9pm. Cash only. ⏰ Open M-F 2pm-3am, Sa and Su 3pm-3am.

## Begine

BAR, GLBT

Potsdamer Str. 139

☎030 215 14 14; www.begine.de

In a neighborhood dominated by male gay clubs, Begine is a welcome retreat for women. Named after a now-defunct Lesbian WC, Berlin's biggest lesbian community center has a popular, low-key cafe and bar with comfortable sofas and features readings and live music at night. Dim yellow lighting and an acre of empty floor space make for a quiet bar that offers a short and unremarkable list of beers, coffee, and cocktails. The bar is far removed from the nightlife center over by Nollendorfpl., but maybe that's precisely the point. An older crowd proudly patronizes this respectable neighborhood rarity.

▶ 🚏 U2: Bülowstr. ⏰ Open M-F 5pm-late, Sa 3pm-late, Su 7pm-late.

## Train

BAR

On the corner of Potsdamer Str. and Willmanndamm

☎030 017 734 441 23

You know those terrible restaurants that our parents took you to when you were a kid, ya know, the ones inside of old train cars? Well, this cocktail bar, located inside a good ol' locomotive, may bring back those mundane memories. Sure, it's gimmicky, but it's also decked out in aluminum foil ceilings and chandeliers, and totally packed with sexy 20-somethings! With a ton of train-themed drinks listed in the sleek black menu, like the fruity Train Fever (rum, lime juice, lemon juice, maracuja syrup, mango juice; €6), you might easily wake up the next morning feeling like you were run over by several trains. Choo choo!

▶ 🚇 U7: Kleistpark. 💲 All cocktails €6, €5 on M-Tu and Su nights. Cash only. 🕙 Open daily 1pm-late.

### Heile Welt
BAR, GLBT

Motzstr. 5

☎030 219 17 507

Even with the addition of two enormous, quiet sitting rooms, the 20-something clientele still pack the bar and take over the street. As a foil to the frenetic energy of **Hafen,** which lies a little further down Motzstr., Heile Welt keeps its cool with a fur-covered wall, chandeliers, gold tassels darkening the street window, and a row of comfy armchairs. But without much of the glamor or volume of its competitors, Heile Welt can seem dull at times, so arrive once your buzz has begun to mellow.

▶ 🚇 U1, U3, U4, or U9: Nollendorfpl. 💲 Beers €2.50 per liter. Cash only. 🕙 Open daily 6pm-4am, sometimes later.

# MITTE

### 🏅 Cookies
CLUB

Friedrichstr. 158

☎030 274 92 940; www.cookies-berlin.de

Hot, sweaty, sexy, and packed, Cookies is housed in a former Stasi bunker that operates as a restaurant during the day. Locals claim that this party originally started in some guy's basement before moving to more permanent digs. Three bars lubricate your dancing joints with a long list of trendy, expensive cocktails, such as the Watermelonman (Smirnoff, watermelon liqueur, grenadine, lemon juice, orange juice; €7.50). Once you're all messy and unbalanced, choose between a huge dance floor with light, clean techno and a tiny room with heavy American hip hop. The party don't start 'til 1am, so save your tears if you show up alone at midnight. Also, invest in some plaid or a cardigan beforehand, because the bouncers tend to select the more hipsterly attired.

▶ 🚇 U6: Französische Str. From the Metro, head north on Friedrichstr. along the left side of the street. The club is unmarked, so look for a group of darkly dressed dudes around a door as you near Dorotheenstr. 💲 Cover €5-15. Cocktails €7.50-€10. Coat check €1. Unfortunately, no baked goods. 🕙 Open Tu 10:30pm-6am, Th 10:30pm-6am.

## Levee CLUB

Neue Promenade 10

www.levee-club.com

This dark and smoky techno club, hidden under the S-Bahn tracks in a nook just off of Hackescher Markt, is tremendously popular among 20-something locals. And there's no wonder why. There are two very different dance floors: the one on the ground floor is large and surrounded by a huge bar, while the one downstairs is cramped (or intimate, depending on your tastes) and better dressed. The ground floor's techno is heavy; upstairs it's heavier. The cover can be difficult to, well, cover at popular hours, but you'll want to stay here all night once it gets packed around 1 or 2am. Check the website for guest DJs, concerts, and special events.

▶ 🚏 S5, S7, S9, or S75: Hackescher Markt. From the Metro, walk west and enter the 1st street that runs under the S-Bahn tracks. $ Cover free-€20. Beer €4. Cash only. ⏰ Open F-Sa 11pm-late.

## Kaffee Burger CLUB

Torstr. 58-60

☎030 280 46 495; www.kaffeeburger.de

So it's a Wednesday night and you're buzzed from the hostel bar, but can't find anywhere to show off your moves: Kaffee Burger is the perfect place to stumble into. There's a small dance floor packed by 20-year-olds in band T-shirts and scarves right next to 40- and 50-year-olds showing off how crazy they can still be. With a quieter, smokier "Burger Bar" next door with plenty of cushy furniture to lounge on and a cocktail called the "Drunken Rihanna" (€7), Kaffee Burger will transform your weeknight from a bleak night into a freak night. Weekly programs include poetry readings, film screenings, and drunken sloppiness.

▶ 🚏 U6: Rosa-Luxemburg-Pl. From the Metro, walk 1 block to the east on Torstr. $ Cover M-Th €1, F-Sa €5, Su €1. Beer €2.50. Shots €3-4. Cocktails €6-7. Cash only. ⏰ Open M-F 8pm-late, Sa 9pm-late, Su 7pm-late.

## Week End CLUB

Alexanderpl. 5

☎030 246 31 676; www.week-end-berlin.de

Two words: rooftop bar. It may not be the rooftop of the Park Inn nearby, but this club with the neon "Sharp" sign in the smaller skyscraper just off Alexanderpl. lets you cool off from the bangin' dance floor while enjoying a spectacular view of Mitte's nightscape. Downstairs in the actual club, a tremendous bar borders a small dance floor with some of the coolest lighting you'll find outside of a Lady Gaga concert. One downside is the annoyingly large tourist population invited by this club's central location, none of whom are adequately acclimated to the heavy techno. Plus, with skyscraping cover and drink prices, you may not want to spend every weekend at Week End.

▶ ⚌ U6: Alexander Pl. From the Metro, head northeast to the "Sharp" building. Ⓢ Cover €10-20. Coat check €1.20. 🕐 Open F-Su 11pm-late.

### Clärchens Ballhaus                                               CLUB
Auguststr. 24
☎030 282 92 95; www.ballhaus.de

For travelers who enjoy the type of dancing that gets worse as the night wears on, this 1930s-style ballroom has cha cha, salsa, and other programs Sunday through Thursday. Friday and Saturday DJs play "hipper" music. Come early for a drink in the beautiful patio garden, or come late to watch the surprisingly talented steppers of all generations kick it old school in a tremendous hall surrounded by silver tassels.

▶ ⚌ U8: Oranienburger Str. From the Metro, head north on Tucholsky Str. and turn right on Auguststr. Ⓢ M-Th, Su programs €8, students €6, after

Nightlife

midnight free; F-Sa €3. ⏰ Open daily 10am-late. Dance programs start 7-8:30pm, depending on the day of the week. Check the website for more details.

## 8mm Bar

BAR

Schönhauser Allee 177B

☎030 405 00 624; www.8mmbar.com

8MM is a dim, smoky hipster bar where you can chat about how ironic you are or just play a round of pool. Art films projected on the wall, guest performers, and live DJs make this more than just a place to wear flannel and look disaffected, although there's still plenty of that to go around. Crowd levels vary, but when it's bustling, it's bustling.

▸ 🚏 U2: Senefelderpl. From the Metro, head south on Schönhauser Allee. $ Beer €2.50-6. Mixed drinks €4-7. Cash only. ⏰ Open M-Th 8pm-late, F-Su 9pm-late.

## Delicious Doughnuts

CLUB

Rosenthaler Str. 9

☎030 280 99 274; www.delicious-doughnuts.de

No, it's not a doughnut shop. Yes, it's a hip backpacker hangout with a late-20s crowd of locals. There's not much room to dance here, but there are plenty of couches and space enough to relax, talk, drink, and smoke. Plus, there's a gigantic bar with pretty much any drink you can think of, all under a mess of tree branches and a stuffed owl. If your friends are boring, escape to the pinball machine in the corner. After all, a small steel ball is friend enough for anyone.

▸ 🚏 U8: Rosenthaler Pl. From the Metro, head south on Rosenthaler Str. It's the club on the corner of Rosenthaler Str. and Auguststr. labeled with a donut with three crosshatches. $ Cover €5-10. Cocktails €6-8. ⏰ Open daily 10pm-late.

## Neue Odessa Bar

BAR

Torstr. 89

☎017 183 98 991

Black-and-white-striped wallpaper, dimly lit vintage parlors furnished with cushy, classy furniture, and a dazzling bar invite you to this glamorous and heavily populated hipster bar. The bar is small and there will constantly be several layers of the perfectly dressed keeping you from it, but plenty of table space spread across two large rooms and lining the sidewalk outside means that it won't be difficult to find a niche. A live DJ spinning electropoppy American indie rock completes the scene.

▶ 🚇 U6: Rosa-Luxemburg-Pl. From the Metro, walk 2 blocks east on Torstr. to the corner of Torstr. and Chorinerstr. $ No cover. Beer €3. Cocktails €6-8. Cash only. ⏰ Open daily 7pm-late.

### Tape

CLUB

Heidestr. 14

☎030 284 84 873; www.tapeberlin.de

The huge open spaces of this converted warehouse keep it cool when the party hits a hard boil. And it always does. The party starts (and goes) very late. Tape derives some of its hip powers from its remote location: be sure to check the website calendar before making the long trek, because after an hour-long quest, you don't want to find it closed for the night.

▶ 🚇 U8: Hauptbahnhof. From the Metro, walk north on Heidestr. for about 10min. Tape will be on your right, in an old warehouse building. $ Cover varies. Cash only. ⏰ Open F-Sa 11pm-late.

## PRENZLAUER BERG

With less techno, more lounging, and far earlier quiet hours (midnight-1am) than other parts of Berlin, Prenzlauer Berg's nightlife is calm but worth checking out. The bars are some of the most unforgettable in town, and, since they fill and empty a bit earlier, they're perfect before you head out to later, clubbier climes.

### 👍 The Weinerei: Forum

BAR

Fehrbelliner Str. 57

☎030 600 53 072; www.weinerei.com

This unmarked wine bar has been catapulted from local secret to local legend thanks to its comfortable elegance and unique payment system. Pay €2 for a glass, sample all the wines, and then sample again and again. Before leaving, just pay what you think you owe. Only in Berlin! Enjoy your vintage at an outdoor table or on an indoor sofa, but be warned: this place is so absurdly (and understandably) popular that you'll definitely have trouble finding a seat.

▶ 🚇 U2: Senefelderpl. From the Metro, exit by the northern stairs, then head west on Schwedter Str. Turn left on Kastanienalle, then veer right onto Veteranenstr. a block down the hill. The bar is on the corner of Veteranenstr. and Fehrbelliner Str. $ Depends on how drunk you get. Cash only. ⏰ Open M-Sa 10am-late, Su 11am-late, but the wine flows 8pm-midnight every night, so let that guide you.

## 👍 Dr. Pong

BAR, PING-PONG

Eberswalder Str. 21

www.drpong.net

Under falling fluorescent lights, in the middle of a concrete room with peeling paint, stands a single ping-pong table, the centerpiece of this minimal bar. Intense hipsters ring the table, gripping their paddles, motivated by nothing other than the thrill of victory over a ring of unsteady strangers. All are welcome, including beginners and the severely intoxicated.

▶ 🚏 U2: Eberswalder Str. From the Metro, head east on Eberswalder Str. The bar is on the left. $ Cover €3.50; includes 1 beer. Beer €2.70. Cocktails €4.50-5.50. Cash only. ⏰ Open M-Sa 8pm-late, Su 6pm-late.

## 👍 Klub Der Republik (KDR)

CLUB

Pappelallee 81

www.myspace.com/klubderrepublik

There are few museums that have as many authentic Soviet artifacts as KDR has hanging on its walls. Once the showroom of a DDR carpet and linoleum supplier, KDR kept the old Formica bar and leaded glass, and added lamps from the original Palast Republik, as it was being torn down. The furniture is from the DDR landmark Café Moscow. Eclectic DJs play everything from punk to trance to something known as "cosmic disco," which is probably as ahead-of-its-time as Sputnik. Huge crowds of P'Berg's hippest comrades arrive late and stay late, so end your night at KDR, and you won't be disappointed.

▶ 🚏 U2: Eberswalder Str. Turn into what looks like a deserted parking lot and climb the metal stairs. ℹ DJs W-Su. Check the website for a schedule of events. $ Long drinks €5-6. Beer €2.30-3. Spirits €3.50-5. Cash only. ⏰ Open from "dark to light." In more definite terms, that's around 9pm-late in the summer, 8pm-late in the winter.

## Scotch and Sofa

BAR

Kollwitzstr. 18

☎030 440 42 371

Exactly what the name promises. This bar channels gold-foiled '70s glamour and serves classic drinks on vintage sofas. Far from stuffy, Scotch and Sofa relaxes to some mellow tunes—big band and reggae sound especially refreshing in a land of house—and grand French doors open up to a quiet street lined with patio seating.

▶ 🚏 U2: Senefelderpl. From the Metro, exit by the northern stairs, then head southeast on Metzer Str. After passing the grocery store, turn left on Kollwitzstr. The bar is on the right, about half a block up Kollwitzstr. ℹ Happy hour cocktail of the day €3.80. $ Scotch from €5. ⏰ Open daily 6pm-very late. Happy hour daily 6-7pm.

## Wohnzimmer BAR

Lettestr. 6

☎030 445 54 58; www.wohnzimmer-bar.de

Wohnzimmer means "living room," and it's not hard to see why this bar goes by that name, given its wide wood-planked floors, glassware cabinets, and vintage lounge chairs. Settle into a velvety Victorian sofa with a mixed drink among a crowd split between nostalgic 50-year-olds and 25-year-olds wishing they had something to feel nostalgic about.

▶ 🚏 U2: Eberswalder Str. From the Metro, head east on Danziger Str., turn left on Lychener Str., then turn right on Lettestr., just past the park. The bar is on the left, at the corner of Lettestr. and Schliemannstr. $ Cocktails €4-5. Beer €2.50-3. Cash only. ⏰ Open daily 9am-4am.

## Duncker CLUB

Dunckerstr. 64

☎030 445 95 09; www.dunckerclub.de

Suits of armor, chainmail, and retro bead curtains hang from the high ceilings of this horse-stable-turned-club. A gigantic metal bat keeps a watchful perch above the small corner stage—who knows, it may even come alive on "Dark Monday." Duncker heats up at around 1am, when it draws punkish crowds with an insider vibe and great sound. Ring the bell for entry.

▶ 🚏 U2: Eberswalder Str. From the Metro, head east on Danziger Str., then turn left on Dunckerstr. Walk north on Dunckerstr. until you reach the bridge over the train tracks. The club is on the left, in the darkened building, immediately past the bridge. ℹ Goth music on M. Eclectic DJs Tu-W. Live bands on Th. "Independent dance music" F-Sa. Throwback DJs on Su. "Dark Market" goth flea market on Su 1pm. $ Cover M-W €2.50, F €4, Sa €4.50, Su €2.50. No cover on Th. Beers €2.50. Long drinks €4.50. F-Sa all drinks max €2. Cash only. ⏰ Open M-W 9pm-late, Th 10pm-late, F-Sa 11pm-late, Su 10pm-late.

## White Trash Fast Food BAR, CLUB, TATTOOS

Schönehauser Allee 6-7

☎030 503 48 668; www.whitetrashfastfood.com

White Trash Fast Food cakes the irony on so disgustingly thick that it may be hard to tell whether you're actually enjoying yourself. Four floors filled with intentionally kitschy paintings, obscene Americanisms, and dark, candlelit hallways mean that entering this restaurant/bar/club/tattoo parlor complex feels like descending into some haunted funhouse. Fortunately, it can be a lot of fun. International punk bands, rock bands, and DJs fill the place with distorted noise every night of the week, and the wide, greasy, hilarious menu is worth sampling. Is this how Americans seem to the world? Hell yeah.

▶ � U2: Senefelderpl. From the Metro, exit by the southern steps, then head south on Schönhauser Allee. The bar is on the left as you approach Torstr. ⑤ Cover €5. Beers €2.80-3.50. Specialty drinks from €8. Burgers €7.50-13. Cash only. ⏰ Open M-F noon-late, Sa-Su 6pm-late.

## Morgenrot                                                              BAR

Kastanienallee 85

☎030 443 17 844; www.cafe-morgenrot.de

This little cafe is trying to save the world, and they're having a great time doing it. Owned by a five-person work collective, Morgenrot makes vegan, organic, fair-trade food by day (including a weekend brunch buffet where guests pay €5-9, according to what they can afford) and serves beer, frosty vodka shots, and live house music by night. Deep teal walls and climbing plants on the outside pull in black-clothed crowds to brood over how much capitalism has destroyed their souls.

▶ ✧ U2: Eberswalder Str. From the Metro, head southwest on Kastanienallee. The bar is about halfway down the 2nd block on the left. ⑤ Shots €2. Beer €2.50-3. Spirits €3.60. Cash only. ⏰ Open Tu-Th noon-1am, F-Sa 11am-3am, Su 11am-1am.

# FRIEDRICHSHAIN

With its heavily graffitied walls and blinding floodlights, industrial Friedrichshain may not be the most inviting neighborhood to navigate in the dead of night, but it hides some of Berlin's biggest and most bangin' techno clubs. The old warehouses along **Revaler Strasse** hold the lion's share of sprawling dance floors, but you might want to branch out a little to avoid a double-digit cover. Fortunately for those with two left feet (or three for that matter) Friedrichshain isn't only about its *Diskotheken:* the area around **Simon-Dach-Strasse** provides plenty of popular bars to liven your night without stretching your legs.

**Nightlife**

## ◪ Rosi's                                                    CLUB

Revaler Str. 29
www.rosis-berlin.de

Walking into this indoor-outdoor club complex is like a kid walking into a candy store with great house music playing over the speakers: there are a ton of things to do, and, like we said, there's great house music playing over the speakers! Outdoor features include a fire pit, ping-pong, a small dance floor, and a tiny grill. Indoor features include Indiana Jones pinball, a high-ceilinged dance floor, and, still, great house music playing over the speakers. Rosi's is way at the opposite end of Revaler Str. from the main club complex, meaning that natural selection weeds out most of the tourist riff-raff on the dark walk over. Plus, parties start and end super late, so this is a perfect place to end your night.

▶ ⚡ U1, S3, S5, S7, S9, or S75: Warschauer Str. From the Metro, walk north on Warschauer Str., turn right on Revaler Str., and walk for about 10min; Rosi's will be on your right. Ⓢ Cover €3-7. Cash only. ⏰ Open Th-Sa 11pm-late.

## Astro-Bar                                                    BAR

Simon-Dach-Str. 40
www.myspace.com/astrobar

If your religion requires that you only enter houses of debauchery with Transformers action figures nailed behind the bar, then enter Astro-Bar with ease. Light-years of lounge and table space line the walls, while the dim lighting from orb-shaped lamps may make you feel lost in space. With a new DJ every night, Astro-Bar provides a ton of tunage, from punk to powerpop to Britfunk to every head-scratching subgenre under the sun. Astro-Bar is an extremely popular bar with the 20-something set; the kids just keep coming back for the booze, the tunes, and the feeling that they're floating in space.

▶ ⚡ U5: Frankfurter Tor. From the Metro, head south on Warschauer Str., turn right on Grünberger Str., and then turn right on Simon-Dach-Str. Ⓢ Beer from €2.50. Mixed drinks from €5. Cash only. ⏰ Open daily 6pm-late.

## K-17                                                         CLUB

Pettenkoferstr. 17
www.k17.de

This towering club has a spacious dance floor and bar on each of its four floors. It's a long trip from any of the nightlife centers in Friedrichshain, but this ensures fewer tourists on the hunt for their first *Diskothek* experience. Metal and all things loud and crunchy blast from the speakers of each floor, attracting a mostly black-clad crowd that will inevitably think you're preppy. Concerts are usually once per week, so keep an eye on the website for dates and prices.

▶ U5: Frankfurter Allee. Once you're on Pettenkoferstr., keep an eye out for signs; the club is off the road on your right. $ Cover €6. Beer €2.50. Vodka and coke €3.50. ⏰ Open F-Sa 10pm-late.

## Abgedreht BAR

Karl-Marx-Allee 140

☎030 293 81 911; www.abgedreht.net

Though it caters particularly to a metal crowd, with enough churning guitars on the speakers to make any grandma faint, this dim and dark wooden bar serves up enough good beer and loud company to attract a wider set of locals than just the ones wearing black. Sheet music papers the walls, and leather couches clump around antique sewing tables, all of which are puzzling in a bar whose name means "high" in colloquial German. Though its crowd generally falls in the 30+ range, and though you might get a couple of disapproving stares when you walk in wearing that lime-green button-up that your mom bought you, this is one of the more accessible points of entry into F'Hain's metal scene.

▶ U5: Frankfurter Tor. From the Metro, walk west on Karl-Marx-Allee until you pass the building with the huge, copper tower. $ Beer €3-4 per 0.5L. Happy hour cocktails €4. Traditional German foods like bratwurst and *wienerschnitzel* around €9. Cash only. ⏰ Open daily 5pm-late. Happy hour 7-9pm.

## Sanitorium 23 BAR

Frankfurter Allee 23

☎030 420 21 193; www.sanatorium23.de

If you're looking to experience the techno scene but don't know if you're ready for the Revalerstr. riot, get your feet wet at Sanitorium 23. This bar plays light, almost clinical techno to guests that lounge on sleek, backless couches shaped like cubes. It's almost like they're all sitting on a life-sized version of the menu, which is cleverly designed to look like the periodic table of elements.

▶ U5: Frankfurter Tor. $ Cocktails €5.50-8. Beer €2.50-3.50. Cash only. ⏰ Open M-Th 3pm-2am, F-Sa 4pm-4am, Su 4pm-2am.

## Fritz Club

CLUB

Prinzessinnenstr. 1

☎030 698 12 80; www.fritzclub.com

It's a testament to how touristy this place is that the American Top 40 dance floor is constantly and completely packed, while the techno floor remains sparsely attended. That said, the club's three tremendous dance floors—the other one plays American arena rock, which is not quite a dealbreaker in our book—provide plenty of space and opportunity for you to try your feet at some different dance cuisine, and the whole place is a constant bustle of activity and colored lights. A huge outdoor rock garden that's more desert than oasis provides some space to lounge and let your sweat evaporate, while bars strewn liberally about the complex prevent you from going dry. Though it's a bit far and we have our reservations, a relatively cheap cover and a constant stream of 20-year-olds ready to pump their fists make this one of the highlights off Mühlenstr.

▸ 🚏 S3, S5, or S75: Ostbahnhof. From the Metro, walk south on Str. der Pariser Kommune, turn left on Mühlenstr., and take the first left toward the big complex of warehouses. The club will be on the right side of these warehouses. $ Beer €3-3.50. Cover €6. Cash only. ⏰ Concerts start at 9pm. Club open F-Su 11pm-late and select weekdays. Check the website for a calendar of events.

## Red Rooster

BAR

Grünbergerstr. 23

☎030 290 03 310; www.redroosterbar.de

Since it's linked to the Odysee Hostel next door, the Red Rooster fills every night with an international crowd of backpackers, who spill out onto the outdoor patio and porch swing. Inside, from behind an old wood countertop and under exposed brick ceilings and pipelines, bartenders serve cider and Czech beers from the tap. For the particularly outgoing or desperate backpacker, "perform 4 stay" events invite you to sing for a free beer—or even a free bed! The drunken crowing that results is where we assume the name comes from.

▸ 🚏 U5: Frankfurter Tor. Walk south on Warschauer Str. and turn right on Grünberger Str. $ Beer from €2.50-3. Cash only. ⏰ Open M-Th 5pm-1am, F-Sa 5pm-3am, Su 5pm-1am.

### Cassiopeia
CLUB, BEER GARDEN, RESTAURANT, LIVE MUSIC

Revaler Str. 99

☎030 473 85 949; www.cassiopeia-berlin.de

A sprawling nightlife oasis in an abandoned train factory with space for about 3000 guests, this all-in-one entertainment complex may as well have its own government. Outdoor couches and a climbing wall let you take a break from the huge indoor dance floor, not that you'll want to—the tunes are unstoppable. Occasionally, the club hosts concerts, usually starting around 8pm; check out the list of bands you've never heard of on the website. Unfortunately, with a cover that can move into the high teens during prime time, the budget traveler may have to remain content with gazing at the Cassiopeia in the sky, rather than gaining entry to this piece of club heaven on earth.

▶ 🚏 U1, S3, S5, S7, S9, or S75: Warschauer Str. $ Cover €5-16. Beer €2.50-3. Vodka €2.50. Cash only. ⏰ Open W-Sa 11pm-late.

### Jägerklause
BAR, BEER GARDEN

Grünbergerstr. 1

☎017 622 286 892; www.jaegerklause-berlin.de

Jägerklause is frequented by pin-up stylers, leather-clad bikers, and the old T-shirt and ripped-jeans crowd. Hence the mounted antlers and disco ball combo. This bar is known for its large beer garden lined with tall shrubs, where guests can lounge in canvas chairs under strands of outdoor lights while sniffing the bratwurst and steaks sizzling on the grill. The connected pub has a dance floor, and features live bands, like the chart-topping stylings of a band called Cannabis Corpse from Wednesday to Saturday. Check the website calendar for dates and deets.

▶ 🚏 U5: Frankfurter Tor. ⏰ Beer garden open daily 3pm-late. Pub open daily 6pm-late.

## KREUZBERG

Kreuzberg is world-renowned for its unbelievable techno scene. Converted warehouses, wild light displays, destructive speaker systems, and dance floors so packed they look like Dante's *Inferno* cluster around **Schlesisches Tor,** but some of the best are scattered more widely. Kreuzberg is one of Berlin's most notoriously nocturnal neighborhoods, so expect the parties to rage from about 2am to well past dawn.

## Club Tresor

CLUB

Köpenicker Str. 70

☎030 629 08 750; www.tresorberlin.com

Club Tresor, like many of Berlin's best, contains two dance floors in an old warehouse. Apart from that, there is no comparison to be made between this superb club and its peers. The basement dance floor manages to provide plenty of dancing and breathing room in one of the most oppressive environments of any Berlin club. Intense strobe lights cut up the time continuum, exposed pipeline caverns hide unseen techno monsters, and the beats are so heavy, they practically dislodge the drywall. Upstairs, a brighter, redder, and more comfortable floor plays tight house tracks, which serve as a perfect warm-up or cool-down. Make the trek, stay all night, and have your nightmares later.

▸ 🚏 U8: Heinrich Heinestr. $ Cover €8-15. Cash only. ⏰ Usually open W 10pm-late, F-Sa 10pm-late.Check the website for a schedule.

## Club der Visionaere

CLUB, BAR

Am Flutgraben 1

☎030 695 18 942; www.clubdervisionaere.com

Though this riverfront cabana/bar/club/boat is packed, the experience is well worth the sweaty armpits. A DJ spins inside a mini indoor club, but the fun's definitely outside, where you can sip rum drinks, dip your feet in the river, and share large pizzas (€8) with friends, preferably all at once. This club is like a mix of the Bayou, New York, and Cancun, but it could never exist in any of them. So relaxing, so visionary, so Berlin.

▸ 🚏 U1: Schlesisches Tor. From the Metro head southeast on Schlesischestr. Cross the 1st canal, and, when you reach the 2nd, the club will be on the left next to the bridge. $ Cover €4-15. Beer €2.50-3.50. Long drinks €5.50. Cash only. ⏰ Open M-F 2pm-late, Sa-Su noon-late.

## Horst Krzbrg

CLUB

Tempelhofer Ufer 1

www.horst-krzbrg.de

Though it's not a tremendous, multi-level, self-sufficient community like many of Kreuzberg's clubs, Horst Krzbrg offers an excess of two club fundamentals: delicious beats and room to dance. This club is the place to be when you're fed up with the incessant pulse of house that hounds you from every bar and club you pass. The drum kicks here are all over the place and not necessarily where you expect them to be, yielding music that's just as unsettling as it is danceable—that is, extremely. The spacious, black-and-white tiled dance floor allows a young, bohemian crowd to spread out and go crazy—think punks, scene kids, and misplaced dudes in baggy jeans and old Adidas flailing their limbs. Though it'll take some commuting, Horst Krzbrg is a worthy place to spend any (or all) of your weekend nights.

▶ ⚥ U1, U6: Hallesches Tor. From the Metro, cross to the south side of the river, then turn right on Tempelhofer Ufer. ⓢ Cover €8-12. Shots €2.50-3. Beer €3. Long drinks €6-7. Cash only. ⏰ Hours vary, but normally open Th-Sa midnight-late.

## Arena Club                                                        CLUB
Eichenstr. 4
☎030 533 20 30; www.arena-club.de

Part of the awesome indoor/outdoor complex of Arena, which includes a pool floating on the Spree and a gigantic venue for concerts and events, Arena Club inhabits an old, two-story factory building, in which some of the old machinery is still intact. Plenty of lounge space, with cushy, square booths for snuggling, fills every corner of the labyrinthine floor plan, along with two bars and two dance floors that spin a wide range of techno. The factory aesthetic is good retro fun (check out the throwback glass tiles on the second floor), the tunes are some of Kreuzberg's finest, and the whole place promises a memorable night of raging and relaxing in alternation.

▶ ⚥ U1: Schlesisches Tor. From the Metro, head south on Schlesischestr. across both canal bridges. The Arena complex is the large industrial set of buildings on the left after the 2nd bridge. ⓢ Cover €5-10. Cash only. ⏰ Party hours vary but usually open F-Sa midnight-late.

## Watergate                                                         CLUB
Falckensteinstr. 49
☎030 612 80 396; www.water-gate.de

Even if we don't recommend it, we understand: you'll probably end up going anyway. As Berlin's most exclusive club, this is a must for anyone who needs something to brag about on Facebook. From about 1am on (and we mean *on*), a long line (30min.-1hr.) will greet you at the door. If not perfectly gender-balanced or heavy on the women, groups should split up: the bouncer is ruthless. Inside, you'll find a gorgeous Spree-level view, a boat to cool off on, and a dance floor that's so packed, so loud, and so long, that you'll probably momentarily forget the world while you're there. The whole place is spectacular and enticing, but for authenticity's sake, we urge you to seek some other Kreuzberg clubs. Watergate is like Nixon's presidency: ruined by nosy Americans. So if you're looking for somewhere more local, look around.

▶ ♯ U1: Schlesisches Tor. From the Metro, head toward the bridge. It's the unmarked door at the top of the stairs just before the river. There'll be a line. Ⓢ Cover €8-20. Mixed drinks €6.50. Cash only. ⏰ Open W midnight-late, F-Sa midnight-late.

**Nightlife**

## Ritter Butzke CLUB

Ritterstr. 24

www.ritterbutzke.de

One of Berlin's only clubs to feature a *Gästeliste,* or guest list, in addition to regular admission for n00bs and natives without friends in high places, Ritter Butzke's three-dance-floor complex nestled in the alleyways of an old factory building is one of Kreuzberg's most well-known and best-kept secrets. Word about this place doesn't often reach tourists, so it's one of your best bets for kickin' it with local *Volk.* Floors vary from small and intimate to medium-sized and cramped to expansive and accommodating of even the most notorious toe steppers.

▶ ♯ U1: Prinzenstr. From the Metro, head northeast on Prinzenstr. for 2 blocks, then turn left on Ritterstr. Halfway down the block, turn into the courtyard shaded by trees on the right. The entrance to the club is at the end of this courtyard. Ⓢ Cover around €10. Shots €2-2.50. Beer €2-3. Long drinks €5-6. Cash only. ⏰ Hours vary, but generally open F midnight-late, Sa 10pm-late. Check the website for a full calendar of events.

## Luzia BAR, CAFE

Oranienstr. 34

☎030 817 99 958; www.luzia.tc

This huge bar is tremendously popular among a 20-something, hipster clientele, and understandably so. Gold-painted walls glow softly in a dim space flickering with candles. A huge, L-shaped design allows for long lines of vintage, threadbare lounge chairs, cafe tables, and a bar so long that it can easily fit even the crowd that swarms at peak hours. The tables out on the sidewalk are always packed, with skinny-jeaned barhoppers replacing skinny-jeaned cafe-dwellers at sundown. Sipping absinthe in a dilapidated armchair to '80s synth? Yeah, you're in Berlin.

▶ ♯ U1 or U8: Kotbusser Tor. From the Metro, head northeast up Aldabertstr.

and turn left on Oranienstr. The bar is on the right. The only sign is a large, black rectangle with a gold coat-of-arms in the middle. $ Beer €2.50-3.50. Long drinks €5-6. Absinthe €3-7. Cash only. ⏰ Open daily noon-late.

## Magnet Club

CLUB, LIVE MUSIC

Falckensteinstr. 48

☎030 440 08 140; www.magnet-club.de

This club's guests break down into two groups: cool locals who come for the DJs and frequent live bands, and angry tourists who got rejected from Watergate next door. Indie bands play on a short, shallow stage that makes it seem as though they're part of the crowd, and DJs spin a much lighter mix than their Kreuzberg counterparts—think indie electropop. A little too "indie" for its own good, Magnet Club repels the vicious dancers, but its softer steps and three-bar complex attract those looking for a quieter night than Kreuzberg normally allows.

▶ 🚏 U1: Schlesisches Tor. From the Metro, head toward the bridge. An "M" hangs above the door. $ Cover €3-7. Beer Shots €2-2.50. €2.50-3. Long drinks €6-6.50. ⏰ Usually open Tu-Su from 10pm. Check online for exact schedule.

## SO36

BAR, CLUB, LIVE MUSIC

Oranienstr. 190

☎030 614 01 306; www.so36.de

SO36 sees itself less as a club, and more as an organization with an attitude. The various parties, live shows, and cultural presentations that fill this huge hall attract a mixed gay/straight clientele whose common denominator is that they like to party hardy. Gayhane, a gay cabaret that performs the last Saturday of every month, has become a staple of the Berlin GLBT scene and can get pretty epic.

▶ 🚏 U1 or U8: Kottbusser Tor. From the Metro, walk north on Adalbertstr. and turn right on Oranienstr. The club is on the right. $ Cover varies. Shots €2.20. Beer €2.80-3.50. Wine €3. Long drinks €5.50, with Red Bull €6. Cash only. ⏰ Hours vary, but usually open F-Sa 10pm-late.

## Roses

BAR, GLBT

Oranienstr. 187

☎030 615 65 70

Fuzzy pink walls, a fuzzy pink ceiling, ubiquitous tiger print, and a curious collection of Christian iconograpy make this small gay bar a real treat. Gay men, some lesbian women, and a couple of straight groups (there to camp out in campy glory)

**Nightlife**

join together for small talk over some clean electro. The bar's small size makes mingling easy, and the endless assortment of wall trinkets (glowing mounted antlers, twinkling hearts, a psychedelic Virgin Mary) keeps everyone giggling.

▶ ⚉ U1 or U8: Kottbusser Tor. From the Metro, head northwest on Oranienstr. past Mariannenstr. The bar is on the left. Ⓢ Beer €2.50. Cocktails €5, with Red Bull €6. Cash only. 🕐 Open daily 9pm-late.

## Milchbar                                                             BAR

Manteuffelstr. 40/41

☎030 611 70 67; www.milchbar-berlin.de

Despite an unfortunate lack of *Clockwork Orange* references to match its milky title, Milchbar draws a sampling of the punk spectrum to lounge, drink, and listen to hardcore music throughout the night. For some inexplicable reason the walls are painted blue and covered by murals of sea creatures. Foosball and pinball in a back room provide some entertainment in case you get lost at sea.

▶ ⚉ U1: Görlitzer Bahnhof. From the Metro, head west on Skalitzer Str., then turn right on Manteuffelstr. The bar is on the left. Ⓢ Beer €3. Spirits €2-5. 🕐 Open M-Sa 9am-late.

# Arts and Culture

As the old saying goes, "where there be hipsters, there be Arts and Culture." Though the saying's origins are unclear, it certainly applies to Berlin. Whether it's opera, film, or Brecht in the original German that you're after, Berlin has got you covered. For a magical evening at the symphony, grab a standing-room-only ticket to see the Berliner Philharmoniker or grab a rush seat to see the Deutsche Oper perform Wagner's four-opera cycle, *The Ring of the Nibelung*. If rock, pop, indie, or hip hop are more your style, head to Kreuzberg to check out Festsaal Kreuzberg and Columbiahalle. Nearby English Theater Berlin will satisfy any Anglophone's theater cravings, while the Deutsches Theater in Mitte hosts performances of the German classics as well as the English canon in translation. The truly hip should head straight to Lichtblick Kino or Kino Babylon to find radical documentaries, avant-garde films, and a sea of flannel and retro frames.

## Budget Arts and Culture

Berlin battles the stereotype that opera and classical music are over your head and your budget. Standing-room tickets for the **Berliner Philharmonie,** available 90min. before the show, cost only €7. The **Deutsche Staatsoper,** East Berlin's finest opera house, has a similar deal 30min. before each show, in which tickets only cost €13.

# MUSIC AND OPERA

### Berliner Philharmonie MITTE

Herbert-von-Karajan-Str. 1

☎030 254 88 999; www.berlin-philharmonic.com

It may look strange from the outside, but acoustically, this yellow building is pitch-perfect. Every audience member seated around the massive pentagonal hall gets a full view and even fuller sound. But the hall can only be as good as the music that fills it: fortunately, the **Berliner Philharmoniker,** led by the eminent Sir Simon Rattle, is one of the world's finest orchestras. It's tough to get a seat, so check the website for availability. For sold-out concerts, some tickets and standing room may be available 90min. before the concert begins, but only at the box office. Stand in line, get some cheap tickets if you're lucky, and enjoy some of the sweetest sounds known to mankind.

▶ 🚉 S1, S2, S25, or U2: Potsdamer Pl. From the Metro, head west on Potsdamer Str. $ Tickets for standing room from €7, for seats from €15. ⏰ Open from July to early Sept. Box office open M-F 3-6pm, Sa-Su 11am-2pm.

### Deutsche Staatsoper MITTE

Unter den Linden 7

☎030 203 54 555; www.staatsoper-berlin.de

The Deutsche Staatsoper is East Berlin's leading opera theater. Though it suffered during the years of separation, this opera house is rebuilding its reputation and its repertoire of classical Baroque opera and contemporary pieces. Unfortunately, it's exterior is under extensive renovation until 2013, but performances will continue as usual. Recent performances have included productions of Mozart and Strauss, so you know you're in good hands.

## Doing it in Public

Had too many beers and can't make it back to the hotel in time? No worries. Berlin has various public facilities that cater to your needs. Some are paid, some are free, but all will get the job done.

- **Mean, green pissing machines.** These *pissoirs* conceal their function behind their elegant octagonal walls, but the rust and smell probably give it away. Historically significant (who knew urinals could be landmarks?), they were established in the 19th century and are now privately run. Toilet-goers-to-be beware: of the 30 *pissoirs* left standing, some are only for men.
- **Do it in style.** In front of the C&A Store in Mitte's Alexanderpl., a modern temple to bodily fluids flatters worshippers with stainless steel, glass, and artsy photographs of the city.
- **Keep it in your pants.** No matter how badly you have to go, always remember where you are. In the few months after its 2005 opening, drunken fans and opportunistic visitors availed themselves behind the privacy of the 2711 concrete slabs at Berlin's Holocaust Memorial. Not cool.



▶ U6: Französische Str. Or bus #100, 157, or 348: Deutsche Staatsoper. $ Tickets €14-260. For certain seats, students can get a ½-price discount, but only within 4 weeks of the performance, and only at the box office. Unsold tickets €13, 30min. before the show. ⏰ Open from Aug to mid-July. Box office open daily noon-7pm and 1hr. before performances.

### Deutsche Oper Berlin — CHARLOTTENBURG

Bismarckstr. 35

☎030 343 84 343; www.deutscheoperberlin.de

The Deutsche Oper Berlin's original home, the Deutsches Opernhaus was built in 1911 but decimated by Allied bombs. Today performances take place in Berlin's newest opera house, which looks like a gigantic concrete box. If you have the chance, don't pass up a cheap ticket to see one of Berlin's most spectacular performances. The 2011-2012 season includes Wagner's four-opera cycle, *The Ring of the Nibelung,* and Puccini's *Tosca,* along with a variety of other canonical German and Italian productions.

▶ U2: Deutsche Oper. $ Tickets €16-122. 25% student discount when you buy tickets at the box office. Unsold tickets €13, 30min. before the show. ⏰

Open Sept-June. Box office open M-Sa 11am until beginning of the performance, or 11am-7pm on days without performances; Su 10am-2pm. Evening tickets available 1hr. before performances.

### Festsaal Kreuzberg

KREUZBERG

Skalitzerstr. 130

☎030 611 01 313; www.festsaal-kreuzberg.de

Free jazz, indie rock, swing, electropop—you never know what to expect at this absurdly hip venue. A tremendous chasm of a main hall accommodates acts of all shapes and sizes, plus an overflowing crowd of fans packed together on the main floor and hanging from the mezzanine. A dusty courtyard out front features a bar, some busy chill-out space, and novelty acts like fire throwers. Poetry readings, film screenings, and art performances fill out the program with some appropriately eclectic material, making this one of Berlin's most exciting venues.

▶ 🚏 U1 or U8: Kottbusser Tor. From the U-Bahn, head east on Skalitzerstr. The venue is on the left. $ Tickets €5-20. Shots €2. Long drinks €6. ⏰ Hours vary. Usually open F-Sa 9pm-late. Check website for details.

### Columbiahalle

KREUZBERG

Columbiadamm 13-21

☎030 698 09 80; www.columbiahalle.de

Any venue that features Snoop Dogg, The Specials, and Bon Iver in a matter of a couple months has a special place in our hearts. With a wildly eclectic collection of superstars and indie notables from all over the world, Columbiahalle's calendar is bound to make you gasp and say, "Oh I definitely wanna see that," at least twice. Once a gym for American service members in south Kreuzberg, Columbiahalle may look dated and innocuous, but its standing-room-only floor and mezzanine sure can rage.

▶ 🚏 U6: Pl. der Luftbrücke. From the Metro, head east on Columbiadamm. The venue is in the 1st block on the right. $ Tickets €20-60, depending on the act. ⏰ Hours and dates vary, but concerts tend to start at 8pm. Check the website for more details.

## FILM

Finding English films in Berlin is almost as easy as finding the Fernsehturm. On any night, choose from over 150 different films, marked **O.F.** or **O.V.** for the original version (meaning not dubbed in German), **O.m.U** for original version with German subtitles, or **O.m.u.E.** for original film with English subtitles.

## Lichtblick Kino                                    PRENZLAUER BERG

Kastanienallee 77

☎030 440 58 179; www.lichtblick-kino.org

> This 32-seat theater specializes in avant-garde films and radical documentaries, with a range of movies that crosses decades, borders, and the lines of polite society. English films are intermixed with all sorts of other international fare, and all films are shown with the original sound and accompanied by German subtitles, so you won't need to perform any amazing feats of lip-reading in order to enjoy a movie whose dialogue is in a language you can actually understand. Directors stop by frequently. This is the quintessential art-house experience.

▶ ⚐ U8: Eberswalder Str. From the Metro, walk southwest on Kastanienallee, past Oderberger Str. The theater is near the end of the next block on the left. Ⓢ Tickets €5, students €4.50. Ⓩ 2-5 films shown every night, usually 5-10pm. Check the website for a full calendar.

## Kino Babylon                                             MITTE

Rosa-Luxemburg-Str. 30

☎030 242 59 69; www.babylonberlin.de

> Americans and Berliners alike flock to this spunky independent film house with a commitment to classic international cinema. Silent films, fiction readings, and constant themed retrospectives—like a recent exposition of Lithuanian films—guarantee that you'll have a chance to see something new and interesting alongside the classics. Occasional summer screenings happen outdoors on the beautiful Rosa-Luxemburg-Pl.—and epic screenings of *Rocky Horror Picture Show* go down regularly. Unfortunately, outside of the frequent American classics, English is a bit hard to come by, as most subtitles are in German.

▶ ⚐ U2: Rosa-Luxemburg-Pl. From the Metro, walk south on Rosa-Luxemburg-Str. Ⓢ Tickets €4-8. Ⓩ The schedule changes daily; check website for details. Box office open M-F from 5pm until the 1st film of the evening.

## Arsenal                                                 MITTE

In the Filmhaus at Potsdamer Pl.

☎030 269 55 100; www.arsenal-berlin.de

> Run by the founders of Berlinale and located just below the **Museum for Film and Television**, Arsenal showcases independent films and some classics. Discussions, talks, and frequent appearances by guest directors make the theater a popular meeting place for Berlin's filmmakers. With the majority of films in the original with English subtitles, the English "purist" can get her fix.

▶ ⚐ U2, S1, S2, or S25: Potsdamer Pl. From the Metro, head west on Potsdamer Str. and go into the building labeled "Deutsche Kinemathek." Take the elevator down to the 2nd basement level. Ⓢ Tickets €6.50, students €5. ⏲ 3-5 films shown each night. Films usually start 4-8pm. Check the website for a full calendar.

# THEATER

### English Theater Berlin KREUZBERG

Fidicinstr. 40

☎030 693 56 92; www.etberlin.de

For over 20 years, Berlin's only completely English-language theater has been defying German-language totalitarianism with everything from festivals of 10min. contemporary shorts to full-length canonical productions. Leave your *umlauts* at home.

▶ ⚐ U6: Pl. der Luftbrücke. From the Metro, head north on Mehringdamm for 2 blocks and turn right on Fidicinstr. The theater is on the left within the 1st block. Ⓢ €14, students €8. ⏲ Box office opens 1hr. before show. Shows are at 8pm unless otherwise noted. Check the website for a calendar of performances.

### Deutsches Theater MITTE

Schumann Str. 13a

☎030 284 41 225; www.deutschestheater.de

Built in 1850, this world-famous theater that legendary director Max Reinhardt once controlled is still a cultural heavy hitter in Berlin. With even the English drama in translation (Shakespeare and Beckett are rockstars here), English speakers shouldn't expect to understand any of the words, but the productions are gorgeous enough that they're worth seeing in spite of the language barrier.

▶ ⚐ U6: Oranienburger Tor. From the U-Bahn, head south on Friederichstr., take a right on Reinhartstr. and another right on Albrecthstr. Ⓢ €5-30. ⏲ Box office open M-Sa 11am-6:30pm, Su 3-6:30pm. Shows at 8pm unless otherwise noted.

# Shopping

Though you'll probably have trouble finding room in your pack for new merch, Berlin's shopping scene is worth several broken zippers. Appropriate to its opulent West Berlin background, Ku'Damm in Charlottenburg is considered Berlin's quintessential shopping center, although the stores are generally high-class franchises, and the prices are more western than Plato in a cowboy hat. Friedrichstraße in Mitte is Ku'Damm's East Berlin twin, although with more glamorous marble colonnades, and the book/music chain behemoth Dussmann. Kastanienallee in Prenzlauer Berg or Hackescher Markt in Mitte are the places to prowl if you want to return home several degrees hipper than you left, with genitalia-crushing skinny jeans and ill-fitting v-necks in every stark storefront. Kastanienallee quakes with record stores as well—it's the place to go for either new CD releases or vintage LPs. In line with its "street"-ier reputation, Kreuzberg is strewn with some impressive skate shops, which are pricey, but offer the best selection of hoodies and threads to wear while robbing a gas station. Thrift stores are spread widely without a specific "thrift-strict," where you can hunt for secondhand clothes, books, and music, but the best options are located in Schöneberg and Prenzlauer Berg. Otherwise, any flea market will oblige, with the exception of the Turkish Market, which is more focused on food. If you want a more complete, although less discerning, guide to clothes shopping in Berlin, ask the clerk at any clothing store for a free Berlin shopping guide. Meanwhile, here are our favorites:

Berlin welcomes anything that could make it—is it possible?—hipper. Therefore, thrift stores, embraced with open arms, can be found just about everywhere. For the best deals, head to **Garage,** where Happy Hour (W 11am-1pm) offers 30% off of prices that already make us weak in the knees. And honestly, *Let's Go* is down for literally anything that can be purchased (like the clothes at Garage) for €15 per kg.

# CLOTHING

## Department Stores

### KaDeWe                                    CHARLOTTENBURG
Tauentzienstr. 21-24
☎030 212 10

If a zombie infestation occurs, KaDeWe is the place to hole up with the rest of the uninfected. With seven floors of food, groceries, books, toys, make-up, and clothes, you'll have at least a year's worth of stuff to begin rebuilding human civilization before supplies start running out. But, zombie invasions aside, we question KaDeWe's worth. Due to the unrelenting prices, it serves only as a jaw-dropping spectacle to anyone who has any budget conscience whatsoever. But with Chanel, Prada, and Cartier flashing from every window display, it may be worth checking out if you don't feel quite poor enough after a visit to **Schloß Charlottenburg.**

▶ ♯ U1, U2, or U3: Wittenbergpl. ☒ Open M-Th 10am-8pm, F 10am-9pm, Sa 9:30am-8pm.

### Overkill                                    KREUZBERG
Köpenicker Str. 195a
☎030 695 06 126; www.overkillshop.com

This two-story shoe store lives up to its name by offering an uncommonly excessive selection of two quintessentially Kreuzbergian accessories: bright shoes and even brighter spray paint. Until you have these in tow, you may as well be a pathetic tool on a bus tour in the eyes of most Kreuzbergers, so Overkill is a good place to start out on the right foot. On the sleek ground level, a floor-to-ceiling display of the hippest kicks by Nike, New

*Shopping*

Balance, Adidas, Fred Perry, and other big names squares off against another floor-to-ceiling display of the largest spray-paint rainbow you'll ever lay eyes on. The second floor is an abrupt contrast, with more shoes and some expensive skater clothes spread around a gorgeous old Berlin apartment, bearing vintage leather furniture, stained wood floors, and intricate wallpaper. It's a beautiful home to a dazzling collection of merchandise.

▶ ♯ U1: Schlesiches Tor. From the Metro, begin walking west on Köpenicker Str. The store is on the left. Ⓢ Shoes €90-180. Shirts €45. ⏰ Open M-Sa 11am-8pm.

## Secondhand

Unfortunately, there's no central grouping of secondhand stores in Berlin where you can go and spend an entire vintage afternoon: the best ones are spread all over the place, and the *best* one happens to be located in rich, old West Berlin (lots of rich old ladies donating their rich old clothes). You'll definitely find the largest number in Prenzlauer Berg, particularly around **Kastanienallee,** but otherwise, you should plan on hitting our recommendations one at a time as you navigate the different neighborhoods. Request a free Berlin shopping guide at any of these places: your wardrobe will thank you.

### Garage                                                    SCHÖNEBERG
Ahornstr. 2
☎030 211 27 60

American Apparel wishes it were this legit. With quirky posters (Beastie Boys tour '92!), silver tassels hanging from the ceiling, shopping carts full of socks, disaffected mannequins, and a sea of circular racks arranged neatly by color, Garage will raise your hipster cred simply by walking in. And with one of the best deals in town (€15 per kg of clothes from the largest portion of the store), it'll make you want to return again and again, extra-large shopping bags in tow.

▶ ♯ U1, U2, U3, U4, or U9: Nollendorfpl. ⓘ "Happy Hour" W 11am-1pm add an extra 30% off to those criminally low prices you're already enjoying. ⏰ Open M-F 11am-7pm, Sa 11am-6pm.

### Stiefelkombinat-Berlin                        PRENZLAUER BERG
Eberswalder Str. 21/22
☎030 510 51 234; www.stiefelkombinat.de

This packed, double-address thrift store (one for men, one for women) hawks merch from the '40s through the '90s, including the usual quirky options to complete your outfit, plus a hilarious collection of all sorts of eclectic antiques, many of them inexplicably pertaining to vintage American cartoons. This means you can finally get that Garfield shirt (the comic strip, not the movie), gigantic Smurf action figure (the TV show, not *Avatar*), or plastic Snoopy with an electric fan in his nose you were deprived of during childhood. The shoe selection, though mostly dress shoes priced in the upper double-digits, is unbeatably wide for anyone looking to put some class in his step.

▶ 🚇 U2: Eberswalder Str. From the Metro, head west on Eberswalder Str. The thrift store is about a quarter of the way down the block on the left. Ⓢ Garfield shirts €10-25. Dress shoes €50-100. Blazers €40-80. 🕐 Open M-Th 10am-10pm, F-Sa 10am-midnight.

## Macy'z                                    WILMERSDORF
Mommsenstr. 2
☎030 881 13 63

Mommsenstr. is Berlin's secondhand designer-label mecca, and Macy'z may have the best collection around. Everything the store carries is less than two years old, and designed by the biggest names in the industry—think Gucci bags and Prada shoes for half the original price or less. (Just to clarify, half-price on a Burberry coat might still set you back €500.) But for the truly devoted, a (very relative) deal can be found.

▶ 🚇 U1: Uhlandstr. 🕐 Open M-Sa noon-6:30pm, Su noon-4pm.

# Flea Markets

Basically, if there is a Berlin square and it's warm out, come early afternoon on a weekend or holiday and you can pretty much guarantee a flea market. Most are small, and many contain the same boring assortment of books, LPs, and kitchenware, so if you want to find a wide selection of good, cheap merchandise—plus extra features like free fruit and street musicians—stick with our recommendations.

## 🔲 Turkish Market                          KREUZBERG
Along the south bank of the Landwehrkanal

Entering this market is like entering a shouting match in several different languages you don't understand. Fruit sellers scream melon prices in Turkish-infused German, and clothes hawkers announce deals on shoes in German-infused Turkish. Some shop owners even sing, overflowing with enthusiasm at the prospect of an incessantly dense crowd. The Turkish Market is not just an amazing place to find great deals on fruit and clothing—it's one of the best experiences of the entire city. The fruit stands have fruits you've never seen (that may cost as little as €1), and many of them feature free samples, meaning an agile traveler can assemble a free fruit salad during a spin through the market. The clothing stands have deals like three pairs of socks for the price of one, and confectionary stands serve substantial hunks of Turkish delight for gutter prices (€1 per 100g).

▶ ⚑ U1: Kottbusser Tor. From the Metro, head south toward the canal. 🕐 Open Tu noon-6pm, F noon-6pm.

## 🔲 Flea Market on Mauerpark     PRENZLAUER BERG

Bernauerstr. 63-64

☎017 629 250 021; www.mauerparkmarkt.de

The Flea Market on Mauerpark is the biggest and best-known in all of Berlin. A labyrinth of booths and stalls hides everything from hand-ground spices to used clothing to enamel jewelry to old power tools. Hordes of bargain hunters, hipsters, and gawking tourists crowd the park, drinking fresh-squeezed orange juice and listening to street musicians. Like all secondhand stores in Prenzlauer Berg, Mauerpark's prices are hardly secondhand. You can still find good values, but don't expect to come away feeling like you just legally robbed several people.

▶ ⚑ U2: Eberswalden Str. From the Metro, head west on Eberswalder Str. The flea market will be on your right, immediately after you pass Mauerpark. 🕐 Open Sunday 9am-5pm.

## Arkonaplatz     PRENZLAUER BERG

Arkonapl.

☎030 786 97 64; www.troedelmarkt-arkonaplatz.de

Craftsmen sell jewelry. Farmers juice oranges. That guy down the street hawks his CDs from a towel. Arkonapl. brings out the weird, the old, the desperate, and the people who want to buy stuff from all of them. Despite the modest size of the square, the market itself is packed together and features an incredible range of wares: DDR relics, bolts of fabric, pictures of vendors' babies, antique space hats, etc. Stick around in the afternoons when the Irish guy comes by with a karaoke machine on his bike. He's been doing it for years.

▶ ⚑ U8: Bernauerstr. From the Metro, walk south on Brunnenstr. and take the

1st left on Rheinsberger Str. Take the 3rd right on Wolliner Str. Arkonapl. is on the right. 🕑 Open Su 10am-6pm.

## Am Kupfergraben                                    MITTE
On Am Kupfergraben, across from the Bodemuseum

Stroll along Museum Island while you shop at secondhand tents, and cross your fingers that you'll come across Nefertiti's Bust among the wares. The market is tiny and consists of almost exclusively books and LPs, but if you're looking to pick up a cheap German book the selection is unrivalled and extremely cheap. A requisite collection of steins will remind you that Berlin happens to be located in Germany.

▶ 🚊 S3, S5, S7, or S75: Hackescher Markt. From the Metro, walk south on Burgstr., turn right on Bodestr. After you pass across Museum Island and cross the Spree for the 2nd time, Am Kupfergraben is on the right. 🕑 Open Sa-Su 11am-5pm.

---

# BOOKS

Finding English books in Berlin is about as easy as finding someone who speaks English: they're everywhere, but they're not always very good. Secondhand is the way to go to offset the extra cost of English books.

## 🔖 St. George's Bookstore                  PRENZLAUER BERG
Wörtherstr. 27

☎030 817 98 333; www.saintgeorgesbookshop.com

You'll be hard-pressed to find a better English-language bookstore on the continent. St. George's owner makes frequent trips to the UK and the US to buy the loads of titles that fill the towering shelves so that his customers can find anything they're looking for and then some. Over half of the books are used and extremely well-priced (paperbacks €4-8), with a number of books for just €1. This shop also carries new books and can order absolutely any title they don't already carry. If you're searching for a book to make you look mysterious in your hostel's lobby, there's absolutely no better place. Pay in euro, British pounds, or American dollars (oh my!).

▶ 🚊 U2: Senefelderpl. From the Metro, head southeast on Metzerstr. and turn left on Prenzlauer Allee. Follow Prenzlauer Allee for 3 blocks, then turn left on Wörtherstr. The bookstore will be halfway down the block, on your right. 💲 Used hardcovers €10. 🕑 Open M-F 11am-8pm, Sa 11am-7pm.

### Another Country                    KREUZBERG

Riemannstr. 7

☎030 694 01 160; www.anothercountry.de

Browsing this cluttered secondhand English bookstore feels a little like walking around some guy's house, but a wide and unpredictable collection rewards searching, especially since all books are €2-5. Another Country doesn't just want to be that forgettable place where you can buy a cheap copy of *Twilight* (€5); it wants to be a local library and cultural center. Ten to fifteen percent of the books are labeled "lending only," meaning they're priced a little higher (around €10), and you get back the entire price minus €1.50 when you return them. Plus, live acoustic performances, readings, and trivia add a further incentive to return again and again. Check out the wide selection of "Evil Books," which includes a copy of L. Ron Hubbard's *Dianetics, The Quotable Richard Nixon,* and a book entitled *Bradymania*.

▶ 🚇 U7: Gneisenaustr. 🕐 Open Tu-F 11am-8pm, Sa-Su noon-4pm.

---

# MUSIC

### 🔲 Space Hall                    KREUZBERG

Zossenerstr. 33, 35

☎030 694 76 64; www.spacehall.de

They don't make them like this anymore in the States—maybe they never did. With two addresses (one of just CDs, the other strictly vinyl), Space Hall makes it nearly impossible *not* to find what you're looking for, plus 1001 things you aren't looking for. The vinyl store never misses a beat, with the longest interior of any Berlin record store (painted to resemble a forest, of course), and easily one of the widest selections to boot. They also have an inspiring collection of rubber duckies.

▶ 🚇 U7: Gneisenaustr. From the Metro, head south on Zossenerstr. The record store is on the left. Ⓢ CDs regular €10-20, discounted €3-10. LPs €10-30. 🕐 Open M-W 11am-8pm, Th-F 11am-10pm, Sa 11am-8pm.

### 🔲 Hard Wax                    KREUZBERG

Paul-Lincke-Ufer 44a

☎030 611 30 111; www.hardwax.com

Walk down a silent alleyway, through an eerily quiet courtyard, up three flights of dim, graffitied stairs, and suddenly, you're in one of Berlin's best record stores for electronic music. Bare brick and concrete walls make it feel aggressively nonchalant, while an entire back room dedicated to private listening stations for patrons show that Hard Wax is dedicated to helping you get out of the House. Dubstep, IDM, ambient, and subgenres upon subgenres of all shapes and sizes confound you from the shelves, but fortunately, nearly every CD and LP bears a short description in English courtesy of Hard Wax's experts, so you never feel like you're randomly flipping through a lot of crap. Though the selection is small compared to some of Berlin's other electro record stores, the offerings seem hand-picked.

▸ 🚇 U1 or U8: Kottbusser Tor. From the U-Bahn, head south on Kottbusserstr. Take a left just before the canal, then enter the courtyard on the left just after crossing Mariannenstr. $ Records €5-30, but mostly €8-12. CDs €10-20. ⏰ Open M-Sa noon-8pm.

## Fidelio

SCHÖNEBERG

Akazienstr. 30

☎030 781 97 36

For those looking to develop their finer tastes, or seeking to butcher the names of the world's greatest composers (give Rozhdestvensky a try—we dare you), Fidelio is the place to go. An extensive selection of classical CDs lines the walls, along with a smaller, but still impressive collection of jazz. If you've only just recently been inspired to give Wagner a listen, the staff here are more than happy to point newcomers in the right direction. Here and there, some vintage vinyl makes an appearance, but the major commodities are the CDs. Prices vary widely, but most CDs fall between €12 and €20.

▸ 🚇 U7: Eisenacherstr. From the Metro, head east on Grunewaldstr. and turn right on Akazienstr. Follow Akazienstr. for 2 blocks. The store will be on your right near the end of the 3rd block. ⏰ Open M-F 11am-7pm, Sa 10am-3pm.

## Melting Point

PRENZLAUER BERG

Kastanienallee 55

☎030 440 47 131; www.meltingpoint-berlin.de

Berlin DJs frequent this small, whitewashed storefront for one of the most tremendous selections of international techno vinyl in Berlin. The records you can flip your grimy little fingers through are only the tip of the iceberg: a packed library extends back behind the clerk. If your techno tastes are obscure enough, you may have a chance to plumb the depths.

▸ 🚇 U8: Rosenthaler Pl. From the Metro walk northeast up Weinbergsweg, which becomes Kastanienallee. The store is at the corner of Kastanienallee and Fehrbelliner Str. $ Records €5-30. Cash only. ⏰ Open M-Sa noon-8pm.

## Franz and Josef Scheiben PRENZLAUER BERG

Kastanienallee 48

☎030 417 14 682

If you're looking for '80s punk and rock, this secondhand vinyl store will have what you're looking for. If you're looking for anything else, you're pretty much out of luck (sorry, bro-fi fans). The owner will tell you to expect to pay somewhere between €1 and €1000 for the vinyl, but most records thankfully fall into the lower part of that range (€10-30). Some real antiques hide in the €1-5 bins out front: they feature a wide selection of embarrassing Christmas albums that you can bring home for your grandma.

▶ 🚇 U2: Senefelderpl. From the Metro, exit from the northern steps, and head northeast on Schwedter Str. Walk 4 blocks and turn left on Kastanienallee. The store will be on your right. $ Cash only. ⏰ Open M-Sa 1-8pm.

# Excursions

Though it could take years to see all of Berlin's sights, try all of its cafes, and dance in all of its clubs, sometimes you just need to get away. So if you're ready for a change of scenery and a change of pace, head to the quaint village of Lübbenau, kayak down the Spree, or explore the winding paths and peaceful meadows of the Spreewald. If you prefer a more regal daytrip, we suggest Potsdam, where you'll encounter the exquisitely manicured gardens and richly gilded halls of Schloß Sanssouci. Both of the excursions in this chapter are within easy commuting distance of Berlin, but if you're looking for a longer country escape in the Spreewald, your cheapest option may be to camp.

## Budget Excursions

These two excursions can be easily done in one day each, meaning you don't have to worry about finding and paying for a hostel bed in Potsdam or Lübbenau. To save some more dough, pack a bag lunch and avoid over-priced, touristy food options. Spreewald's (free) forest is a great spot for a picnic. In Potsdam, your budget sightseeing options are more limited, but a Premium *Tageskarte* will get you student-discounted access to all of the sights. If you really want to cut back on expenses, take an architectural tour of Potsdam by simply gaping at all of the buildings from the outside: most have plaques with historical explanations, which means the cheapskate's tour can even be somewhat educational!

# SPREEWALD AND LÜBBENAU

So you've been in Berlin for a couple of days. You love it, and you've declared several times that you want to stay here forever, but you're secretly getting a little tired of the constant hangovers, the incessant ringing of bikes alerting you that you're in the way, and the fact that you can just never seem to catch the right train. Where can you find some respite to rekindle your *Feuer?* Look about 100km to the southeast. There, the Spree River (pronounced "shpray") splits into a vein-like network of small streams and canals, slicing up the meadows and forests that were once home to the **Sorbs** (roughly pronounced "zoe-awbz"), Germany's native Slavic minority. This 1000 sq. km area is called the **Spreewald** (Spree Forest). Of the many small villages scattered around the area, the most famous is **Lübbenau.**

The Spreewald draws German tourists seeking to get momentarily lost among its meandering paths and streams, and Lübbenau is their hub. In a fleet of gondolas and kayaks mobilized every morning, tourists drift lazily down narrow Spree tributaries lined with thatched roofs and birch trees and consume pounds of pickles (a Lübbenau specialty) and rivers of beer when they return to town. After being a tourist in their home, watch how Germans spend their vacations. Lübbenau is not only the gateway to the forest, but a charming relic of a time before Starbucks ruled the world. To the northwest, **Altstadt** features cobblestone roads, the tiny **Nikolaikirche,** more sausage than your heart can handle, and rows of tiny pensions where you can sleep soundly all night with the assurance that you won't be woken up by a passing siren.

A small, second town, officially considered part of Lübbenau, is three green kilometers away from the Altstadt and easily accessible by bike, boat, and foot. **Lehde** is truthfully less of a town and more of a sight.

## Accommodations

Though Lübbenau itself can be fully experienced in a day (or even an hour or two), if you want to penetrate more than a couple of kilometers into the Spreewald, you might want to stay overnight—many do. Expect to pay €45-55 for a double, or about €25-40 per person. Your best bet is to check out the comprehensive catalog of pension listings available in the tourist office. In the busy summer months, it's likely that your decision will be determined by availability, but there will always be the option of **camping.** If you didn't pack your tent in your carry-on, renting one from the **Campingplatz Am Schloßpark** is the cheapest and potentially most rewarding way to enjoy the Spreewald.

### Campingplatz Am Schloßpark — CAMPGROUND $

Schloßbezirk 20

☎03542 35 33; www.spreewaldcamping.de

This beautiful campground, settled between Lübbenau and Lehde and surrounded by the meandering Spree, has 125 tent plots, cooking and bathing facilities, and a convenience store.

▸ From the tourist information office, follow Ehm-Welk-Str. to the left as it turns into Schloßbezirk. Then, follow the road as it passes by the Schloß and curves left. The campground will be on the left at the end of the curve. $ €6 per person; tents €5-6; 2- to 4-person bungalows €20-50. Bikes €1.50 per hr. Cash only. ⏰ Reception 7:30am-12:30pm and 2-9pm.

### Pension Am Alten Bauernhafen — PENSION $$$$

Stottof 5

☎03542 29 30; www.am-alten-bauernhafen.de

Huge windows and vaulted ceilings brighten up the spacious rooms at this two-story riverside pension. Plus, a huge breakfast room and shady outdoor patio along a beautiful creek will let you eat, drink, and relax.

▸ From the tourist information office, follow Ehm-Welk-Str. to the right as it becomes Karl-Marx-Str., and then turn left onto Stottof. The pension is on the left. $ Singles from €35; doubles from €45; triples from €69. Cash only.

### Pension Scherz

PENSION $$

Bergstr. 9A

☎03542 46 578; www.pensionscherz.de

Coral walls, mismatched lawn furniture, and a shady courtyard perfect for lazing about in your early afternoon beer coma give this pension the feel of a laid-back family lake house. Rooms are cozy with light colors (yellow curtains are nice things to see when you open your eyes) and contain couches and lounge chairs in case your bed isn't comfy enough.

▶ From the tourist information office, walk down Ehm-Welk-Str. until it becomes Karl-Marx-Str. Turn right onto Bergerstr. The pension is at the end of the street. *i* Breakfast included. $ Singles €40; doubles €49. Per-person rates €19-24 per night. Cash only.

## Sights

Luckily for travelers, Lübbenau's biggest sight is always free and open. The winding paths and quaint canals of the **Spreewald** are yours for the taking, so explore at will. If you want to hike or bike far enough and have some time to kill, there are even some old castles and windmills several forested kilometers away from Lübbenau. If you're looking to relax and enjoy Spreewald in true Sorb fashion, and don't mind the company of many a German senior citizen, **gondola rides** are a popular option that might show you some splendid stretches of forest but will cost you several hours and a great deal of boat-confined boredom. Tours of the forest (in German, without exception) depart from the **Großer Hafen** (larger port) and the **Kleiner Hafen** (smaller port). The Großer Hafen, along Dammstr. behind the church, offers a wider variety of tours, including 2-3hr. trips to Lehde. Boarding starts at 9-10am and depart when full (about 20 passengers) throughout the day. **Genossenschaft der Kahnfährleute** is the largest gondola company in Lübbenau. They offer 2hr. round trips to Lehde. (Dammstr. 77a. ☎03542 22 254; www.grosser-kahnhafen.de $ €8.50, children €4.25; 3hr. €10/5. 5hr. tour of the forest €13, children €6.50. ⏰ Open Mar-Oct daily 9:30am-6pm.) From the Kleiner Hafen, less tourist-ridden but nearly identical wilderness trips are run by the **Kahnfährmannsverein der Spreewaldfreunde.** (Spreestr. 10a ☎03542 403 710; www.spreewald-web.de $ 2-10hr. tours €9-21, children €5-11. ⏰ Open Apr-Oct daily 9am-6pm.)

While gondola rides are too restrictive for those looking to explore on their own, and too German for those who like to understand tour guides, paddling your own boat puts you and your biceps in charge. Kayaks, canoes, and paddle boats can be rented from the **Campingplatz Am Schloßpark** for €5 per hr. (per person), or €15 per day. You can also try **Kajak-Sports.** (Dammstr. 76a. ☎03542 37 64; www.bootsverleih-richter.de Ⓢ Single paddle boats €7 per hr., €15 per day; doubles €7 per hr., €21 per day. Kayaks €9 per hr., €18 per day. Ⓩ Open daily from 9am. Boats may run out in the early afternoon, so arrive in the morning.)

## Freilandmuseum Lehde (Open-air Museum Lehde)
MUSEUM
In Lehde, behind the aquarium.
☎03542 29 44; www.spreewald-lehde.de

**Lehde** itself is a sight to behold. Just 3km away from Lübbenau along a tree-shaded path, this UNESCO-protected landmark can be reached by foot, boat, or bike. The Freilandmuseum is a small community of recreated houses and workshops with exhibits that illustrate the 19th-century lifestyle of the Sorbs, when whole families slept in one room and newlyweds would go out back for a literal "romp in the hay." Though the terribly creepy mannequins performing typical Sorbian tasks may intimidate more than educate (where, oh where have their pupils gone?), the overall effect of this small cluster of thatch-roofed shacks is pleasant. The buildings are authentically constructed, and the handicraft is observable in the rough timbers lining the walls and the uneven clay-brick floors. Artisans have set up workshops in some of the buildings, making pots and decorative eggs in the Sorbian tradition. There's even an entire room dedicated to the history of pickles!

▶ ♫ Follow the signs from Altstadt or Großer Harbor to Lehde. Ⓢ €5, students €3.50, under 16 €1. Ⓩ Open daily Apr-Sept 10am-6pm, last entry 5:30pm; from mid-Sept to Oct 10am-5pm. Last entry 30min. before close.

## Spreewaldmuseum                                    MUSEUM
Topfmarkt 12
☎03542 24 72; www.spreewald-web.de/land-leute/spreewald-museum

This erratic collection of Spreewald artifacts includes, but is not limited to, Romantic-era oil paintings of Lübbenau and Lehde, toys from DDR-era Germany, those pottery shards you're probably an expert on by now, Expressionist canvases, a reconstruction of a Sorb settlement, and perhaps even creepier mannequins than the **Freilandmuseum**. One of them has its back turned to you, but, if you look closely, it's not ignoring you: it's staring at you from a mirror on

**Excursions**

the wall! Three stories hide some neat artifacts and a lot of random crap that's not worth seeing. Perhaps it's worth a trip if you can find no other way to spend your time in Lübbenau, but parts of this museum make a 9hr. boat tour in German seem desirable.

▶ From the tourist information office, follow Ehm-Welk-Str. until it turns into Karl-Marx-Str. at a 1-lane gate. The museum is on the right. $ €4, students €3, under 16 €1. ⏰ Open from Apr to mid-Oct Tu-Su 10am-6pm.

## Food

Although virtually every restaurant in Lübbenau caters to tourists, with moderately overpriced menus and hordes of 60-year-olds crowding outdoor patios, there's still plenty of cheap food out there. Check out the *Imbiße* (snack bars) and food stands that line the **Großer Hafen.** The local specialties are pickles and fresh fish, so if you're dying to eat like the Sorbs, give those a try. The irrepressible bratwurst is a good fallback for a filling meal, and the sausage-and-beer combo (around €4) feels fitting in this quintessentially German town.

### Erich Babben Brauhaus — BREWERY $

Brauhausgasse 2

☎03542 21 26; www.babben-bier.de

Half brewery, half pension, the Erich Babben Brauhaus brews sweet and smooth beer that attracts a regular set of locals to the small beer garden every evening. Though the few food options are intended as small snacks to accompany the massive pitchers of liquid bread you'll inevitably glug, they're unbelievably cheap and prove to be large enough to serve as a full meal. The sausage and pickle plate (two large sausages, several sliced pickles; €2.90) is probably the cheapest and most delicious way to enjoy authentic Lübbenau cuisine.

▶ From the train station, walk up Poststr. When you reach the end, turn left onto Ehm-Welk-Str. Then walk until you reach the point where Ehm-Welk-Str. merges with Mittelstr. and Fischerstr. at the metal sculpture of a blue figure on a gold background, and turn onto Fischerstr. The Brauhaus will be at the end of Fischerstr. $ Beer €2.70-3.30. Home-brewed schnapps €1.50. Food €2.90-6.50. Cash only. ⏰ Open Mar-Oct daily 5pm-late.

# Essentials

## Practicalities

- **Tourist office:** Ehm-Welk-Str. 32 ☎03542 36 68 ⇆ From the train station, walk north on Poststr., until it ends at Ehm-Welk-Str. Turn left, and the office will be on the right side of the street. ⏰ Open M-F 10am-6pm, Sa 9am-4pm, Su 10am-4pm.

## Getting There

Lübbenau is a 2hr. bus and train ride away from Berlin, through beautiful farmland and pine forests. Don't let the distance scare you; the trip is pleasant and easy, and the switch from train to bus a quarter of the way through makes it speed by. Take the **Regional Express, line 2** toward **Königs Wusterhausen.** Trains run several times per hour from Zoologischer Garten, Berlin Hauptbahnhof, and Berlin Ostbahnhof (tickets €13). At Königs Wusterhausen, you'll need to transfer to a bus; exit the train station, turn right, and then take the first right (about 30m from the train station), walk under the bridge, and turn right once you emerge from under the bridge. **Bus B,** the second leg of the trip, departs from there (dir. Lübbenau). Lübbenau is the last stop on the bus line (about 1hr. from the station).

## Getting Around

There's not much to be said for internal transportation in little Lübbenau. Buses run Monday to Friday from early morning to 3pm (single ride €1.30), but, luckily, you won't need them. The whole area is easily covered on foot or, if you prefer, by bike. Bike rentals are all over the city; expect to pay €8-10 per day. For rentals, try **Kowalsky's,** near the train station (Poststr. 6. ☎0354 22 835 $ €8 per day. ⏰ Open M-F 9am-12:30pm and 2-6pm, Sa 9am-noon, Su call in advance.), or **Michael Metzdorf,** across from the tourist office. (Ehm-Welk-Str. 32 ☎03542 46 647 $ €8 per day. ⏰ Open M-F 9:30am-noon and 2-6pm, Sa 10am-noon.)

# POTSDAM

Do you like forests? What about palaces that look like cakes? What about intricate gilding? Or perfectly cut hedges? Or glowing 17th-century portraits? If you answered yes to any or all (or even none) of these questions, then lock your pack up for the day, board the nearest S-Bahn, and make the 30-45min. trip to Potsdam. Oh yeah, and get as excited as a five-year-old on Christmas morning, because Potsdam has all of these things in unbelievable excess. In contrast to a decidedly un-royal Berlin, Potsdam is the glittering home of Friedrich II and his successors, where royal residences, court gardens, private art galleries, and celebratory palaces compete for your attention among shady paths, grassy fields, and jaw-dropping lake vistas. Plus, the low cost of the trip and Potsdam's accessibility means there's no excuse to miss it while you're in Berlin. The most extraordinary sights are concentrated in the **Park Sanssouci,** but the **Neuer Park** to the northeast also packs a heavy Old-World punch, with enough pastoral lake scenes to keep a landscape painter busy through several careers. The town center, though riddled by American franchises and dubious fashion stores, is all brick, cobblestone, and copper towers, making a stroll through town a pleasant break in your hikes through palaces and paths.

## Accommodations

Budget options are extremely limited in Potsdam. Luckily, it's easy to commute from your hostel in Berlin, meaning you most likely won't need accommodations. Nonetheless, here are some suggestions if you want to stay overnight.

### Jugendherberge Potsdam (HI) — HOSTEL $$

Schulstr. 9

☎0331 581 31 00; www.jh-potsdam.de

Potsdam's best-valued hostel is one S-Bahn stop before the Hauptbahnhof, so there's still a train ride to reach Potsdam's greatest hits—but a 5-10min. train ride rather than the 30-45min. from Berlin. Far less sterile than many HI hostels, Jugendherberge Potsdam cooks up the foolproof recipe of pine bunks and yellow walls to give you the impression of home cooking. Rooms are a little crowded, but clean and neat, with personal lockers and ensuite baths.

▶ 🚉 S7: Babelsberg. ℹ Breakfast and linens included. Wi-Fi €2 per hr. [$] Dorms from €15, over age 27 €19; singles €22/26; doubles €53. ⏰ Reception 24hr.

## Campingplatz Sanssouci  CAMPGROUND $

An der Pirschhiede 41

☎0331 951 09 88; www.campingpark-sanssouci-potsdam.de

Located on the banks of the idyllic Templiner See, this campsite is not a convenient place from which to explore Potsdam or Berlin, but its relaxed lakeside lifestyle might make it a destination in itself. A load of extra features, like boat rentals, a restaurant, and a hairdresser, ensure that you'll have plenty to do despite your remoteness from any city center.

▶ 🚆 S7: Potsdam Hauptbahnhof, then tram 91 to Bahnhof Pirschheide. From 8:45-10:45am or 5:30-9pm, call for free shuttle to the campground from Pirschheide. *i* Free Wi-Fi. Ⓢ €13 per person. Boats €17 per night. 🕐 Phone reception 8am-1pm and 3-8pm.

# Sights

The **Premium Tageskarte** (Premium Day Pass; €19, students €14) will get you into all the sights in the parks, including Schloß Sanssouci; the **Tageskarte** (€14/10) will get you in everywhere except the Schloß. While the Tageskarte can be purchased at any of the different sights, the Premium Tageskarte is only for sale at Schloß Sanssouci, so head here first if this option appeals to you. And frankly, why wouldn't it? Schloß Sanssouci is Potsdam's central destination, and admission to the Schloß alone is €12, so unless you're really set on seeing only the Schloß or everything *but* the Schloß, the Premium Tageskarte is the way to go. The **Premium Family Ticket** (€49) is good for two adults and up to three children, as is the **Family Ticket Without Schloß** (€24). Finally, there's the option of skipping entry to any of these places and simply experiencing Potsdam from the outside. While this may not feel quite as "enriching," it will allow you to see a lot more buildings during your daytrip, and you can always fork out a couple of bucks if there's a building you're really drawn to. Also, most of these sights conveniently bear a sign out front with an explanation of the historical context and a description (with pictures) of most of what's inside. It's almost as if the museums *wanted* you to skirt by.

## Park Sanssouci Sights

If you only go to one place in Potsdam, make it **Park Sanssouci.** Every bend in the path reveals a new, tremendous palace, each more impressive than the last, and each surrounded by neat gardens, gilded teahouses, and green gazebos. Next to the Schloß Sanssouci, a spellbinding array of Friedrich II's painting collection crowds one wall of the football-field-sized **Bildergalerie,** which includes works by Caravaggio, van Dyck, and Reubens. (☎0331 969 41 81 $ €3, students €2.50. Audio tour €1. ⏰ Open May-Oct Tu-Su 10am-5:30pm.) The stunning **Sizilianischer Garten** (Sicilian Garden) is next door, featuring hedge-enveloped walkways that feel like the entry to the belly of some gigantic plant monster. Overlooking the park from the north, the pseudo-Italian **Orangerie,** Park Sanssouci's last and largest addition, is famous for its 67 dubious Raphael imitations that replace originals swiped by Napoleon. Climb to the top of the tower for a view of the whole park. ($ Tours €3, students €2.50. Tower only €2. ⏰ Open from mid-May to mid-Oct Tu-Su 10am-12:30pm and 1-5pm.) Little **Schloß Charlottenhof,** whose park surroundings were a Christmas gift from Friedrich Wilhelm III to his son Friedrich Wilhelm IV, is a dinky palace worth little more than a jaunt through its delicate grape arbors. ($ €4, students €3; includes mandatory guided tour. ⏰ Open May-Oct Tu-Su 10am-6pm.) Nearby, the **Römische Bäder** (Roman baths) sit beside a reedy pond spanned by small bridges. ($ €3, students €2.50. ⏰ Open May-Oct Tu-Su 10am-6pm.) The park's single and mystifyingly Asian-inspired building, the **Chinesisches Teehaus,** is complete with a parasol-bearing Buddha on the rooftop and 18th-century Chinese pottery inside. Gold statues of 18-century musicians jam around the periphery. ($ €2. ⏰ Open May-Oct Tu-Su 10am-6pm.)

## Park Sanssouci — PARK

Access the park from Hegelallee, Weinbergstr., or Gregor-Mendal-Str.
☎0331 969 42 00

Schloß Sanssouci's 600-acre "backyard" puts Versailles to shame. The park sports two distinct styles: half is Baroque, with geometric paths intersecting at topiaries and statues of nude nymphs, and the other half is a rolling landscape of wheat fields, rose trellises, and lush gardens. The beauty is addicting; be warned that once you start walking, you may never want to leave. For information on the park's many attractions, from Rococo sculptures to beautiful fountains, head to the visitors center behind the *Schloß* next to the windmill.

▶ 🚏 Buses #606, 612, 614 or 692: Luisenpl. Nord/Park Sanssouci. $ Free. ⏰ Open daily Mar-Oct 8am-10pm; Nov-Feb 9am-8pm.

### Schloß Sanssouci

PALACE

Off Zur Historischen Mühle

☎0331 696 42 00

The park's main attraction, the turquoise-domed Schloß Sanssouci sits atop a terraced hill, looking out over fountains and manicured gardens. Designed in 1747, the palace is small and airy, with ethereal paintings and carvings of the Greek gods in pinks and light greens. Frescoes of Dionysus are right at home: after all, "Sanssouci" is French for "without worry," or, more familiarly, "hakuna matata." The brainchild of Francophile Friedrich II, Sanssouci also holds the small, exotically decorated **Voltairezimmer** (Voltaire Room), outfitted with carved reliefs of parrots and tropical fruit that climb around walls and down the chandelier. The library reveals another of Friedrich's eccentricities: whenever he wanted to read a book, he had a copy printed for each of his palaces *en français*. Andy Warhol's magnificently magenta-and-lime modern interpretation of the king's portrait is also on display.

▸ 🚏 Bus #695 or X15: Schloß Sanssouci. $ €12, students €8. Audio tour (available in English) included. ⏰ Open Tu-Su Apr-Oct 10am-6pm, last entry 5:30pm; Nov-Mar 10am-5pm, last entry 4:30pm.

### Neues Palais

PALACE

Am Neuen Palais

☎0331 969 43 61

Because sometimes one beautiful palace just isn't enough. Friedrich the Great built Sanssouci's fourth and largest palace in celebration of the Prussian victory in the Seven Years' War. And because nothing says masculine-military-power like pale magenta, the Neues Palais is an expansive, 200-room, proudly pink *Schloß*, featuring royal apartments, festival halls, and the impressive Grottensaal, whose shimmering walls are covered with seashells.

▸ 🚏 X5: Neues Palais. $ €5, students €4. Audio guide €1. ⏰ Open Apr-Oct M 10am-6pm, W-Su 10am-6pm; Nov-Mar daily 10am-5pm. Last entry 30min. before close.

## Other Sights

### Neuer Garten                                                  GARDEN
Schloß Cecilienhof
☎0331 969 42 44
Bordered by Holy Lake on the east, and Am Neuen Garten on the west

Neuer Garten, the smaller, attraction-thin counterpart to Park Sanssouci that lies to the east, is all flowering meadows and beautiful lake beaches. Scattered through the park are several royal residences, including the **Schloß Cecilienhof.** Built in the style of an English Tudor manor, this *Schloß* houses exhibits on the Potsdam Treaty, signed at the palace in 1945. Visitors can see the table where the Big Three bargained over Europe's fate and stand in the room Stalin used as his study. The garden's centerpiece is the **Marmorpalais** (Marble Palace). Designed from rust-colored marble in a Neoclassical style, the palace includes a bite-sized concert hall. Also in the Neuer Garten is the inexplicable **Egyptian Pyramid,** which was once used for food storage. At the far north end of the lake, beachgoers bare all and relieve themselves from the summer humidity in the cool water.

▶ ✚ Bus #692: Schloß Cecilienhof. Ⓢ Garden free. Schloß Cecilienhof €5, students €4. Marmorpalais €4, students €3. Ⓩ Schloß Cecilienhof open Tu-Su Apr-Oct 10am-6pm; Nov-Mar 10am-5pm. Marmorpalais open Apr-Oct Tu-Su 10am-6pm; Nov-Mar Sa-Su 10am-4pm.

## Food

The Altstadt, especially **Brandenburger Straße** and **Friedrich-Ebert-Straße,** is lined with cafes and restaurants, but, unfortunately, the intensely touristy territory entails unacceptably high prices. For budget options, your best bets are to try ethnic restaurants or venture far north of the Altstadt. For fresh produce, try the **flea market** in Bassinpl. (Ⓩ Open M-F 9am-6pm.), or stock up at the massive **Kaufland** grocery store in the Hauptbahnhof. (Ⓩ Open daily 6am-8pm.)

### Meierei im Neuen Garten                                  BREWERY $$$
Im Neuen Garten 10
☎0331 704 32 11; www.meierei-potsdam.de

Way up north at the peak of the Neuer Garten, this yellow-brick brewery, established in the 1860s, serves some unbeatable brews alongside some unbeatable views. Right on the Heiliger See (as in, you could easily jump in for a dip after one too many liters), a huge beer garden allows, nay, requires a gaze over one of Potsdam's most gorgeous vistas. Though the entrees are a slight let-down for the budget-savvy, the food is delicious, authentic, and far cheaper than its traditional German counterparts in the Altstadt.

▶ ♯ Bus #603: Höhenstr. From the bus stop, head east on Im Neuen Garten and follow it as it curves right. The brewery is on the left after the curve. Ⓢ Wienerschnitzel €11. Appetizers €3-8; entrees €9-12. Beer 0.5L €3.20, 1L €6. Cash only. ⏰ Open M-Th 11am-10pm, F-Sa 11am-11pm, Su 10am-10pm.

## Mea Culpa                                          TAPAS $
Dortustr. 1
☎0331 201 17 80

Spanish wine, candlelight, and older crowds usually indicate something far beyond our price range, but not when tapas are on the menu. Who says tapas have to be ordered in large quantities to make a full meal? We say order one, round out your meal with the basket of bread that's served alongside, and go on your merry way having only dropped €2-6 on a sizeable portion of tasty food. The *Tortillaecken* (a sort of quiche with spinach and tomato; €2.60) is a surprisingly large and tasty option and one of the most inexpensive dishes on the menu.

▶ ♯ Tram 92 or 96: Nauener Tor. From the tram, head west on Hegelallee for 2 blocks. The restaurant is on the corner of Hegelallee and Dortustr. Ⓢ Cocktails €5.50-5.90. Cash only. ⏰ Open daily noon-1am.

## Siam                                               THAI $
Friedrich-Ebert-Str. 13
☎0311 200 92 92

Large portions and small prices make Siam one of the few value havens in the Altstadt. Admittedly, it's more than a little strange to chow down on Thai specialties in a bamboo-heavy restaurant while gazing at such a quintessentially Old-Europe street. But if you embrace the irony, you'll leave Potsdam with a full stomach and wallet.

▶ ♯ Tram 92 or 96: Brandenburgerstr. From the tram, head south on Friedrich-Ebert-Str. The restaurant is on the left. Ⓢ Soups €2.50-5.50. Entrees €4.60-8.80. Cash only. ⏰ Open daily 11:30am-11pm.

# Essentials

## Practicalities

- **TOURIST OFFICES:** In the **S-Bahn station.** (Ⓢ Maps €1. ⏰ Open M-Sa 9:30am-8pm, Su 9:30am-4pm.) 2nd location in the **city center.** (Brandenburgerstr. 3 Ⓢ Maps start at €2. ⏰ Open Apr-Oct M-F 9:30am-6pm, Sa-Su 9:30am-4pm; Nov-Mar M-F 10am-6pm, Sa-Su 9:30am-2pm.) Both offices book rooms at cooperating hotels at no extra charge. The tourist offices run 2hr. tours in English and German. (Ⓢ €9. ⏰ Departs May-Sept daily 3pm.) They also lead 3½hr. tours of Sanssouci Park. (⚲ Depart tourist info center in Potsdam Hauptbahnhof. *i* Reservations required. Ⓢ €16, with Schloß Sanssouci €27. ⏰ 2hr., Tu-Su 11am.)

- **POST OFFICE:** Am Kanal 16-18. ⏰ Open M-F 9am-6:30pm, Sa 9am-1pm.

- **POSTAL CODE:** 14467.

## Getting There

Getting to Potsdam is simple. Take the **S7** toward Potsdam Hauptbahnhof (⏰ 40min.), or the **RE1** from most major stations, including Berlin Ostbahnhof, Friedrichstr., Alexanderpl., Hauptbahnhof, or Zoologischer Garten (⏰ 25min.). You'll need to buy a ticket for Zones A, B, and C (Ⓢ €2.40 single ticket), or, if you already have a day or week-long pass for Zones A and B, supplement it with an extra ticket to Zone C (Ⓢ €1.40).

## Getting Around

### By Public Transportation

Potsdam is in **Zone C** of Berlin's BVG transit network, so all main-city prices are the same. Special passes for Zones B and C can be purchased on any bus or tram. (Ⓢ €2.70 valid 2hr., €6.60 all-day.) The **Berlin Welcome Card** is also valid in Potsdam.

### By Bicycle

Potsdam is best experienced by bike. If you choose to rent for the day, be sure to request a map outlining the best route to see all the sights on two wheels. Also, make sure to heed signs throughout the park that mark where you're allowed to bike. Basically, if you stick to paths with a broken green line painted down the middle, you're in the green to keep riding. Otherwise, most dirt paths bear signs forbidding you to even walk your bike, so be careful and lock it up when necessary. From the Griebnitzsee station, pay to take your bike on the S-Bahn. (ℹ Bike passes available at any BGV ticket office. $ €1.20.)

## Potsdam Per Pedales

Rudolf-Breitscheid-Str. 201

☎0331 748 00 57; www.pedales.de

They offer bike tours in English (reserve ahead) and German, but you can go solo with a rental bike from here too.

▶ 🚏 In the Griebnitzsee S-Bahn station or on the S-Bahn platform at Potsdam Hauptbahnhof. $ Rentals €10, students €8.50. Bike tours €11, students €8.50. Audio guide €6. ⏰ Open daily 9am-6:30pm.

## Cityrad

Weinbergstr. 7b

☎0177 825 47 46; www.cityrad-rebhan.de

Cityrad also offers bike rentals along with a free city map with a recommended tour route.

▶ 🚏 From the Babelsbergerstr. exit of the Hauptbahnhof, turn right at the door and walk down Babelsbergerstr. until you reach the end of the station. Cityrad is across the side street in the parking lot. $ €11 per day. ⏰ Open Apr-Oct M-F 9am-7pm, Sa-Su 9am-8pm.

# Essentials

## RED TAPE

We're going to fill you in on visas and residence permits, but don't forget the most important ID of all: your passport. Don't forget your passport!

### Visas

Those lucky enough to be EU citizens do not need a visa to travel to Germany. You citizens of Australia, Canada, New Zealand, the US, and other non-EU countries do not need a visa for stays of up to 90 days, but this three-month period begins upon entry

### Entrance Requirements

- **PASSPORT:** Required for citizens of Australia, Canada, Ireland, New Zealand, the UK, and the US.

- **VISA:** Required for visitors who plan to stay in Germany for more than 90 days.

- **WORK PERMIT:** Required for all visitors who want to gain employment in Germany.

into any of the countries that belong to the EU's freedom of movement zone. Those staying longer than 90 days may apply for a long-term visa; consult an embassy for more information. US citizens can also consult **http://travel.state.gov.** Entering Germany to **study** requires a special visa. For more information, see **Beyond Tourism.**

### Work Permits

Entry into Germany as a traveler does not include the right to work, which is authorized only by a **work permit** or **residence permit.** For more information, see **Beyond Tourism.**

## EMBASSIES

### At Home

- **AUSTRALIA:** 119 Empire Circuit, Yarralumla ACT 2600, AUS ☎+61 262 70 19 11; www.canberra.diplo.de ☒ Open M-F 9:30am-12:30pm.

- **CANADA:** 1 Waverly St., Ottawa ON, K2P OT8, CAN ☎+1-613-232-1101; www.ottawa.diplo.de ☒ Open M-F 9am-noon.

- **IRELAND:** 31 Trimleston Ave., Booterstown, Blackrock, IRE ☎+353 1 269 3011; www.dublin.diplo.de ☒ Open M-Tu 8:30-11:30am, Th 8:30-11:30am and 1:30-3:30pm, F 8:30-11:30am.

- **NEW ZEALAND:** 90-92 Hobson St., Thorndon 6011 Wellington, NZL ☎+64 473 60 63; www.wellington.diplo.de ☒ Open M-Th 7:30am-4:30pm, F 7:30am-3pm.

- **UK:** 23 Belgrave Sq. SW1X 8PZ London, UK ☎+44 20 7824 1300; www.london.diplo.de ☒ See website for a detailed service schedule.

- **US:** 4645 Reservoir Rd. NW, Washington DC 20007, USA ☎+1-202-298-4000; www.germany.info ☒ See website for a detailed service schedule.

**Essentials**

# In Berlin

- **AUSTRALIAN EMBASSY:** Wallstr. 76-79, 10179 ☎030 880 08 80; www.germany.embassy.gov.au/beln/home.html ⏰ Open M 9am-noon and 1-5pm, Tu 1-5pm, W 9am-noon, Th 1-5pm, F 9am-noon and 1-4pm.

- **CANADIAN EMBASSY:** Leipziger Pl. 17, 10117 ☎030 20 31 20; www.canadainternational.gc.ca/germany-allemagne. ⏰ Open M-F 8:30am-5pm.

- **IRISH EMBASSY:** Jägerstr. 51, 10117 ☎030 22 07 20; www. embassyofireland.de/home/index.aspx?id=29424 ⏰ Open M-F 9:30am-12:30pm and 2:30-4:45pm.

- **NEW ZEALAND EMBASSY:** Friedrichstr. 60, 10117 ☎030 20 62 10; www.nzembassy.com/germany ⏰ Open M-Th 9am-1pm and 2-5:30pm, F 9am-1pm and 2-4:30pm.

- **UK EMBASSY:** Wilhelmstr. 70, 10117 ☎030 20 45 70; www. ukingermany.fco.gov.uk/en ⏰ Open M-Tu 9am-noon and 2-4pm, Th-F 9am-noon and 2-4pm.

- **US EMBASSY:** Clayallee 170, 14191 ☎030 83 050; www. germany.usembassy.gov ⏰ Open M-F 8:30am-noon.

## One Europe

The EU's policy of **freedom of movement** means that most border controls have been abolished and visa policies harmonized. Under this treaty, formally known as the Schengen Agreement, you're still required to carry a passport (or government-issued ID card for EU citizens) when crossing an internal border, but, once you've been admitted into one country, you're free to travel to other participating states. Most EU states (the UK is a notable exception) are already members of Schengen, as are Iceland and Norway.

In recent times, debate over immigration has led to calls for suspension of the freedom of movement policy. Border controls are being strengthened, but this shouldn't affect casual travelers.

# MONEY

Stuff happens. When stuff happens, you might need some money. When you need some money, the easiest and cheapest solution is to have someone back home make a deposit to your bank account. Otherwise, consider one of the following options.

## Wiring Money

Arranging a **bank money transfer** means asking a bank back home to wire money to a bank in Berlin. This is the cheapest way to transfer cash, but it's also the slowest and most agonizing, usually taking several days or more. Note that some banks may only release your funds in local currency, potentially sticking you with a poor exchange rate; ask about this in advance.

Money transfer services like **Western Union** are faster and more convenient than bank transfers—but also much pricier. Western Union has many locations worldwide. To find one, visit www.westernunion.com or call: in Australia }1800 173 833, in Canada }800-235-0000, in the UK }0808 234 9168, in the US }800-325-6000, or in Germany }0800 181 1797. Money transfer services are also available to **American Express** cardholders and at select **Thomas Cook** offices.

## US State Department (US Citizens Only)

In serious emergencies only, the US State Department will help your family or friends forward money within hours to the nearest consular office, which will then disburse it according to instructions for a US$30 fee. If you wish to use this service, you must contact the **Overseas Citizens Services** division of the US State Department. (☎+1-202-501-4444, from US ☎888-407-4747)

## Withdrawing Money

To use a debit or credit card to withdraw money from a **cash machine** (ATM) in Europe, you must have a four-digit Personal Identification Number (PIN). If your PIN is longer than four digits, ask your bank whether you can just use the first four or whether you'll need a new one. Credit cards don't usually come with PINs, so if you intend to hit up ATMs in Europe with a credit card, call your credit card company before leaving to request one.

ATMs are readily available in Berlin, though they will almost always charge a small fee for withdrawals made from accounts with other banks. Check with your bank to see if there are any advantages to using certain ATMs. Bank of America, for instance, has a deal with Deutsche Bank allowing fee-free withdrawals. If you need to cash **traveler's checks,** go to Deutsche Reisebank, which has several convenient locations and will do so free of charge.

---

### The Euro

Despite what many dollar-possessing Americans might want to hear, the official currency of 16 members of the European Union—Austria, Belgium, Cyprus, Finland, France, Germany, Greece, Ireland, Italy, Luxembourg, Malta, the Netherlands, Portugal, Slovakia, Slovenia, and Spain—is the **euro.**

The currency has some positive consequences for travelers hitting more than one eurozone country. For one thing, money-changers across the eurozone are obliged to exchange money at the official, fixed rate and at no commission (though they may still charge a small service fee). Second, euro-denominated traveler's checks allow you to pay for goods and services across the eurozone at the official rate and commission-free. For more info, check a currency converter (such as **www.xe.com**) or **www.europa.eu.int.**

---

# TIPPING AND BARGAINING

In Germany, service staff is paid by the hour, and a service charge is included in an item's unit price. Cheap customers typically just round up to the nearest whole euro, but it's customary and polite to **tip 5-10%** if you are satisfied with the service. If the service was poor, you don't have to tip at all. To tip, mention the total to your waiter while paying. If he states that the bill is €20, respond "€22," and he will include the tip. Do not leave the tip on the table; hand it directly to the server. It is standard to tip a taxi driver at least €1, housekeepers €1-2 per day, bellhops €1 per piece of luggage, and public toilet attendants around €0.50. Germans rarely barter, except at flea markets.

## TAXES

Most goods in Germany are subject to a **value-added tax** (called a *mehrwertsteuer* or MwSt) of 19%. A reduced tax of 7% is applied to books and magazines, foods, and agricultural products. Ask for a **MwSt return form** at points of purchase to enjoy tax-free shopping. Present it at customs upon departure, along with your receipts and the unused goods. Refunds can be claimed at **Tax Free Shopping Offices,** found at most airports, land borders, and ferry stations, or by mail. Be warned that there are sometimes rather high minimum refund amounts, so don't expect to receive tax money back on that I <3 Berlin T-shirt. For more information, contact the Germany VAT refund hotline (☎0228 406 2880; www.bzst.de).

## GETTING THERE

### By Plane

**Capital Airport Berlin Brandenburg International (BBI)** will open in southeast Berlin in June of 2012. Until then, **Tegel Airport** will continue to serve travelers. (☎018 050 00 186; www.berlin-airport.de ⇆ Take express bus #X9 or #109 from U7: Jakob-Kaiser Pl., bus #128 from U6: Kurt-Schumacher-Pl., or bus TXL from S42, S41: Beusselstr. Follow signs in the airport for ground transportation.)

### By Train

International trains (☎972 226 150) pass through Berlin's **Hauptbahnhof** and run to: **Amsterdam, NTH** ([$] €130. ⏰ 7hr., 16 per day); **Brussels, BEL** ([$] €140. ⏰ 7hr., 16 per day); **Budapest, HUN** ([$]€140. ⏰ 13hr., 4 per day); **Copenhagen, DNK** ([$] €135. ⏰ 7hr., 7 per day); **Paris, FRA** ([$] €200. ⏰ 9hr., 9 per day); **Prague, CZR;** ([$] €80. ⏰5hr., 12 per day); **Vienna, AUT** ([$] €155. ⏰ 10hr., 12 per day).

### By Bus

**ZOB** is the central bus station. (Masurenallee 4 ☎030 301 03 80 ⇆ U2: Theodor-Heuss-Pl. From the Metro, head southwest on Masurenallee; the station is on the left. Alternatively, S4, S45, or S46: Messe Nord/ICC. From the Metro, walk west on Neue Kantstr. The station is on the right. ⏰ Open M-F 6am-9pm, Sa-Su and holidays 6am-8pm.)

# GETTING AROUND

## By Public Transportation: The BVG

The two pillars of Berlin's Metro are the **U-Bahn** and **S-Bahn** trains, which cover the city in spidery and circular patterns, (somewhat) respectively. **Trams** and **buses** (both part of the U-Bahn system) scuttle around the remaining city corners. (BVG's 24hr. hotline ☎030 194 49; www.bvg.de.) Berlin is divided into three transit zones. **Zone A** consists of central Berlin, including Tempelhof Airport. The rest of Berlin lies in **Zone B; Zone C** covers the larger state of Brandenburg, including Potsdam. An **AB** ticket is the best deal, since you can later buy extension tickets for the outlying areas. A **one-way** ticket is good for 2hr. after validation. (Ⓢ Zones AB €2.30, BC €2.70, ABC €3, under 6 free.) Within the validation period, the ticket may be used on any S-Bahn, U-Bahn, bus, or tram.

Most train lines don't run Monday through Friday 1-4am. S-Bahn and U-Bahn lines do run Friday and Saturday nights, but less frequently. When trains stop running, 70 night buses take over, running every 20-30min. generally along major transit routes; pick up the free Nachtliniennetz **map** of bus routes at a **Fahrscheine und Mehr** office. The letter "N" precedes night bus numbers. Trams continue to run at night.

Buy tickets, including monthly passes, from machines or ticket windows in Metro stations or from bus drivers. **Be warned:** machines don't give more than €10 change, and many machines don't take bills, though some accept credit cards. **Validate** your ticket by inserting it into the stamp machines before boarding. Failure to validate becomes a big deal when plainclothes policemen bust you and charge you €40 for freeloading. If you bring a bike on the U-Bahn or S-Bahn, you must buy it a child's ticket. Bikes are prohibited on buses and trams.

Single-ride tickets are a waste of money. A **Day Ticket** (Ⓢ AB €6.30, BC €6.60, ABC €6.80) is good from the time it's stamped until 3am the next day. The BVG also sells **7-day tickets** (Ⓢ AB €27.20, BC €28, ABC €33.50) and **month-long passes** (Ⓢ AB €74, BC €75, ABC €91). The popular tourist cards are another option. The **WelcomeCard** (sold at tourist offices) buys unlimited travel ($ 48hr. AB €17, ABC €19; 72hr. €23/26) and includes discounts on 130 sights. The **CityTourCard** is good within zones AB ($ 48hr. €16, 72hr. €22) and offers discounts at over 50 attractions.



## By Taxi

Call 15min. in advance. Women can request female drivers. Trips within the city cost up to €30. (☎030 261 026, toll-free ☎0800 263 00 00)

## By Bike

Biking is one of the best ways to explore the city that never brakes. Unless your hostel is out in the boonies, few trips will be out of cycling distance, and given that U-Bahn tickets verge on €3 and that the average long-term bike rental costs €8 per day, pedaling your way can be a better deal and a simpler way to navigate.

### Fat Tire Bike Rental — MITTE

Panorama Str. 1a

☎030 240 47 991; www.berlinfahrradverleih.com

Fat Tire rents bikes for half and full days.

▶ 🚉 East location U2: Alexanderpl. Directly under the TV Tower. West location U2 or U9: Zoological Garten. $ €7 per ½-day, €12 per day. €10 for a 2nd day, €8 for each day thereafter. ⏰ Open Apr 10-Sept 30 daily 9:30am-8pm; Oct 1-Nov 30 daily 9:30am-6pm; Mar 1-Apr 9 daily 9:30am-6pm.

### Prenzlberger Orange Bikes — PRENZLAUER BERG

Kollwitzstr. 35

☎016 389 26 427

You may not want to ride a bright orange bike with a small sign on the back advertising the rental place, but at €6 per 24hr., this is about the cheapest form of transportation available that isn't walking.

▶ 🚉U2: Senefelder Pl. Head slightly east on Metzer Str., then turn left onto Kollwitzstr. The rental place is on the left within the 1st block. $ €6 per 24hr. ⏰ Open daily noon-6pm.

## Beware of Bikes

Painted or paved in red, Berlin's bike lanes skip the roads and take up space on or right next to the sidewalks. When walking, stay off the red and stick to the gray pedestrian paths to avoid nasty looks, ringing bells, and loss of life and limb.

# PRACTICALITIES

For all the hostels, cafes, museums, and bars we list, some of the most important places you'll visit during your trip may be more mundane. Whether it's a tourist office, internet cafe, or post office, these practicalities are vital to a successful trip, and you'll find all you need right here.

- **Tourist Offices:** Now privately owned, tourist offices merely give you some commercial flyer or refer you to a website instead of guaranteeing human contact. Visit **www.berlin.de** for reliable info on all aspects of city life. **Tourist Info Centers.** (Berlin Tourismus Marketing GmbH, Am Karlsbad 11 ☎030 25 00 25; www.visitberlin.de ⇄ On the ground floor of the Hauptbahnhof, next to the northern entrance. *i* English spoken. *Siegessäule, Blu,* and *Gay-Yellowpages* have GLBT event and club listings. $ Transit maps free; city maps €1-2. The monthly *Berlin Programm* lists museums, sights, restaurants, and hotels as well as opera, theater, and classical music performances, €1.75. *Tip* provides full listings of film, theater, concerts, and clubs in German, €2.70. *Ex-Berliner* has English-language movie and theater reviews, €2. ⏰ Open daily 8am-10pm.) **Alternate location.** (Brandenburger Tor. ⇄ S1, S2, S25, or bus #100: Unter den Linden. On your left as you face the pillars from the Unter den Linden side. ⏰ Open daily 10am-6pm.)

- **Student Travel Offices: STA** books flights and hotels and sells ISICs. (Dorotheenstr. 30 ☎030 201 65 063 ⇄ S3, S5, S7, S9, S75, or U6: Friedrichstr. From the Metro, walk 1 block south on Friedrichstr., turn left onto Dorotheenstr., and follow as it veers left. STA will be on the left. ⏰ Open M-F 10am-7pm, Sa 11am-3pm.) **2nd location.** (Gleimstr. 28 ☎030 285 98 264 ⇄ S4, S8, S85, or U2: Schönhauser

Allee. From the Metro, walk south on Schönhauser Allee and turn right on Gleimstr. ⏰ Open M-F 10am-7pm, Sa 11am-4pm.) **3rd location.** (Hardenbergstr. 9 ☎030 310 00 40 🚏 U2: Ernst-Reuter-Pl. From the Metro, walk southeast on Hardenbergstr. ⏰ Open M-F 10am-7pm, Sa 11am-3pm.) **4th location.** (Takustr. 47 ☎030 831 10 25 🚏 U3: Dahlem-Dorf. From the Metro, walk north on Brümmerstr., turn left onto Königin-Luise Str., and then turn right onto Takustr. ⏰ Open M-F 10am-7pm, Sa 10am-2pm.)

- **Tours: Terry Brewer's Best of Berlin** is legendary for vast knowledge and engaging personalities, making the 6hr. walk well worth it. (Tours leave daily from in front of the Bandy Brooks shop on Friedrichstr. ☎017 738 81 537; www.brewersberlintours.com 🚏 S1, S7, S9, S75, or U6: Friedrichstr. $ €12. ⏰ Tours start at 10:30am.) **Insider Tour** offers a variety of fun, informative walking and bike tours that hit all the major sights. More importantly, the guides' enthusiasm for Berlin is contagious, and their accents span the English-speaking world. (☎030 692 3149; www.insidertour.com ℹ Offers tours of Cold War Berlin, Jewish Berlin, Nazi Berlin, and Potsdam as well as a Berlin Pub Crawl and daytrips to Dresden. $ €12, under 26 €10, WelcomeCard or ISIC €9. Bike tours €22, under 26 €20, with WelcomeCard or ISIC €20. 5% discount for online booking. ⏰ Starts daily from the McDonald's outside the Hauptbahnhof Apr-Oct 10am, 2:30pm; from the A.M.T. Coffee Apr-Oct 10:30am, 3pm; from the Hauptbahnhof Nov-Mar 10am; from A.M.T. Coffee Nov-Mar 10:30am. Bike tours meet at the A.M.T. Coffee at [M]Hackescher Markt. 4hr.; June-Sept 10:30am, 3pm.) **Original Berlin Walks** offers a range of English-language walking tours, including Discover Potsdam, Infamous Third Reich Sites, Jewish Life in Berlin, and Nest of Spies. (☎030 301 91 94; www.berlinwalks.de 🚏 Tours meet at the taxi stand in front of Bahnhof Zoo and outside Restaurant Weihenstephaner opposite ĆHackesher Markt. $ Discover Berlin walk €12, under 26 €10, with WelcomeCard or ISIC €9. ⏰ Tours depart the Bahnhof Zoo Apr-Oct 10am, 1:30pm; Nov-Mar 10am. Tours depart [M]Hackescher Markt Apr-Oct 10:30am, 2pm; Nov-Mar 10:30am.) **New Berlin** offers free tours of Berlin's biggest sights (guides work for tips; expect some pandering) and special tours (Sachsenhausen, Third Reich tour, Eco City tour, pub crawl, etc.) for a fee. The "free" tour is recommended as a starting point for backpackers with little cash, but you may find some of their coverage a little cursory. The company now offers bike tours as well. (☎030 510 50 030; www.newberlintours.com ⚑ Tours leave from either the Brandenburg Gate Starbucks or the Zoologischer Garten Deutsche Bank. Bike tours depart the Friedrichstr. Starbucks. S3, S5, S7, S9, S75, or U6: Friedrichstr. From the Metro, head south on Friedrichstr. The Starbucks is on the left. Ⓢ Bike tours €12, with bike rental €15. Ⓩ Tours depart the Brandenburg Gate Starbucks 9, 11am, 1, 4pm; the Zoologischer Garten Deutsche Bank 10:30am, 12:30, 3:30pm. Bike tours depart 11am, 2pm.)

- **Currency Exchange and Money Wires:** The best rates are usually found at exchange offices with **Wechselstube** signs outside, at most major train stations, and in large squares. For money wires through Western Union, use **ReiseBank.** (Ⓜ Hauptbahnhof. ☎030 204 53 761 Ⓩ Open M-Sa 8am-10pm.) **2nd location** (Ⓜ Bahnhof Zoo. ☎030 881 71 17). **3rd location** (Ⓜ Ostbahnhof. ☎030 296 43 93).

- **Luggage Storage:** In the ĆHauptbahnhof. (⚑ "DB Gepack Center," 1st fl., east side. Ⓢ €4 per day.) Lockers also at Ⓜ Bahnhof Zoo, Ⓜ Ostbahnhof, and Ⓜ Alexanderpl.

- **Internet Access:** Free internet with admission to the **Staatsbibliothek.** During its renovation, Staatsbibliothek requires a €10 month-long pass to the library. (Potsdamer Str. 33 ☎030 26 60 Ⓩ Open M-F 9am-9pm, Sa 9am-7pm.) **Netlounge.** (Augustistr. 89 ☎030 24 34 25 97; www. netlounge-berlin.de ⚑ Ⓜ Oranienburger Str. Ⓢ €2.50 per hr. Ⓩ Open daily noon-midnight.) **Easy Internet** has several locations throughout Berlin. (Unter den Linden 24, Rosenstr. 16, Frankfurter Allee 32, Rykestr. 29, and Kurfürstendamm 18.) Many cafes throughout Berlin offer free Wi-Fi, including **Starbucks,** where the networks never require a password.

- **Post Offices: Bahnhof Zoo.** (Joachimstaler Str. 7 ☎030 887 08 611 ⚑ Down Joachimstaler Str. from Bahnhof Zoo, on the corner of Joachimstaler Str. and Kantstr. Ⓩ Open M-Sa 9am-8pm.) **Alexanderplatz.** (Rathausstr. 5, by

## Emergency

Hopefully you never need any of these things, but, if you do, it's best to be prepared.

- **POLICE:** Pl. der Luftbrücke 6. ♯ U6: Pl. der Luftbrücke.

- **EMERGENCY NUMBERS:** ☎110. **Ambulance and Fire:** ☎112. **Non-emergency advice hotline:** ☎030 466 44 664.

- **MEDICAL SERVICES:** The American and British embassies list English-speaking doctors. The **emergency doctor service** (☎030 31 00 31 or ☎018 042 255 23 62) helps travelers find English-speaking doctors. **Emergency dentist.** (☎030 890 04 333)

- **CRISIS LINES:** English spoken at most crisis lines. **American Hotline** (☎017 781 41 510) has crisis and referral services. **Poison Control.** (☎030 192 40) **Berliner Behindertenverband** has resources for the disabled. (Jägerstr. 63d ☎030 204 38 47; www.bbv-ev.de ☒ Open W noon-5pm and by appointment.) **Deutsche AIDS-Hilfe.** (Wilhelmstr. 138 ☎030 690 08 70; www.aidshilfe.de) **Drug Crisis Hotline.** (☎030 192 37 ☒ 24hr.) **Frauenkrisentelefon** women's crisis line. (☎030 615 42 43; www.frauenkrisentelefon.de ☒ Open M 10am-noon, Tu-W 7-9pm, Th 10am-noon, F 7-9pm, Sa-Su 5-7pm.) **Lesbenberatung** offers counseling for lesbians. (Kulmer Str. 20a ☎030 215 20 00; www.lesbenberatung-berlin. de) **Schwulenberatung** offers counseling for gay men. (Mommenstr. 45 ☎030 194 46; www.schwulenberatungberlin.de.) **Maneo** offers legal help for gay victims of violence. (☎030 216 33 36; www.maneo.de ☒ Open daily 5-7pm.) **LARA** offers counseling for victims of sexual assault. (Fuggerstr. 19 ☎030 216 88 88; www.lara-berlin.de ☒ Open M-F 9am-6pm.) **Children's emergency helpline.** (☎030 610 061)

the Dunkin' Donuts. ☒ Open M-F 9am-7pm, 9am-4pm.) **Tegel Airport.** (☒ Open M-F 8am-6pm, Sa 8am-noon.) **Ostbahnhof.** (☒ Open M-F 8am-8pm, Sa-Su 10am-6pm.) To find a post office near you, visit the search tool on their website, www.standorte.deutschepost.de/filialen_verkaufspunkte, which is confusing and in German, but could eventually help.

- **Postal Code:** 10706.

# SAFETY AND HEALTH

In any type of crisis, the most important thing to do is **stay calm.** Your country's **embassy** is usually your best resource in an emergency; it's a good idea to register with the embassy upon arrival. The government offices listed in the **Travel Advisories** feature below can provide information on the services they offer their citizens in case of emergencies.

## Local Laws and Police

Certain regulations may seem harsh and unusual (practice some self-control, city-slickers; **jaywalking** is a €5 fine), but abide by all local laws while in Germany, as your respective embassy won't necessarily get you off the hook. Be sure to carry a valid passport with you, as police have the right to ask for identification.

### Travel Advisories

The following government offices provide travel information and advisories:

- **AUSTRALIA: Department of Foreign Affairs and Trade.** (☎+61 2 6261 1111; www.smartraveller.gov.au)

- **CANADA: Department of Foreign Affairs and International Trade.** Call or visit the website for the free booklet *Bon Voyage, But...* (☎+1-800-267-6788; www.international.gc.ca)

- **NEW ZEALAND: Ministry of Foreign Affairs and Trade.** (☎+64 4 439 8000; www.safetravel.govt.nz)

- **UK: Foreign and Commonwealth Office.** (☎+44 845 850 2829; www.fco.gov.uk)

- **US: Department of State.** (☎+1-888-407-4747 from the US, +1-202-501-4444 outside the US; www.travel.state.gov)

## Drugs and Alcohol

The **drinking age** in Germany is 16 for beer and wine and 18 for hard alcohol. The maximum blood alcohol content for drivers is 0.05%. It's 0.00% for drivers who have only recently gotten their licenses. Avoid public drunkenness: it can jeopardize your safety and earn the disdain of locals.

If you use insulin, syringes, or any prescription drugs, carry a copy of the prescriptions and a doctor's note. Needless to say, illegal drugs are best avoided. While possession of **marijuana** or **hashish** is illegal, possession of small quantities for personal consumption is decriminalized in Germany. Each region has interpreted "small quantities" differently; the limit in Berlin is 10g. Carrying drugs across an international border—considered to be drug trafficking—is a serious offense that could land you in prison.

## Pre-Departure Health

Matching a prescription to a foreign equivalent is not always easy, safe, or possible, so if you take **prescription drugs,** carry up-to-date prescriptions or a statement from your doctor stating the medications' trade names, manufacturers, chemical names, and dosages. Be sure to keep all medication with you in your carry-on luggage. It is also a good idea to look up the German names of drugs you may need during your trip.

### Immunizations and Precautions

Travelers over the age of two should make sure that the following vaccines are up to date: MMR (for measles, mumps, and rubella), DTaP or Td (for diphtheria, tetanus, and pertussis), IPV (for polio), Hib (for *Haemophilus influenzae* B), and HepB (for Hepatitis B). For recommendations on immunizations and prophylaxis, check with a doctor and consult the **Centers for Disease Control and Prevention (CDC)** in the US (☎+1-800-232-4636; www.cdc.gov/travel) or the equivalent in your home country.

# KEEPING IN TOUCH

## By Email and Internet

Hello and welcome to the 21st century, where you're rarely more than a 5min. walk from the nearest **Wi-Fi hot spot,** even if sometimes you'll have to pay a few bucks or buy a drink for the privilege of using it. **Internet cafes** and free internet terminals are listed in **Practicalities.** Starbucks is a good bet, as it usually offers Wi-Fi without any sort of fee or "buy something and get a code" deal. For lists of additional cybercafes in Berlin, check out **www. hotspot-locations.com.**

Wireless hot spots make internet access possible in public and remote places. Unfortunately, they also pose security risks. Hot spots are open, public networks that use unencrypted, insecure connections. They are susceptible to hacks and "packet sniffing"—the theft of passwords and other private information. To prevent these breaches, disable "ad hoc" mode, turn off file sharing and network discovery, encrypt your email, turn on your firewall, beware of phony networks, and watch for over-the-shoulder creeps.

# By Telephone

### Calling Home from Berlin

If you have internet access, your best—i.e., cheapest, most convenient, and most tech-savvy—means of calling home is our good friend Skype (www.skype.com). You can even videochat if you have a webcam. Calls to other Skype users are free; calls to landlines and mobiles worldwide start at US$0.023 per minute, depending on where you're calling.

For those still stuck in the 20th century, **prepaid phone cards** are a common and relatively inexpensive means of calling abroad. Each one comes with a Personal Identification Number (PIN) and a toll-free access number. You call the access number and then follow the directions for dialing your PIN. To purchase prepaid phone cards, check online for the best rates; **www. callingcards.com** is a good place to start. Online providers generally send your access number and PIN via email, with no actual "card" involved. You can also call home with prepaid phone cards purchased in Berlin.

Another option is a **calling card,** linked to a major national telecommunications service in your home country. Calls are billed collect or to your account. Cards generally come with instructions for dialing both domestically and internationally.

Placing a collect call through an international operator can be expensive but may be necessary in an emergency. You can frequently call collect even without a company's calling card just by calling its access number and following the instructions.

**Essentials**

## International Calls

To call Germany from home or to call home from Germany, dial:

1. **THE INTERNATIONAL DIALING PREFIX.** To call from from Germany, dial ☎00. To call from **Australia,** ☎0011; **Canada** or the **US,** ☎011; and from **Ireland, New Zealand,** or the **UK,** ☎00.

2. **THE COUNTRY CODE OF THE COUNTRY YOU WANT TO CALL.** To call Germany, dial ☎49; **Australia,** ☎61; **Canada** or the **US,** ☎1; **Ireland,** ☎353; **New Zealand,** ☎64; the **UK,** ☎44.

3. **THE CITY/AREA CODE.** *Let's Go* lists the city/area codes for cities and towns in Germany opposite the city or town name and next to a ☎ and in every phone number.

4. **THE LOCAL NUMBER.** If the area code begins with a zero, you can omit that number when dialing from abroad.

### Cellular Phones

Cell phones are easy to purchase and helpful to have in Berlin. Pay-as-you-go phone plans with phone cards are available from **02** and **Vodafone,** though many travelers opt to buy a German SIM (Subscriber Identity Module) card for their US phones.

The international standard for cell phones is **Global System for Mobile Communication (GSM).** To make and receive calls in Germany, you will need a GSM-compatible phone and a SIM card, a country-specific, thumbnail-size chip that gives you a local phone number and plugs you into the local network. Many SIM cards are prepaid, and incoming calls are frequently free. You can buy additional cards or vouchers (usually available at convenience stores) to "top up" your phone. For more information on GSM phones, check out **www.telestial.com.** Companies like **Cellular Abroad** (www.cellularabroad.com) and **OneSimCard** (www.onesimcard.com) rent cell phones and SIM cards that work in a variety of destinations around the world.

## By Snail Mail

### Sending Mail from Berlin

**Airmail** is the best way to send mail home from Berlin. Write "airmail," *"par avion,"* or *"die Luftpost"* on the front. For simple letters or postcards, airmail tends to be surprisingly cheap, but the price will go up sharply for packages. **Surface mail** is by far the cheapest, slowest, and most antiquated way to send mail. It takes one to two months to cross the Atlantic and one to three to cross the Pacific—good for heavy items you won't need for a while, like souvenirs that you've acquired along the way.

### Receiving Mail in Berlin

There are several ways to arrange to pick up letters sent to you while you are in Berlin, even without a mailing address of your own. Mail can be sent via **Poste Restante** (General Delivery; *Postlagernde Briefe* in German) to Berlin, and it is pretty reliable. Address Poste Restante letters like so:

> Albert Einstein
> Postlagernd Briefe
> Post Office Street Address, Zipcode Berlin
> Germany

The mail will go to a special desk in the central post office at **Zimmermannstrasse 22, 12163 Berlin,** unless you specify a local post office by street address or postal code. It's best to use the largest post office, since mail may be sent there regardless. Bring your passport (or other photo ID) for pickup; there should not be a fee. If the clerks insist that there is nothing for you, ask them to check under your first name as well. *Let's Go* lists post offices in **Practicalities.** It is usually safer and quicker, though more expensive, to send mail express or registered. If you don't want to deal with Poste Restante, consider asking your hostel or accommodation if you can receive mail there. Of course, if you have your own mailing address or a reliable friend to receive mail for you, that may be the easiest solution.

# TIME DIFFERENCES

Berlin is 1hr. ahead of Greenwich Mean Time (GMT) and observes Daylight Saving Time. This means that it is 6hr. ahead of New York City, 9hr. ahead of Los Angeles, 1hr. ahead of the British Isles, 8hr. behind Sydney, and 10hr. behind New Zealand.

# CLIMATE

Germany has a temperate seasonal climate dictated by the North Atlantic Drift. The climate is oceanic, with maximum rainfall during the summer.

| MONTH | AVG. HIGH TEMP. | | AVG. LOW TEMP. | | AVG. RAINFALL | | AVG. NUMBER OF WET DAYS |
|-------|------|------|------|------|-------|---------|-----|
| January | 2°C | 36°F | -3°C | 27°F | 46mm | 1.8 in. | 17 |
| February | 3°C | 37°F | -3°C | 27°F | 40mm | 1.6 in. | 15 |
| March | 8°C | 46°F | 0°C | 32°F | 33mm | 1.3 in. | 12 |
| April | 13°C | 55°F | 4°C | 39°F | 42mm | 1.7 in. | 13 |
| May | 19°C | 66°F | 8°C | 46°F | 49mm | 1.9 in. | 12 |
| June | 22°C | 71°F | 12°C | 53°F | 65mm | 2.6 in. | 13 |
| July | 24°C | 75°F | 14°C | 57°F | 73mm | 2.9 in. | 14 |
| August | 23°C | 73°F | 13°C | 55°F | 69mm | 2.7 in. | 14 |
| September | 20°C | 68°F | 10°C | 50°F | 48mm | 1.9 in. | 12 |
| October | 13°C | 55°F | 6°C | 43°F | 49mm | 1.9 in. | 14 |
| November | 7°C | 45°F | 2°C | 36°F | 46mm | 1.8 in. | 16 |
| December | 3°C | 37°F | -1°C | 30°F | 43mm | 1.7 in. | 15 |

To convert from degrees Fahrenheit to degrees Celsius, subtract 32 and multiply by 5/9. To convert from Celsius to Fahrenheit, multiply by 9/5 and add 32. The mathematically challenged may use this handy chart:

| °CELSIUS | -5 | 0 | 5 | 10 | 15 | 20 | 25 | 30 | 35 | 40 |
|----------|-----|-----|-----|-----|-----|-----|-----|-----|-----|------|
| °FAHRENHEIT | 23 | 32 | 41 | 50 | 59 | 68 | 77 | 86 | 95 | 104 |

# MEASUREMENTS

Like the rest of the rational world, Germany uses the metric system. The basic unit of length is the meter (m), which is divided into 100 centimeters (cm) or 1000 millimeters (mm). One thousand meters make up one kilometer (km). Fluids are measured in liters (L), each divided into 1000 milliliters (mL). A liter of pure water weighs one kilogram (kg), which is divided into 1000 grams (g). One metric ton is 1000kg.

Essentials

Essentials

| MEASUREMENT CONVERSIONS ||
|---|---|
| 1 inch (in.) = 25.4mm | 1 millimeter (mm) = 0.039 in. |
| 1 foot (ft.) = 0.305m | 1 meter (m) = 3.28 ft. |
| 1 yard (yd.) = 0.914m | 1 meter (m) = 1.094 yd. |
| 1 mile (mi.) = 1.609km | 1 kilometer (km) = 0.621 mi. |
| 1 ounce (oz.) = 28.35g | 1 gram (g) = 0.035 oz. |
| 1 pound (lb.) = 0.454kg | 1 kilogram (kg) = 2.205 lb. |
| 1 fluid ounce (fl. oz.) = 29.57mL | 1 milliliter (mL) = 0.034 fl. oz. |
| 1 gallon (gal.) = 3.785L | 1 liter (L) = 0.264 gal. |

# LANGUAGE

## German (Deutsch)

Most Germans speak some basic English, but you will encounter many who don't. Preface any question with a polite *Sprechen Sie Englisch?* (Do you speak English?) When out at restaurants, bars, and attractions, *Bitte* (please) and *Danke* (thank you) are the magic words. Even if your handle on German is a little loose, most locals will appreciate the effort.

## Pronunciation

German pronunciation, for the most part, is consistent with spelling. There are no silent letters, and all nouns are capitalized.

An umlaut over a letter (e.g., ü) makes the pronunciation longer and more rounded. An umlaut is sometimes replaced by an "e" following the vowel, so that "schön" becomes "schoen." Germans are generally very forgiving toward foreigners who butcher their mother tongue, but if you learn nothing else in German, learn to pronounce the names of cities properly. Berlin is "bare-LEEN," Hamburg is "HAHM-boorg," Munich is "MEUWN-shen," and Bayreuth is "BUY-royt."

Different pronunciations for certain letters and diphthongs are listed below. The German "ß" is referred to as the *scharfes S* (sharp S) or the *Ess-tset*. It is shorthand for a double-s, and is pronounced just like an "ss" in English. The letter appears only in lower case and shows up in two of the most important German words for travelers: *Straße*, "street," which is pronounced "SHTRAH-sseh" and abbreviated "Str."; and *Schloß*, "castle," pronounced "SCHLOSS."

**Essentials**

| PHONETIC UNIT | PRONUNCIATION | PHONETIC UNIT | PRONUNCIATION |
|---|---|---|---|
| a | AH, as in father | j | Y, as in young |
| e | EH, as in bet | k | always K, as in kelp |
| i | IH, as in wind | r | guttural RH, like French |
| o | OH, as in oh | s | Z, as in zone |
| u | OO, as in fondue | v | F, as in fantasy |
| au | OW, as in cow | w | V, as in vacuum |
| ie | EE, as in thief | z | TS, as in cats |
| ei | EY, as in wine | ch | CHH, as in loch |
| eu | OI, as in boil | qu | KV, as in kvetch |
| ä | similar to the E in bet | sch | SH, as in shot |
| ö | similar to the E in perm | st/sp | SHT/SHP, as in spiel |
| ü | close to the EU in blue | th | T, as in time |

## Phrasebook

Nothing can replace a full-fledged phrasebook or pocket English-German dictionary, but this phrasebook will provide you with a few essentials. German features both an informal and formal form of address; in the tables below, the polite form follows the familiar form in parentheses. In German, nouns can be one of three genders: masculine (taking the article **der;** pronounced DARE), feminine (**die;** pronounced DEE), and neuter (**das;** pronounced DAHSS). All plural nouns take the article *die,* regardless of their gender in the singular. (Revolution girl-style!)

### GREETINGS

| ENGLISH | GERMAN | ENGLISH | GERMAN |
|---|---|---|---|
| Good morning. | Guten Morgen. | My name is... | Ich heiße... |
| Good afternoon. | Guten Tag. | What is your name? | Wie heißt du (heißen Sie)? |
| Good evening. | Guten Abend. | Where are you from? | Woher kommst du (kommen Sie)? |
| Good night. | Guten Nacht. | How are you? | Wie geht's (geht es Ihnen)? |
| Excuse me/Sorry. | Enthschuldigung/ Sorry. | I'm well. | Es geht mir good. |
| Could you please help me? | Kannst du (Können Sie) mir helfen, bitte? | Do you speak English? | Sprichst du (Sprechen Sie) Englisch? |
| How old are you? | Wie alt bist du (sind Sie)? | I don't speak German. | Ich spreche kein Deutsch. |

Essentials

## USEFUL PHRASES

| ENGLISH | GERMAN | PRONUNCIATION |
|---|---|---|
| Hello!/Hi! | Hallo!/Tag! | Hahllo!/Tahk! |
| Goodbye!/Bye! | Auf Wiedersehen!/Tschüss! | Owf VEE-der-zain!/Chuess! |
| Yes. | Ja. | Yah. |
| No. | Nein. | Nine. |
| Sorry! | Es tut mir leid! | Ess toot meer lite! |
| **EMERGENCY** | | |
| Go away! | Geh weg! | Gay veck! |
| Help! | Hilfe! | HILL-fuh! |
| Call the police! | Ruf die Polizei! | Roof dee Pol-ee-TSEI! |
| Get a doctor! | Hol einen Arzt! | Hole EIN-en Ahrtst! |

### CARDINAL NUMBERS

| 0 | 1 | 2 | 3 | 4 | 5 | 6 | 7 | 8 | 9 | 10 |
|---|---|---|---|---|---|---|---|---|---|---|
| null | eins | zwei | drei | vier | fünf | sechs | sie-ben | acht | neun | zehn |

| 11 | 12 | 20 | 30 | 40 | 50 | 60 | 70 | 80 | 90 | 100 |
|---|---|---|---|---|---|---|---|---|---|---|
| elf | zwölf | zwan-zig | dreißig | vier-zig | fün-fzig | sechzig | sie-bzig | achtzig | neun-zig | hun-dert |

### ORDINAL NUMBERS

| 1st | erste | 5th | fünfte | 9th | neunte |
|---|---|---|---|---|---|
| 2nd | zweite | 6th | sechste | 10th | zehnte |
| 3rd | dritte | 7th | siebte | 20th | zwanzigste |
| 4th | vierte | 8th | achte | 100th | hunderte |

### DIRECTIONS AND TRANSPORTATION

| (to the) right | rechts | (to the) left | links |
|---|---|---|---|
| straight ahead | geradeaus | Where is...? | Wo ist...? |
| next to | neben | opposite | gegenüber |
| How do I find...? | Wie finde ich...? | It's nearby. | Es ist in der Nähe. |
| How do I get to...? | Wie komme ich nach...? | Is that far from here? | Ist es weit weg? |
| one-way trip | einfache Fahrt | round-trip | hin und zurück |
| Where is this train going? | Wohin fährt das Zug? | When does the train leave? | Wann fährt der Zug ab? |

### ACCOMMODATIONS

| Rooms available | Zimmer frei | I would like a room... | Ich möchte ein Zimmer... |
|---|---|---|---|
| No vacancies | besetzt | ...with sink. | ...mit Wasch-becken. |
| Are there any vacancies? | Gibt es ein Zimmer frei? | ...with shower. | ...mit Dusche. |
| Single room | Einzelzimmer | ...with a toilet. | ...mit WC. |
| Double room | Doppelzimmer | ...with a bathtub. | ...mit Badewanne. |
| Dormitory-style room | Mehrbettzimmer/Schlafsaal | nonsmoker | Nichtraucher |

| TIME AND HOURS | | | |
|---|---|---|---|
| open | geöffnet | closed | geschlossen |
| morning | Morgen | opening hours | Öffnungszeiten |
| afternoon | Nachmittag | today | heute |
| night | Nacht | yesterday | gestern |
| evening | Abend | tomorrow | morgen |
| What time is it? | Wie spät ist es? | break time, rest day | Ruhepause, Ruhetag |
| It's (seven) o'clock. | Es ist (sieben) Uhr. | At what time? | Um wieviel Uhr? |

| FOOD AND RESTAURANT TERMS | | | |
|---|---|---|---|
| bread | Brot | water | Wasser |
| roll | Brötchen | tap water | Leitungswasser |
| jelly | Marmelade | juice | Saft |
| meat | Fleisch | beer | Bier |
| beef | Rindfleisch | wine | Wein |
| pork | Schweinfleisch | coffee | Kaffee |
| chicken | Huhn | tea | Tee |
| sausage | Wurst | soup | Suppe |
| cheese | Käse | potatoes | Kartoffeln |
| fruit | Obst | milk | Milch |
| vegetables | Gemüse | sauce | Soße |
| cabbage | Kohl | french fries | Pommes frites |
| I would like to order... | Ich hätte gern... | Another beer, please. | Noch ein Bier, bitte. |
| It tastes good. | Es schmeckt gut. | It tastes awful. | Es schmeckt widerlich. |
| I'm a vegetarian. | Ich bin Vegetarier (m)/ Vegetarierin (f) | I'm a vegan. | Ich bin Veganer (m)/ Veganerin (f). |
| Service included. | Bedienung inklusiv. | Daily special | Tageskarte |
| Check, please. | Rechnung, bitte. | Give me a Nutella sandwich. | Geben Sie mir ein Nutellabrötchen. |

| RIDICULOUS(LY) USEFUL PHRASES | | | |
|---|---|---|---|
| Here's looking at you, kid. | Schau mich in die Augen, Kleines. | Many thanks for the pleasure ride in your patrol car. | Vielen Dank für den Ausritt in Ihrem Streifenwagen. |
| May I buy you a drink, darling? | Darf ich dir ein Getränk kaufen, Liebling? | I'm hungover. | Ich habe einen Kater. |
| Cheers! | Prost! | There is a disturbance in the force. | Es gibt eine Störung in der Kraft. |
| You're delicious. | Du bist lecker. | Inconceivable! | Quatsch! |
| That's cool. | Das ist ja geil/ crass. | Hasta la vista, baby. | Bis später, Baby. |

**Essentials**

## Let's Go Online

Plan your next trip on our spiffy website, **www.letsgo.com.** It features full book content, the latest travel info on your favorite destinations, and tons of interactive features: make your own itinerary, read blogs from our trusty Researcher-Writers, browse our photo library, watch exclusive videos, check out our newsletter, find travel deals, follow us on Facebook, and buy new guides. Plus, if this Essentials wasn't enough for you, we've got even more online. We're always updating and adding new features, so check back often!

# Berlin 101

A city for hipsters and history buffs alike, Berlin is brimming with relics of the past and reminders of the city's youth. As you walk the streets munching your *currywurst*, you can't help but notice the city's unique vibe. From gallery openings to indie bands, opera houses to grungy clubs, Berlin is a combination of rich history and avant-garde expression. So go ahead—explore the memorials that are scattered throughout the city and snap photos of the art on the crumbling Wall. Try to find five bands you've never heard of (and probably will never hear again). Imagine how things used to be, or just live in the moment and enjoy your beer.

# HISTORY

## Back in the Day (750-1700)

In 750 CE, a settlement named **Spandau** was founded in the region now known as Berlin. Control over this town flip-flopped between Slavic and German rule for the next 350 years until the Germans finally gained power in the 12th century.

In 1150, Albert the Bear inherited most of the region and, under his reign, the Slavic and German tribes began to intermarry, slowly diminishing the distinctions between the two. In fact, it turns out they really enjoyed each other's company—as things proceeded relatively peacefully, the population grew steadily, reaching roughly 8000 in the 15th century.

The 16th century, on the other hand, was not Berlin's happiest. Thirty-eight Jews were burned in 1510 after allegedly stealing the bread of the Holy Communion. Further persecution took place as Berlin was officially declared Lutheran during the **Protestant Reformation** of 1540. The **Bubonic plague**—always a hit—struck the city in 1576. Just when Berlin had replenished its population, the **Thirty Years' War**—another favorite—rolled in from 1618 to 1648. What began as a religious conflict grew into a war of no purpose resulting in mega-destruction and the death of half of Berlin's population. The French saw this as a rare real estate opportunity, and, by 1700, 20% of the population was French. *C'est la vie.*

## One Frederick After Another (1700-1870)

In the aftermath of the Thirty Years' War, Elector Frederick III decided that he would like to be called **Frederick I, King of Prussia.** He built himself a castle, renamed the region the "Royal Capital and Residence of Berlin," and did little else for the city. Things changed during the rule of his son, **Frederick William I,** and Prussia began to emerge as an important military force. Enlightenment thinking reached Berlin during the rule of **Frederick the Great,** but his son, **Frederick William II,** enforced censorship and repression after he came to power in 1786. Berlin did see some liberalization, with its first public elections, the founding of the **Berlin University,** and reforms that allowed Jews to hold any job. Also, the revolution fever spreading across Europe reached Berlin in the mid-1800s, where it was quelled by

Frederick William IV. In 1861, **Kaiser Wilhelm I** took the reins and so began the events that any student of modern European history is painfully familiar with.

## It Gets Worse: From the Empire to the Third Reich (1871-1940)

Wilhelm I appointed **Otto von Bismarck** as Chancellor in 1871. Bismarck had been instrumental in winning the **Danish-Prussian** and **Austro-Prussian Wars,** in 1864 and 1866 respectively, and completed German unification by defeating France in 1871. The rest of the 19th century was a time of development in Germany: important infrastructure such as the **U-Bahn** and **S-Bahn** was built, the economy grew, and, in 1884, the **Reichstag** was built. At the end of WWI, the Weimar Republic was declared and conflicts between the Social Democrats (SPD) and the communist party (KDP) began to brew.

   In 1933 **Adolf Hitler** was appointed Chancellor of Germany, and Berlin became the capital of the **Third Reich.** In the years leading up to WWII, Hitler made sure all Berlin citizens knew who was boss. He disbanded the Weimar Constitution, increased his power immensely, showed off the Nazi regime for the rest of the world during the **1936 Olympics,** and ordered the murder of 11 million European Jews, homosexuals, gypsies, socialists, and others.

## War and No Peace (1940-45)

WWII hit Berlin hard. 1940 saw the first Allied **air raid** on Berlin. By 1943, Berlin had become a major target for bombardment. Thousands of Jews around Germany continued to be sent to concentration camps, and Berlin was a major site of deportation. By 1943, only 1200 (out of a previous 160,000) Jews were left in Berlin. As the war came to a close, the Allied powers raced each other to reach Berlin, an obvious political target. The **Red Army** got there first, and, soon after they moved in, Hitler committed suicide.

## The Aftermath (1945-90)

Conflict didn't end with the declaration of peace. Berlin was divided into four sectors, one each for the US, the UK, France, and the Soviet Union. Tensions rose in 1948, and, angered by the fact that the Americans wouldn't pay reparations and that the Allies wanted to join their sectors, the Soviets blocked off ground access to West Berlin, in a move known as the **Berlin Blockade.** Though the blockade was eventually lifted, the Soviets decided they didn't want to share the city anymore. In 1949, they announced that they would independently govern their sector, now known as **East Berlin.** For years, the Soviets struggled to keep people from fleeing to West Berlin. They eventually decided a physical separation was necessary, and, on August 13, 1961, the first brick of the **Berlin Wall** was laid, essentially putting East Berlin in a permanent time-out. In the 28 years that the Wall stood, there were only 5000 successful escapes to West Berlin, while 192 people were murdered and 200 seriously wounded as they tried to cross. Meanwhile, the popularity of **student movements** increased, with young radicals starting parties in the shadow of the Wall. Riots and revolts were common, especially in the **Kreuzberg.**

The Wall stood strong until November 9, 1989. After a misleading press statement that led guards to believe the Wall would be opened, hundreds rushed the Wall, dancing and celebrating. Almost immediately, citizens took to the structure with hammers and chisels, and it was rapidly destroyed. Germany was officially declared reunited on October 3, 1990, after the Soviet Union collapsed throughout Europe.

## Life After the Wall (1990-Present Day)

After the fall of the Wall, **Chancellor Helmut Kohl** led a unified Germany and, in 1994, Russian and Allied troops finally withdrew from Berlin. The rest of the 20th century and the start of the 21st was a somewhat tumultuous time politically for the country, with various resignations and transfers of power. In 1999, the German parliament made the move from Bonn to Berlin, restoring the city to its pre-war status as the nation's capital. Although it has come far since then—2005 saw **Angela Merkel** become the first female Chancellor—Berlin still struggles with many of the same issues facing the rest of the world. The economic slump of 2008 forced Germany into recession (from which it is still, understandably, recovering), and, in May 2011, the German government announced plans to phase out nuclear power over the next 11 years. With Germany as a leading world power, Berlin continues to be an important player in global affairs.

# CUSTOMS AND ETIQUETTE

In Berlin, as in the rest of Germany, frankness should not be mistaken for rudeness. Simply put, Berliners are nice—just don't expect too much emotion, or get all sappy with them, and you should be fine.

## R-E-S-P-E-C-T

When meeting someone for the first time, it is customary to lock lips. Just kidding. A quick (but firm) handshake will do. Make sure you are on time for your meeting—Germans put an emphasis on punctuality. Titles are also important to Germans, so it's a good idea to use *Herr* (Mr.) and *Frau* (Mrs.) followed by a surname unless invited to use a first name. Don't be intimidated by Berliners' tendency toward intense eye contact—it's just a sign that they're *really* listening (and you would be wise to return the stare).

## Honor the Haus

It is customary to bring a small gift when visiting a German's house—just like pretty much everywhere else in the world, flowers are a common one. Keep in mind that red ones (especially roses) imply romantic intentions. If you bring wine, opt for an imported one—bringing German wine screams, "Whatever you have to offer isn't good enough!"

If you're staying for a meal, don't be the first to seat yourself unless invited to do so. Your host will likely initiate a toast. Some common ones include "*Zum Wohl!*" (Cheers!) when drinking wine and "*Prosit!*" (Toast!) when drinking beer.

## Around Town

When entering a small store, it's polite to say *Guten Tag* to the clerk, even if he is busy with another customer. And though English is spoken in most places, using German phrases such as *bitte* (please) and *danke* (thank you) is considered courteous.

At restaurants, it's preferred to hand your check and money directly to your waiter rather than leaving it on the table. For information on **tipping,** see **Essentials.** When venturing to the bathroom, know that H stands for *Herren* (gentlemen) and D for *Damen* (ladies).

# FOOD AND DRINK

What do Germans eat? In a word, meat. And more meat. And some more meat. **Currywurst,** slices of sausage served in a curry sauce, is an extremely common option throughout the city, sold on street corners and in restaurants alike. **Bratwurst,** another common street food, resembles an American hot dog. Traditionally it is made from pork, but today, it's frequently made from a combination of meats. **Kassler** is a cured and smoked slice of pork. Simple but yummy.

But fret not if meat isn't your thing. **Vegetarian** options are becoming increasingly popular in Berlin restaurants, if not among street vendors. If you look beyond meat and sit-down meals, you'll find a rich **coffeehouse culture** in Berlin. Berliners (and Germans in general) prefer their coffee thin, dark, and bitter. If you're unable to wrap your American head around the idea of a black coffee, you can order a **Milchkaffe** (that's right—coffee with milk); just don't complain when the locals scoff. Berliners also take pride in their pastries, particularly the **jelly-filled donut** (one of JFK's favorites). Outside of Berlin, it's called a *Berliner,* but in the city, they're usually referred to as **Pfannkuchen.**

And of course there's ▓**beer.** Germans take their beer seriously. In fact, all beer is brewed in accordance with *Reinheitsgebot* or "beer purity law," which regulates the ingredients. If you're looking for something uniquely Berlin, order a **Berliner Weisse.** This pale, sour wheat beer is often served with a shot of flavored syrup to cut the tartness and presented in a bowl-shaped glass. And if your beer comes with a straw, ditch it. It's your waiter's way of saying, "I can tell you're a tourist."

# ART AND ARCHITECTURE

## Museums, Manifold and Multifarious

Europe and art go together like Alfalfa and Darla, and Berlin is no exception. The city boasts over 170 museums visited by millions of people each year. A good place to start is **Museumsinsel**—a mini island nested in the middle of the city that is home to some of its most famous museums. The **Bode Museum** holds a collection of sculptures, coins, medals, and Byzantine art. The **Alte Nationalgalerie** contains works from the eras of Classicism, Romanticism, and Impressionism as well as some early modern work. The collection at the **Altes Museum** is focused on classical antiquities, while the **Neues Museum** contains ancient Egyptian and prehistoric works. Last but not least, there's the **Pergamon Museum**, the most visited museum in Germany. The antiquities collection boasts actual sections of the **Pergamon Altar,** the Gate of **Miletus,** and the **Ishtar Gate.** Don your best sandals and loincloth a la King Nebuchadnezzar II (who commissioned the Ishtar Gate in Babylon in 575 BCE) for the full effect.

If art's not your thing, first reconsider traveling in Europe, then check out Berlin's other cultural museums that deal with everything from Jewish history to sex and eroticism. For more on museums in Berlin, flip to **Sights.**

## History: It's All Around You

As you walk around the city it's hard to ignore its striking monuments. The nave of the Berlin Cathedral, better known as the **Berliner Dom**, is spectacular in its own right, but be sure to head downstairs if you enjoy the company of dead guys—it's home to the sarcophagi of roughly 90 Prussian royals. Other monuments of note include the **Victory Column,** representing the unification that followed the Prussian wars, the **Brandenburg Gate,** representing the unification of East and West Germany, and the **Reichstag,** which, after being razed by Nazi supporters, bombed by the Allies, and stormed by Russian troops, was renovated in 1999 as a symbol of—you guessed it—German unification. The **Olympia-stadion** is a particularly eerie sight. A relic from Nazi Germany, the venue still has a circle on the facade that once contained a giant swastika.

## Important Graffiti (Not an Oxymoron)

Perhaps the most famous and extravagant graffiti in Berlin today is on the crumbling fragments of the Wall, which acts as a canvas for social, political, and artistic thoughts. There are paintings from before and after the fall that include sayings ("Crack is Wack" and "We Are The Wall"), cartoons (everything from raindrops to penises), and truly beautiful artwork by artists from around the world. The Wall embodies the youthful spirit that is quickly enveloping Berlin while simultaneously paying homage to the city's rich history. The **East Side Gallery** in Friederichshain preserves a portion of the Wall with graffiti by international artists made at the time of its fall in 1989.

# HOLIDAYS AND FESTIVALS

| HOLIDAY OR FESTIVAL | DESCRIPTION | DATE |
|---|---|---|
| Berlinale Film Festival | Berlin's version of the Oscars—but with trophies shaped like bears instead of little men. | February |
| Labor Day/May Day | An internationally recognized holiday honoring workers. | May 1 |
| Berlin Carnival of Cultures | An annual celebration of the melting pot that is Berlin. (Also, an excuse to dress up and get drunk.) | June |
| Berlin Beer Festival | Pretty self-explanatory, this festival is a good warm-up for Oktoberfest. | August |
| Jewish Cultural Days | An annual event honoring Berlin's Jewish population and educating the community about Jewish heritage. | September |
| Unity Day | This national holiday marks the official anniversary of German reunification in 1990. | October 3 |
| Berlin Festival of Lights | A citywide celebration that involves laser displays and fireworks around major monuments, squares, towers, streets... and, of course, lots of beer. | October |
| Oktoberfest | Head to Munich for this world-famous beer fest. Book your tickets and hostel far in advance. | October |

Berlin 101

# Beyond Tourism

If you are reading this, then you are a member of an elite group—and we don't mean "the literate." You're a student preparing for a semester abroad. You're taking a gap year to save the trees, the whales, or the dates. You're an 80-year-old woman who has devoted her life to egg-laying platypuses and what the hell is up with that. In short, you're a traveler, not a tourist; like any good spy, you don't just observe your surroundings—you become an active part of them.

Your mission, should you choose to accept it, is to study, volunteer, or work abroad as laid out in the dossier—er, chapter—below. We leave the rest (when to go, whom to bring, and how many changes of underwear to pack) in your hands. This message will self-destruct in five seconds. Good luck.

# STUDYING

Between centuries-old Humboldt University, Freie Universitat Berlin, and a variety of international programs, your biggest challenge will be choosing *where* to study. Those already fluent in the language can enroll directly in classes with German students; if your *Deutsch* doesn't go much further than politely ordering a Berliner Weisse, there are plenty of language programs to bring you up to speed as well as a number of English-speaking study-abroad programs. Almost all programs provide housing, although some options are not conveniently located for your classes.

## Universities

### Freie Universitat Berlin

70 NW Couch St., Ste. 242, Portland, OR 97209, USA

☎+1-800-654-2051; www.ahastudyabroad.org

Through AHA Study Abroad and the University of Oregon you can study at FU—that's Freie Universitat Berlin. AHA offers an intensive language immersion or a language and culture program. Students live with families or in homes and take daytrips and weekend excursions to other parts of Germany including Dresden, Hamburg, and Weimar.

▶ *i* 4- to 6-week summer programs. Ⓢ Courses US$3840-6030.

### Humboldt University

9 W. Broad St., Stamford, CT 06902, USA

☎+1-800-727-2437; www.aifsabroad.com

Founded in 1810, Humboldt is Berlin's oldest university. The American Institute for Foreign Study (AIFS) runs a four-week study-abroad program for rising college freshmen through college seniors that offers classes in everything from Musicology to Agrarian Studies to Image History.

▶ *i* Must take at least 1 course in German language during the program. Min. GPA 2.5. Ⓢ US$5695; includes tuition, housing, meal allowance, cultural activities, excursions, 1-month travel pass, and insurance. Non-refundable application fee US$95. Refundable damage deposit US$250.

Beyond Tourism

## Metropolitan Studies Summer Program

33 N. LaSalle St., 15th fl., Chicago, IL 60602, USA

☎+1-800-995-2300; www.iesabroad.org

> The Institute for the International Education of Students (IES) has a summer program in Berlin with classes in English or German that cover everything from "Sex, Drugs, and Rock and Roll" to "The Politics of Gender."

▶ *i* Apartment housing. Ⓢ US$5995.

## NYU Berlin

110 E. 14th St., Lower Level, New York, NY 10003, USA

☎+1-212-998-4433; www.nyu.edu/global/global-academic-centers1/berlin.html

> New York University offers a study-abroad program for students enrolled at accredited colleges and universities. You can take classes in fields like German, art history, architecture, and political theory.

▶ *i* Students stay in apartments in central Berlin, about 15-20min. from the NYU academic center. Ⓢ Approximately US$26,000 per year.

---

# Language Schools

As renowned novelist Gustave Flaubert once said, "Language is a cracked kettle on which we beat out tunes for bears to dance to." While we at *Let's Go* have absolutely no clue what he is talking about, we do know that the following are good resources for learning German.

## A2Z Berlin

3219 E. Camelback Rd., Ste. 806, Phoenix, AZ 85018, USA

☎+1-888-417-1533; www.a2zlanguages.com/berlin.htm

> A2Z teaches courses of every level and organizes activities in and around Berlin. Only German is spoken in the classroom.

▶ *i* Ages 16 and up. Program provides housing, 2 meals per day, internet access, and books.

## Eurocentres Berlin

Bernburgerstr. 30-31

☎+1-866-869-3520; www.eurocentres.com

> This language center is centrally located with good access to public transportation. One-on-one lessons for students age 16 and older.

▶ *i* Ages 16+. Ⓢ €110. Private lessons €268 per week. Accommodations €221 per week.

**Beyond Tourism**

## Culinary Schools

### Kochen und Würzen

Goltzstr. 51

☎030 219 96 669; www.kochenundwuerzen.de

Chances are you won't be able to bring that delicious German food home with you. So why not learn to recreate it at home with a few classes at Kochen und Würzen?

▶ $ Classes €59-75. ⏰ Classes Th-Sa 7pm.

### Versuchs und Lehranstalt für Brauerei in Berlin (VLB)

Seestr. 13

☎030 45 08 00; www.vlb-berlin.org

Who doesn't love a nice cold brew? Put down that Natty Light and learn how to brew your own. VLB teaches classes in all aspects of brewing, including raw materials, malting technology, water and waste treatment, sensory evaluation, logistics, microbiology, and brewing technology.



## Visa Information

Those planning to study in Berlin for more than three months will need a **student visa.** Germany has three types of visas:

- **STUDENT APPLICANT VISA:** for those who have applied but not yet received acceptance to a university.
- **STUDENT VISA:** for those who have been accepted to a university.
- **VISA FOR PARTICIPATION IN A LANGUAGE COURSE:** for those enrolled in a German language program.

To obtain a visa you will need a valid passport, two passport photos, and proof of a school leaving certificate (which entitles you to study in Germany) or proof of acceptance to a German university. Some applicants also need proof of previous studies, German skills, and sufficient funds to finance their stay. German regulations require foreign students to have at least €643 per month (€7716 per year). Apply for a visa at a German embassy (see **Essentials**).

# VOLUNTEERING

There are plenty of organizations in Berlin that need a helping hand. Spend a few hours or weeks building houses, teaching, or rescuing animals—the party will still be hopping when you're done.

## Habitat for Humanity

Auf Em Berlich 30, Köln, 50667

☎221 579 59 50; www.habitat.org

Spend some time building houses and your biceps with Habitat for Humanity's German chapter.

## International Cultural Youth Exchange

Stralauer Allee 20E

☎030 212 38 252; www.icye.org

ICYE Berlin is a nonprofit youth exchange organization. The company places young people with host families and a volunteer job. Jobs include caring for the elderly or disabled, helping at orphanages, or working on a farm.

## Responsible Travel

☎+44 1273 600 030; www.responsibletravel.com

Responsible Travel mixes—you guessed it—volunteerism and travel. If you have a heart, chances are you feel bad about the destruction of some furry woodland creature's home or a cute little birdie's nest. Volunteers with this German Conservation program work with park rangers in Harz National Park to restore natural habitats.

## United Planet Germany

☎+1-800-292-2316; www.unitedplanet.org

Through United Planet you can volunteer to help young children, the elderly, or the disabled. The program allows you to choose which social issue you feel most passionately about and places you in a volunteer program in Berlin.

# WORKING

So you've blown all your money on bratwurst and schnitzel. Solution? Get a job. In between exploring the city's many pleasures, wipe down a few tables or babysit some rugrats—after all, extra money means extra beer. Some employers may give you room and board, while others pay stipends or salaries.

Beyond Tourism

## Long-Term Work

It's a good idea to research long-term work ahead of time. Start your search at **www.jobsinberlin.eu,** a search engine for English-speaking job seekers. Americans have things a little harder, since they need help from their employers to obtain a **work permit.** Americans planning to stay in Germany for longer than three months will also need to apply for a **visa** in addition to a work permit. EU citizens don't face the same obstacles.

### Teaching English

As a foreigner, you have likely encountered that gem of a local who pretends not to speak English. However, German culture highly encourages people to be bilingual. It should come as no surprise, then, that there are many Germans eager to hire native English speakers to teach the language. Put that God-given talent to good use.

### Aide Abroad Germany

1221 S. Mopac Expressway, Ste. 100, Austin, TX 78746, USA

☎+1-866-6ABROAD; www.aideabroad.org

With Aide Abroad, you live with a German family and teach them English 15hr. per week in exchange for room and board. When each day's work is done, you're free to go off and do all those typical touristy things.

▶ *i* 3-6 months.

### Oxford Seminars

244 5th Ave., Ste. J262, New York, NY 10001, USA

☎+1-800-779-1779; www.oxfordseminars.com

Oxford Seminars hires college graduates to teach English abroad.

▶ *i* 30-40hr. per week teaching. Ⓢ Salary €1500-2400 per month.

### Au Pair Work

### interexchange

161 6th Ave., New York, NY 10013, USA

☎+1-800-597-3675; www.interexchange.org

Interexchange places au pairs with carefully screened host families, who provide a private room and full board. Who knows?

You might just find the Maxwell to your Fran.

▶ *i* Jobs last from 6 months to 1 year. At least 1½ days off per week, and 2 weeks paid vacation. Transportation pass and basic health, accident, and liability insurance provided. Ⓢ Stipends from €260 per month, and €25 per month toward airfare.

## Sunny Au Pairs

☎+1-503-616-3026; www.sunnyaupairs.com

Welcome to the OkCupid of au pair work. Sunny Au Pairs maintains a search engine that lets you browse through families (and their thumbnail photos) who are seeking au pairs.

▶ *i* Ages 17-25. Must know basic German. You will be expected to work no more than 5hr. per day. 4 weeks paid vacation, 1 free day per week, and 4 free evenings per week. Ⓢ Salary approximately €230 per month.

---

### More Visa Information

Anyone planning on working in Germany is required to apply for a **residence permit.** Residence permits can be obtained after entering Germany, even without a visa. You can also get a permit before traveling to Germany through the German Embassy. Applications take one to three months to process, so get a move on. You will need two application forms; two passport photographs; a valid national passport; two copies of the data page, employment contract, or letter of intent from your future employer; a driver's license or other proof of residence; and the visa fee (US$92).

---

**Beyond Tourism**

## Internships

If you're looking for something a little less Mary Poppins for your long-term work experience, consider an internship that caters specifically to your interests.

## The Bundestag

UR/Lattimore 206, PO Box 270375, Rochester, NY 14627, USA

☎+1-585-275-8850; www.epa-internships.org

Through EPA Internships you can get an internship in German politics—specifically Germany's national parliament, the Bundestag. Work might include researching, translating, attending meetings, and dealing with correspondence and the press.

### International Exchange for Students for Technical Experience (IAESTE)

www.iaeste.org

IAESTE runs a training program in Germany. Students can choose positions in industry, research, consulting, or lab work.

▶ *i* Internships typically 8-12 weeks during the summer. Apply for positions through the IAESTE in your home country.

## Short-Term Work

Demand for short-term employees in Berlin is constantly fluctuating. If you're looking to make a quick euro, check local newspapers and keep an eye out for "Help Wanted" signs as you saunter through the city.

### New Berlin Tour Guide

☎030 510 50 030; www.newberlintours.com

New Berlin hires guides to give tours of the city. The tours are free, so your earnings are all tips. Visit the website to find out if they're hiring.

### Pub Crawl Tour Guide

☎030 692 31 49; www.insidertour.com

Your mission, should you choose to accept it, is to lead tourists and locals to Berlin's best venues. Do you think you can handle getting paid to party? We do!

### Saint Christopher's Inns

☎030 814 53 960; www.st-christophers.co.uk/berlin-hostels

At St. Christopher's the staff religiously follows the motto "work

**Beyond Tourism**

## Tell the World

If your friends are tired of hearing about that time you saved a baby orangutan in Indonesia, there's clearly only one thing to do: get new friends. Find them at our website, **www. letsgo.com,** where you can post your study-, volunteer-, or work-abroad stories for other, more appreciative community members to read.

hard, play hard." During your stay in Berlin, they offer you a
spot among their group of hostel workers and bartenders.

▶ *i* Applicants should be fun, easygoing, enthusiastic, patient, and well-
spoken.

# Index

## Accommodations Index

## Restaurants Index

## Nightlife

# Shopping Index

# BERLIN ACKNOWLEDGMENTS

**DOROTHY THANKS:** MPMP for being my favorite and doing more than her share of work. All of the RWs for surviving, and being undaunted by the seemingly endless things asked of them. Pod Sinai for being the best "do your f-ing work-themed" pod of all time. All of Masthead for being sweethearts, especially Sarah. Marykate for being calm and wise. Iya for guerrilla compliments. Grooveshark for being free. Tanjore Tuesdays and Bagel Fridays for providing me with essential nutrients. Finally, the best for last: thanks to the Oxford Commas, for being the harvestest; to Maine, for quickly becoming my favorite state; and to my family, for everything.

**MARY THANKS:** Thank you Dorothy, Graham, Mark, Michal, Patrick, Sarah, and everyone at HQ for all of your hard work.

# ABOUT LET'S GO

## The Student Travel Guide

Let's Go publishes the world's favorite student travel guides, written entirely by Harvard students. Armed with pens, notebooks, and a few changes of clothes stuffed into their backpacks, our student researchers go across continents, through time zones, and above expectations to seek out invaluable travel experiences for our readers. Because we are a completely student-run company, we have a unique perspective on how students travel, where they want to go, and what they're looking to do when they get there. If your dream is to grab a machete and forge through the jungles of Costa Rica, we can take you there. If you'd rather bask in the Riviera sun at a beachside cafe, we'll set you a table. In short, we write for readers who know that there's more to travel than tour buses. To keep up, visit our website, www.letsgo.com, where you can sign up to blog, post photos from your trips, and connect with the Let's Go community.

## Traveling Beyond Tourism

We're on a mission to provide our readers with sharp, fresh coverage packed with socially responsible opportunities to go beyond tourism. Each guide's Beyond Tourism chapter shares ideas about responsible travel, study abroad, and how to give back to the places you visit while on the road. To help you gain a deeper connection with the places you travel, our fearless researchers scour the globe to give you the heads-up on both world-renowned and off-the-beaten-track opportunities. We've also opened our pages to respected writers and scholars to hear their takes on the countries and regions we cover, and asked travelers who have worked, studied, or volunteered abroad to contribute first-person accounts of their experiences.

## Fifty-Two Years of Wisdom

Let's Go has been on the road for 52 years and counting. We've grown a lot since publishing our first 20-page pamphlet to Europe in 1960, but five decades and 60 titles later, our witty, candid guides are still researched and written entirely by students on shoestring budgets who know that train strikes, stolen luggage, food poisoning, and marriage proposals are all part of a day's work. Meanwhile, we're still bringing readers fresh new features, such as a student-life section with advice on how and where to meet students from around the world; a revamped, user-friendly layout for our listings; and greater emphasis on the experiences that make travel abroad a rite of passage for readers of all ages. And, of course, this year's 16 titles—including five brand-new guides—are still brimming with editorial honesty, a commitment to students, and our irreverent style.

## The Let's Go Community

More than just a travel guide company, Let's Go is a community that reaches from our headquarters in Cambridge, MA, all across the globe. Our small staff of dedicated student editors, writers, and tech nerds comes together because of our shared passion for travel and our desire to help other travelers get the most out of their experience. We love it when our readers become part of the Let's Go community as well—when you travel, drop us a postcard (67 Mt. Auburn St., Cambridge, MA 02138, USA), send us an email (feedback@letsgo.com), or sign up on our website (www. letsgo.com) to tell us about your adventures and discoveries.

For more information, updated travel coverage, and news from our researcher team, visit us online at www.letsgo.com.

# LET'S GO BUDGET

## TAKE A LET'S GO BUDGET GUIDE TO EUROPE

**LET'S GO BUDGET AMSTERDAM**
978-1-61237-015-6

**LET'S GO BUDGET ATHENS**
978-1-61237-005-7

**LET'S GO BUDGET BARCELONA**
978-1-61237-014-9

**LET'S GO BUDGET BERLIN**
978-1-61237-006-4

**LET'S GO BUDGET FLORENCE**
978-1-61237-007-1

**LET'S GO BUDGET ISTANBUL**
978-1-61237-008-8

**LET'S GO BUDGET LONDON**
978-1-61237-013-2

**LET'S GO BUDGET MADRID**
978-1-61237-009-5

**LET'S GO BUDGET PARIS**
978-1-61237-011-8

**LET'S GO BUDGET PRAGUE**
978-1-61237-010-1

**LET'S GO BUDGET ROME**
978-1-61237-012-5

ALL LET'S GO BUDGET GUIDEBOOKS ARE $9.99.
*Let's Go also publishes guides to individual countries
that are available at bookstores and online retailers.*

For more information: visit **LETSGO.COM**
JOIN THE DISCUSSION WITH LET'S GO ON **FACEBOOK** AND **TWITTE**

**HELPING LET'S GO.** If you want to share your discoveries, suggestions, or corrections, please drop us a line. We appreciate every piece of correspondence, whether a postcard, a 10-page email, or a coconut. Visit Let's Go at www.letsgo.com or send an email to:

feedback@letsgo.com, subject: "Let's Go Budget Berlin"

## Address mail to:

Let's Go Budget Berlin, 67 Mount Auburn St., Cambridge, MA 02138, USA

In addition to the invaluable travel advice our readers share with us, many are kind enough to offer their services as researchers or editors. Unfortunately, our charter enables us to employ only currently enrolled Harvard students.
Maps © Let's Go and Avalon Travel
Interior design by Darren Alessi
Production by Amber Pirker
Photos © Let's Go, Patrick Lauppe, Sophie Angelis, and Nelson Greaves, photographers

Distributed by Publishers Group West.
Printed in Canada by Friesens Corp.

ISBN-13: 978-1-61237-006-4
ISBN-10: 1-61237-006-3
First edition
10 9 8 7 6 5 4 3 2 1

Let's Go Budget Berlin is written by Let's Go Publications, 67 Mt. Auburn St., Cambridge, MA 02138, USA.

Let's Go® and the LG logo are trademarks of Let's Go, Inc.

# QUICK REFERENCE

## YOUR GUIDE TO LET'S GO ICONS

| | | | | | |
|---|---|---|---|---|---|
| [✓] | *Let's Go* recommends | ☎ | Phone numbers | ⇄ | Directions |
| *i* | Other hard info | $ | Prices | ⏰ | Hours |

## IMPORTANT PHONE NUMBERS

| EMERGENCY: ☎112 | | | |
|---|---|---|---|
| Amsterdam | ☎911 | London | ☎999 |
| Barcelona | ☎092 | Madrid | ☎092 |
| Berlin | ☎110 | Paris | ☎17 |
| Florence | ☎113 | Prague | ☎158 |
| Istanbul | ☎155 | Rome | ☎113 |

## USEFUL PHRASES

| ENGLISH | FRENCH | GERMAN | ITALIAN | SPANISH |
|---|---|---|---|---|
| Hello/Hi | Bonjour/Salut | Hallo/Tag | Ciao | Hola |
| Goodbye/Bye | Au revoir | Auf Wiedersehen/ Tschüss | Arrivederci/Ciao | Adios/Chao |
| Yes | Oui | Ja | Sì | Sí |
| No | Non | Nein | No | No |
| Excuse me! | Pardon! | Entschuldigen Sie! | Scusa! | Perdón! |
| Thank you | Merci | Danke | Grazie | Gracias |
| Go away! | Va t'en! | Geh weg! | Vattene via! | Vete! |
| Help! | Au secours! | Hilfe! | Aiuto! | Ayuda! |
| Call the police! | Appelez la police! | Ruf die Polizei! | Chiamare la polizia! | Llame a la policía! |
| Get a doctor! | Cherchez un médecin! | Hol einen Arzt! | Avere un medico! | Llame a un médico! |
| I don't understand | Je ne comprends pas | Ich verstehe nicht | Non capisco | No comprendo |
| Do you speak English? | Parlez-vous anglais? | Sprechen Sie Englisch? | Parli inglese? | ¿Habla inglés? |
| Where is...? | Où est...? | Wo ist...? | Dove...? | ¿Dónde está...? |

## TEMPERATURE CONVERSIONS

| °CELSIUS | -5 | 0 | 5 | 10 | 15 | 20 | 25 | 30 | 35 | 40 |
|---|---|---|---|---|---|---|---|---|---|---|
| °FAHRENHEIT | 23 | 32 | 41 | 50 | 59 | 68 | 77 | 86 | 95 | 104 |

## MEASUREMENT CONVERSIONS

| | |
|---|---|
| 1 inch (in.) = 25.4mm | 1 millimeter (mm) = 0.039 in. |
| 1 foot (ft.) = 0.305m | 1 meter (m) = 3.28 ft. |
| 1 mile (mi.) = 1.609km | 1 kilometer (km) = 0.621 mi. |
| 1 pound (lb.) = 0.454kg | 1 kilogram (kg) = 2.205 lb. |
| 1 gallon (gal.) = 3.785L | 1 liter (L) = 0.264 gal. |